My Family is Back

My Family is Back challenges conventional methods of eating disorder care by explaining the effectiveness of multi-family therapy (MFT) in helping children recover from anorexia nervosa.

MFT is an intensive method involving a small group of families working together towards recovery. Building on previous work that focuses on mobilising family resources as a major factor in therapeutic change, MFT introduces a new element: encouraging groups of families to work together to rediscover their strengths, overcome feelings of isolation, and find renewed hope. The authors describe how MFT works and how it can enhance the treatment of eating disorders by improving service delivery and reducing costs. Eighteen families serve as the 'voice of experience,' their stories breathing life into the science.

The families provide a long-term perspective and reflection on their MFT participation. Their stories emphasise the importance of early intervention, family involvement, and collaboration in overcoming anorexia nervosa. Strategies for family members, friends, and professionals illustrate the evidence base for this model of care.

This book, offering an accessible guide to MFT, has international appeal for families of children with eating disorders, health professionals, and healthcare providers.

June Alexander, PhD, is an Australian writer whose life and career have been shaped by her experience with anorexia nervosa, which began at age 11. Her PhD investigates diary writing as a therapeutic tool for eating disorders.

Ivan Eisler, PhD, is Emeritus Professor of Family Psychology and Family Therapy at King's College, London. He is also honorary Consultant Clinical Psychologist at the Maudsley Centre for Child and Adolescent Eating Disorders in London.

Julian Baudinet, PhD, is Joint Head and Consultant Clinical Psychologist at the Maudsley Centre for Child and Adolescent Eating Disorders. He is also an Adjunct Senior Lecturer in the Department of Psychological Medicine at King's College London.

My Family is Back

Multi-Family Therapy for Eating Disorders

June Alexander, Ivan Eisler, and Julian Baudinet

Routledge
Taylor & Francis Group

LONDON AND NEW YORK

Designed cover image: Getty Images

First published 2026
by Routledge
4 Park Square, Milton Park, Abingdon, Oxon OX14 4RN

and by Routledge
605 Third Avenue, New York, NY 10158

Routledge is an imprint of the Taylor & Francis Group, an informa business

British Library Cataloguing-in-Publication Data
A catalogue record for this book is available from the British Library

ISBN: 978-0-415-63760-2 (hbk)
ISBN: 978-0-415-63761-9 (pbk)
ISBN: 978-1-003-64107-0 (ebk)

DOI: 10.4324/9781003641070

Typeset in Times New Roman
by Newgen Publishing UK

'This book is a valuable testimonial where many voices inter-weave: a narrator, who herself suffered from anorexia nervosa for over 40 years, specialists of the disorder, and above all, families who have undergone multi-family therapy for anorexia nervosa. Therapy with families is based on the observation that you can't move forward without your family, particularly when you suffer from an illness that binds you together pathologic-ally, but also because scientific research shows that the family is a resource for the sufferer. This book aims to reposition the family and the group as fundamental resources in the process of individual development at a time when "self-fulfilment" has become a mantra.'

Noël Pommepuy, MD, Child and Adolescent Psychiatry
Department 93I05, Ville-Evrard Hospital, France

'This inspiring book is a must-read for any family member who has lived through an eating disorder in their child. Ivan Eisler and Julian Baudinet – expert researchers and clinicians – pro-vide a wealth of evidence on eating disorders and the utility of multi-family therapy that is easy to understand with many examples and practical skills that can be applied to different contexts. June Alexander eloquently brings to life the many stories of families from across the globe who have benefited from MFT. She interviews families about how their experiences with MFT galvanized them to bring their family back from the grips of an eating disorder.'

Gina Dimitropoulos, PhD, MSW, FAED, Professor,
Faculty of Social Work, University of Calgary, Canada

'My Family is Back is set to become a treasured resource for families looking for a way forward to help their child start to recover from the eating disorder. The authors have skillfully gathered stories that give hope and show positive steps towards recovery are possible when a family works together and with other families. This is the special power of multi-family therapy, and it shines brightly through each story. My Family is *Back* beautifully allows the voice and experience of parents, siblings and the young person to be heard. I highly recommend this book to parents as a companion on your journey, and to clinicians to better understand the experience of families.'

Dr Andrew Wallis, *Clinical Social Worker, Family Therapist and Eating Disorder Service Network Lead, Sydney Children's Hospitals Network, Australia*

'It is virtually impossible to understand the difficulty of living under the shadow of anorexia nervosa without having firsthand experience. The illness grips and manipulates both the sufferer and their family members in incomprehensible ways that can feel deeply isolating and de-railing. When these families find each other and undergo the journey of recovery together, some-thing deep and powerful happens that cannot be fully under-stood on an intellectual level alone. In *My Family is Back*, June, Ivan and Julian relentlessly endeavour and commit to capturing these effects for the betterment of professionals, patients and families alike by allowing families to give firsthand accounts of their illness and multi-family treatment experiences. These personal stories provide a deeper and more textured understand-ing of what it is to undergo the journey of illness and recovery and the importance of connecting families via multi-family therapy as a powerful antidote to the isolation and paralysis that can come with anorexia and allow it to fester. Through these accounts, we can begin to understand the immense therapeutic value of treating systemically on both an inter- and intra-family level. This book will serve as an access point for patients and families desperate to connect with others' stories as we contend with our healthcare systems' current limitations in facilitating this work and as a poignant learning tool for providers working with those in recovery.'

Stephanie Knatz Peck, PhD, *Associate Clinical Professor; Director, Intensive Family Treatments; University of California San Diego Eating Disorders Treatment; Department of Psychiatry, USA*

We wish to dedicate this book to the families who share their stories in this joint Dedication:

This book is dedicated to the brave children and their families who have faced the unimaginable with courage and resilience. To the parents, siblings, and caregivers whose stories shine with their love and strength during the darkest times, you remind us of the power of hope, unity, and unconditional love.

May these shared experiences offer comfort, inspire others, and honour the journeys of all families touched by anorexia nervosa.

June Alexander, Ivan Eisler, and Julian Baudinet

Contents

Foreword   *xiii*
Acknowledgements   *xvii*

Introduction   1

SECTION I
Understanding eating disorders and
multi-family therapy   19

1 Understanding eating disorders   21

2 Understanding multi-family therapy   43

SECTION II
Our stories—families with experience of
multi-family therapy   79

3 Introduction   81

4 The importance of being treated with
   respect   83
   REBEKAH

5   Everyone in the family has a role in
    recovery   99
    NATALIE

6   When dad is the primary carer   113
    DAVE

7   A tale of anorexia, two mothers, and
    friendship   119
    LISA AND HARRIET

8   A job in a cheese shop provides a lesson
    in recovery   136
    LYDIA

9   Reshaping daughter–mother dynamics   141
    MATHILDA

10 A mother and son can do this, too   152
    JAMES

11 When MFT is the last in a long list of
    therapies   163
    MILLIE

12 'Only I can get myself out of this illness'   178
    CASSANDRA

13 'There is no cookie cutter for this illness'   189
    AMY

14 When 'doing' with others makes a
    difference   197
    EMILY

15 The sparkle behind a belly button piercing   215
    AMELIA

16 'I am not my mother; I'm me'   227
    CHAROLETTE

17 Understanding the illness helps mother
    take charge   233
    DIANA

18 The getting of communication skills leads
    to breakthrough   240
    SAMANTHA

19 Creating a caring environment at home to
    support recovery   245
    EMMA

20 'Oh, my sister does that, too'   255
    EVA

21 'Can I have some fries, Mummy?'   258
    CATHERINE

22 Anorexia does not care who you are or
    where you are   273
    SHIRA

23 The family stories—reflecting on
   inspiring lessons   278

SECTION III
What can parents do if they are concerned
about their child?   **283**

24 How to tell if your child has an eating
   disorder   285

25 Navigating the search for multi-family
   therapy   296

   Abbreviations   *305*
   Overview of FT-ED   *307*
   Eating disorder-focused family therapy
      manuals   *311*
   Index   *314*

Foreword

Hope is a central theme of *My Family is Back*. Defined as 'to want something to happen or be true, to trust', the concept of hope has been shown to be a vital part of the recovery process. As a clinician-researcher, I have seen hope guide families through difficult times as well as help our field strive to improve outcomes in eating disorder treatment. As a scientific community, we have continued to better understand the role of biology in the development of eating disorders and have refined early intervention approaches and treatments to support those with eating disorders. Despite these advances, I am sadly surprised by the continuation of historical patterns to exclude and blame family members and carers for the development of eating disorders. These erroneous beliefs compound the shame and isolation for young people and their families in the already arduous treatment process. As the field continues to progress, working to represent the voices of those with lived experience, there has been a noticeable shift in how family and carers are included. The direct work of Drs Eisler, Baudinet, and Alexander not only includes families but also empowers them as a unit to build and refine skills, improve communication patterns, and leverage their relationship to support their young person throughout eating disorder recovery. In my clinical role, I am consistently inspired by the power of love, care, and persistence that family members demonstrate when faced with this life-threatening and complicated disease. The importance that family and support people play in the treatment of eating disorders cannot be overstated.

When a young person is diagnosed with an eating disorder, parents and family members are often bewildered, uncertain, and scared. The process of seeking treatment requires bravery and hope for a future without the eating disorder. To 'hold on to hope' may require a suspension of logic, coupled with trust in the idea that things could be different and, perhaps, better. While families continue to face many barriers to accessing treatment, there is evidence to point to the utility and success of family-centred interventions, including multi-family therapy. Early intervention, comprehensive psychoeducation, and access to evidence-based treatment are paramount to sufficiently treat eating disorders.

While the careers and contributions of Drs Eisler, Baudinet, and Alexander cannot be summed in a few short sentences, my relationship with the authors continues to enrich my clinical practice. Each of them has given me new perspectives, shown me new ways of thinking, and has directly impacted my work. Dr Eisler is well known in the field of eating disorders for having developed single and multi-family therapy for anorexia nervosa. His work will continue to inform the way we include families in treatment for decades to come. Dr Baudinet's work on developing and adapting treatments for young people and their families, including a better understanding of how treatment works, will support the field in continuing to refine treatment. Dr Alexander's passion for sharing her lived experience enhances the eating disorders community through her important and profound advocacy work. Together, these authors represent the trifecta of hope for the future of eating disorders: understanding the illness, developing and testing interventions, and advocating for their access and high-fidelity implementation among clinicians and entities that fund research and treatment.

Multi-family therapy (MFT) is a treatment founded on the principle that families' experiences are vital—not only to understanding eating disorders and a patient's history, but as an interactive therapeutic strategy when multiple families in different stages of treatment come together. MFT is a form of group therapy that, over consecutive days, serves to connect families while they learn together and from each other. MFT aims to increase knowledge and support, reduce isolation, and reinforce information and skills through utilising the knowledge of both clinicians and families. This treatment harnesses the resilience of families and utilises families' love, trust, hope, and relationships to improve the outcomes for young people with an eating disorder. Throughout MFT, families have the opportunity to create solidarity, overcome stigmatisation and social isolation, and explore how they may be able to see things from a different perspective, leading to both the discovery and the building of new skills.

The perspectives of parents and young people are valuable resources for understanding and treating eating disorders. While many resources are often centred by the clinician or researcher's perspective, the voices of families and those with lived experience have been undervalued. This book corrects the long-standing missed opportunity to bring this third dimension to the forefront in the field of eating disorders.

Hearing from families that have 'been down this road' is a vital part of the knowledge base related to eating disorder treatment. *My Family is Back* offers a window into the experiences of families participating in MFT. The information in this book helps readers understand eating disorders and the treatment model of MFT, and shares the lived experiences of many families, illuminating their rich and diverse perspectives throughout the non-linear treatment process. This collection of stories embodies the work of Drs Eisler, Baudinet, and Alexander in their continued and lifelong dedication to supporting families through the challenge that is eating disorders and their treatment. This book will be an informative and durable resource for treatment providers, families, carers, and those experiencing eating disorders. Undoubtedly, the authors and many readers alike are grateful to the many families who have contributed to this important resource.

Kristen Anderson, LCSW, CEDC-S

Acknowledgements

This book is a collaboration between Prof. Ivan Eisler and Dr Julian Baudinet, families who have experienced multi-family therapy (MFT) for the treatment of anorexia nervosa, and me.

The seed for *My Family is Back* was sown over a decade ago following a conversation with Prof. Eisler in his consulting suite at the Maudsley Hospital. We agreed there was a need for a book to describe the MFT approach to families and health professionals, similar to *My Kid is Back*, which describes family-based treatment (FBT). Our commitment never waned, but Prof. Eisler had many demands on his time, so in 2024, we welcomed Dr Baudinet to join us as a co-author.

Gratitude is extended to our publishing editor, Grace McDonnell, at Routledge, London, whose patience and belief in this book never waned. We thank Grace and her editorial team for their support and encouragement in creating this book.

We thank Kristen Anderson, the writer of the Foreword. Kristen is a co-founder and therapist at the Chicago Centre for Evidence-Based Treatment. We thank Noël Pommepuy, Gina Dimitropoulos, Andrew Wallis, and Stephanie Knatz Peck for their endorsements.

Above all, our deepest thanks go to the parents and their children who have generously shared their experiences of MFT for *My Family is Back*. They are the leading messengers. Their voices are at the heart of this book, illustrating the transformative potential of this therapeutic approach and offering hope to families facing similar challenges. Their stories reveal not only the intricacies of therapy but also the resilience and courage required to confront anorexia nervosa. Showing great vulnerability, parents openly share their family's private struggles and often long-held feelings of (predictable, albeit unwarranted) guilt and shame. Their words 'Because you have been there, too' often bridged the gap, creating a safe space for these families to trust and share.

My Family is Back honours these families—the parents, caregivers, children, and siblings—whose bravery and willingness to share their personal journeys have made this book possible. Their stories are bound to a specific time frame (2012–2014), reflecting memories from that period. Some families had completed MFT eight years before, while others had just finished a year before. Life beyond this time frame has brought new challenges for some young people, including further mental health struggles and, tragically, loss of life. *My Family is Back* is a tribute to these young people and their families who have shared their stories to educate and give hope to others.

We hope that *My Family is Back* provides reassurance to families that healing and growth are possible and that they can help their child get their life back on track through participating in MFT. We acknowledge that, for some, struggles will continue beyond MFT. Anorexia can be one of several mental health challenges a child might face in their lifetime. For some, the journey beyond MFT involves continued work to manage underlying issues like anxiety, depression, or trauma. My psychiatrist, after many years of patient therapeutic guidance, said, 'You no longer have anorexia, but you still have its forerunner, anxiety'. Currently, I am learning how to manage post-traumatic stress disorder. For people like me, maintaining mental health requires ongoing self-discovery and develop self-help techniques to manage these challenges in healthy ways. Establishing and exploring a healthy 'self-identity' can take time. The young people acknowledge this in their stories.

Importantly, the insights within these pages highlight the invaluable role of family stories in advancing treatment. By listening to families' stories of lived experiences, researchers and therapists can find answers to help others. Many of those answers are contained within *My Family is Back*.

June Alexander

Reference

Alexander, J., & Le Grange, D. (2025). *My kid is back: Empowering parents with family-based treatment for anorexia nervosa* (2nd ed.). Routledge.

Introduction

The role of the family in eating disorder recovery

This book arose from a collaboration between June, who, despite having a painful history of living for many years with anorexia nervosa, found the strength and the courage to fight and overcome this pernicious illness, and Ivan and Julian, clinical psychologists and family therapists who have spent much of their careers trying to help people like June find solutions to overcoming an eating disorder. The main focus of this book is a treatment developed by Ivan Eisler and his colleagues, multi-family therapy (MFT), a treatment that brings together six to eight families to share their experiences, provide support for each other, and for each family to learn new ways of helping their child on the road to recovery.

The heart of the book includes a series of conversations that June was able to have with many families that have taken part in MFT and that provide first-hand accounts of how they, both individually and as families, experienced the devastating impact of anorexia nervosa and how MFT became a vital part of the recovery process.

DOI: 10.4324/9781003641070-1

June's story—about a family who had no help

Ivan: June, you are someone who is an experienced journalist, blogger, and adviser to eating disorders organisations, but you are also someone who has personal
experience of living for many years with an eating disorder. I know this book is not about you but about the
stories of the families you interviewed. However, you
yourself have unique insights into the illness because
you know what it can be like at its worst for the sufferer as well as for their families, but importantly also
that, even at its worst, there is hope. The theme of despair and hope is key to this book, and I think it would
be helpful for readers to know a bit more about your
own experience before they start reading the main part
of the book.

June: At the time of writing, in 2025, my five grandchildren
are thirteen to eighteen in age. At their age, in the 1960s,
I was in the grips of anorexia nervosa. The illness
embedded itself in my brain, progressively devouring
my sense of self and impacting every area of my life,
including family relationships.

   For years, I didn't know I had an illness. I thought I was
'weak' for not coping with life, let alone food. No matter
where I went or what I did, from the age of 11, anorexia
went, too. Hiding in my brain, it accompanied me when
I was 20 and walked down the aisle to be married and, as
the years rolled on, caused increased suffering and havoc
for not only me but also my husband and our four children. With anorexia in the mix, family life was never easy.

Ivan: When you were first developing anorexia, very little was
known about effective ways of helping a child suffering
from an eating disorder. Most treatments were centred

around re-feeding in hospital which was effective in the short term but had very high relapse rates. We now know that, for most children and young people suffering from anorexia nervosa, the key to effective treatment is mobilising the family as a resource, which is beautifully described in *My Kid is Back*, now in its second edition, that you wrote with Daniel Le Grange. This wasn't a route available to your family at the time. I know it took a long time, but tell me how you eventually got help.

June: I was in my early 30s when a psychiatrist diagnosed severe and enduring anorexia nervosa, chronic anxiety, and chronic depression. He patiently listened and guided my recovery over the next 25 years.

Julian: What was it like getting a diagnosis?

June: After years of misdiagnosis, meeting the psychiatrist who could see 'me' beyond my illness was life-changing and life-saving. Immediately we met, even though the initial prognosis was bleak, I thought, 'This man can help me'. Trust and hope were established at that first consultation. My greatest motivation was to recover sufficiently to write my story for my four children, all born by the time I was 25, so they would know the 'real me'. I had been labelled 'the problem' in my family of origin, and I yearned to provide my children with my truth. To do that, I believed I first had to recover at least 51 per cent of my healthy self. This level of recovery was achieved in my mid-fifties, and my authentic life began anew.

Julian: I know that your family wasn't directly involved in your treatment, but it seems they were still an important part of your recovery.

June: 'All I want is a mum', my young daughter said when, in my 30s, I began to try and explain myself to her. My illness did not allow me to be fully present as a mum throughout my children's childhood. However, it has not robbed me of being a grandmother. My first grandchild, Lachlan, was born in 2006 when I was 55, the same year that I became more 'me' than my eating disorder. Lachlan immediately became a priceless member of my therapy team. As a toddler, he would call, 'C'mon, Grandma!' and insist I crawl through the tunnel with him at the playground; today, at 18, he makes time for a regular walk-talk with me on the clifftops above the sea. As Grandma, I am ready to pounce on any sign of an eating disorder symptom covertly developing in any of my grandchildren. I am determined that an eating disorder will not ravage the lives, hopes, and dreams of this new generation in my family.

Ivan: There is no doubt that anorexia causes havoc both with the life of the young sufferer but also has a huge impact on the whole family. You have written about this in some detail in your autobiography *A Girl Called Tim* (which I would highly recommend people to read). I don't think here is the place to go into this in detail, but one of the things I got from your life story is just how destructive the illness can be and how it left scars on you and your family.

June: Yes, for years, the anorexia 'voice' continued to torment me. Its mantra was to isolate and conquer. The 'voice' (silent to others but screaming loud to me) refused to let me feel at peace. I could not understand myself, and close others could not understand me. Over time, I became estranged from my parents and sister. After I left home, got married at 20, and had my children, anorexia remained a self-harming gearbox for trying to manage life. I did not know any other way.

Ivan: Before you continue your story about your eventual recovery (and the important role of your relationship with your children and grandchildren), let's return to two aspects of your life story.

These concern the period in your mid-teens when you experienced a partial remission. In *A Girl Called Tim*, you describe in detail how anorexia controlled your life, your mum's bewilderment and concern about your refusal to eat and her many attempts to tempt you to eat a bit more, but also her anger at your 'stubbornness' and her perception of anorexic behaviour as rudeness and bad manners. You also describe your immense sense of guilt and shame and your desperate wish to reconnect with your family and for your parents to be happy. Yet none of this was sufficient for you to be able to resist the illness. Can you describe what enabled you to change at that time and why it didn't last?

June: About a year after anorexia developed, I was watching Mum baking cakes for my teenage sister's birthday celebration. The summer day was hot, and I wished Mum wasn't so tired. She was lifting two trays of patty cakes from the wood-fired oven when she cried, 'Oh no'. The patty cakes, nothing like Mum's usual little peaked mountains, had collapsed into flat, rubbery pancake shapes.

'No-one will want to eat them', she said, wiping her brow wearily. She was about to cry. My heart went out to her.

'Don't worry, Mum, I'll eat them', I suddenly said. The words popped out, just like that. For more than a year, anorexia had imprisoned my healthy-self voice, and now, suddenly, it broke through.

Mum was thrilled. Her flop had turned out to be a winner, and I ate the entire batch of 12 rubbery cakes before the day was out. Soon, I was eating more than rubbery cakes. I was eating meals, and the urge to hide food and constantly exercise ebbed away.

Edited from *A Girl Called Tim*

Julian: This event was clearly an important turning point, but it seems there were other aspects of what was happening at that time in your life that reinforced the retreat of your anorexia. You mentioned being pleased that mum and dad were happy, and how your mum took you shopping for clothes. Also, as you were slowly gaining weight and your preoccupation with thoughts of food receded somewhat, other things in your life started to change for the better.

June: Following the subsidence of my anorexia, I emerged from being the quietest and most withdrawn student to one of the bubbliest in my Year Seven class. Classmates said, 'June has come out of her shell'. I celebrated my 13th birthday, weighing almost 18kg more than 12 months before.

My sister left home to study when I was 14. For me, this was a time of stability. Home life was less stressful. Anorexic thoughts remained, but I could push them away. It was like I knew the thoughts were there and could call on them to cope if the need arose. I was happy—developing friendships, excelling at school, and helping my parents on the farm.

However, by the age of 16, the word 'depressed' was appearing in my diary. This was in the 1960s when depression was not talked about, most certainly not in rural areas. One possible trigger for my anorexia and associated depression, which I could not verbalise as a child, was an unmet need for my mother's acceptance. My earliest memories were of her calling me 'Tim' when I was good and 'Toby' when not so good. I tried to be the good Tim. But horrors upon horrors, within a week of my 11th birthday, I began to menstruate. My mother had not prepared me for this moment. I thought the sky had fallen in. My future looked bleak. I did not want to be a girl. I hated my breasts. They hurt when I ran when playing football with the boys. I could not be what my mother wanted. Enveloped in a developmental identity crisis, I was unable to share my supreme anxiety with anyone. Within four months, anorexia swept in.

Anorexia harmed my relationship with Mum, especially. I had sensed since early childhood that I was not what she wanted. Her calling me 'Tim' and 'Toby' led to identity confusion, and anorexia compounded the feeling that I was letting her down. My illness behaviours, such as refusing to eat at the dinner table and when visiting neighbours and friends, were misunderstood and interpreted as rudeness and selfishness. I felt punished, for example, when Mum refused to buy a school uniform for me to start the new school year. She said I had to gain weight first. She did not understand that I had anorexia and was too fearful to eat. I wanted to please Mum, but my anorexic behaviours made me a continual disappointment.

As a teenager, I felt unable to share my worrying, shameful food thoughts with my parents or anyone. Mum would infer I was silly. She said things like, 'You think about yourself too much', 'It's all in your mind', and 'Why can't you be like other girls?' I wanted to be carefree like other girls but didn't know how. I didn't know how they could eat food without feeling shame or guilt. The constant inference was that I was weak-minded. Neither my parents nor I knew the problem was anorexia.

Dad was a principled, hands-on, 'doing' man. We rarely talked about feelings, but he was more accepting. He never said: 'You can't do that because you are a girl'. His usual, practical advice was: 'You won't know unless you try'. This seed of self-belief sown by Dad would help me weather many a mental storm in the future. My farm-grown work ethic (cows had to be milked twice daily, every day) and my love of and affinity with the land and the bushland evolved from him. The river, the bush, and my Christian faith nurtured my need for a sense of belonging and helped to suppress anxiety and food thoughts. Almost.

Part of my difficulty was that at the time I developed anorexia in rural Australia, a mental illness was considered a personal failing. A broken leg was acceptable, but not a broken mind. My diary pages were full of self-loathing as I tried and failed, thousands of times over, to manage the loud, tormentuous voice in my mind. Miraculously, my love for my four little children managed to avert a descent into suicidal ideation in my late 20s.

I wanted to see my babies grow up, so, for the first time at age 28, I summoned the courage to share my inner struggles with the local country doctor. I blurted out my inner story, terrified I would be locked up and separated from my children. Instead, the (long) journey began to regain 'me'. Doctors in the 1970s did not know how to help me, but they did not say I was 'mad' or, like a family member, say, 'You have the devil in you'. I am grateful to those early doctors for encouraging me to continue writing in my diary and working as a journalist, thus clinging to a small thread of healthy self in my mind.

My parents had left school at age 14 to work on the land. Although I never saw either parent read a book, they accepted my passion for literature. Their guidance, or lack thereof, helped me to develop resilience, self-motivation, independence, and self-reliance from a young age. My parents did the best they could. I only knew them in the context of our farm environment, as we never had a family holiday. Giving up was never an option on the farm, no matter how hard the times, because 'next season will be better', and this steadfast belief would help me to survive anorexia. Daily diary writing, begun at age 11, was a comfort in sorting thoughts when feeling misunderstood and anxious. Words were my friends (unfortunately, for decades, my anorexia befriended my diaries, too).

At 15, I didn't look thin. I mean, I didn't look like I had a food or weight problem, but the breasts that distressed me when I was 11 had disappeared. Mum, concerned that I'd not had a period for almost three years, took me to a doctor who prescribed tablets (the Pill) for nine months.

I was looking forward to finishing those tablets because, although my breasts were filling out, in 14 weeks I gained about 7kg in weight.

Feeling increasingly stressed, for the first time in three-and-a-half years, I began to count calories to gain a sense of control and security. My diary notes:

I am on a diet! I want to lose 3kg.

I began progressively eating less and exercising more. When I ate, guilt kicked in and I would have to go for a long run to regain my sense of control.

Edited from *A Girl Called Tim*

Outwardly, I looked 'well', but the illness in my brain would remain for decades.

Ivan: Let's return to the story of your recovery.

June: My eating disorder caused a disconnection from my healthy self for 44 years, from age 11 to 55. The friendship I developed with steady, reliable George at age 16 (to become my husband four years later) has endured despite anorexia destroying our marriage soon after I began treatment in my 30s. At 36, in a moment of deep reflection, I wrote in my diary:

… for years, I have been seeking my identity, purpose, and meaning in life. Years. I am a prisoner to myself. If I don't take a stand, I will live my life feeling frustrated, and unfulfilled; I will not know the joy of inner peace, or the achievements I can enjoy if my energies are set free.

> *... since falling prey to anorexia, much of my creative energy has been wasted; this private obsession with food has robbed me of my true self. I (must) accept my mistakes and bad experiences (so they) can be the catalyst, the seed, for new beginnings and fulfilment.*

Restoration of my healthy self was a hard slog, but the reward was priceless—the freedom to embrace a new beginning. Through it all, George has remained an anchor. He has been a solid emotional and calming support, for example, in the latter years when secrets about my family of origin and childhood abuse were revealed. We have remained united as parents and now, in our seventies, as grandparents. We regularly chat on the phone. Sometimes, we catch up for a coffee and enjoy a conversation, just the two of us. That's special. Knowing George is 'there' even though we live miles apart is comforting. We share Christmas Day and family birthdays as 'Mum and Dad' and 'Grandma and Grandpa'.

My illness impacted George and our children, now aged 48–52. Unfortunately, when my therapy began in the early 1980s, I was placed on strong medications that had difficult side effects. Partners were not included in the therapy sessions, and George felt left out. Today, I try to appease my deep regret for my family's suffering by focusing on self-care and positivity. We make the most of each moment, and if one of us has a challenge, we work together to help them get back on track. During my recovery, when I felt most hopeless and guilt-ridden, my psychiatrist said to tell my children, 'I love you', and I continue to say this at every opportunity. Until my parents died in 2009 and 2010, I told them I loved them, too.

Sadly, my parents had no chance to understand my illness when I was a child, and upon my recovery in adulthood, my efforts to encourage family healing were disregarded. For my parents, my recovery had come too late. They had become set in their ways and family decisions were made without me.

Nevertheless, until their deaths, I continued to hope for their acceptance, understanding and inclusiveness.

After my parents died, George, who escorted me to the funerals, said as we headed home, 'Now you are free'. He said to 'focus on our children' because 'they are your family now'.

I needed time to heal, but George was right. Family is everything, and the family I created with George has been essential to my survival, recovery, and rejuvenation into a healthy self.

Ideally, having family-of-origin support when recovering from anorexia is a great help—not only for the child with the illness but also for each member of the family. Everyone benefits, and the family unit is strengthened. Recovering from anorexia without family-of-origin support is more difficult, but my experience shows it is possible if a family of choice is established. (A family of choice can comprise one or more people whom you know you can trust and who have your best interests at heart.)

My life became more stable and secure after my parents' deaths because I was no longer hoping for something that doctors had been telling me would never happen. In the years preceding their deaths, I had written many letters explaining how anorexia had affected my life and that their acceptance and understanding would help my recovery. I'd got to the point where I could say, 'June is back'. I'd got me back and wanted my family back, too. My psychiatrist offered to attend a family meeting to explain. However, all attempts to achieve inclusiveness and family healing were ignored. My long-time label as 'the problem' stuck. Doctors tried and failed for years to convince me I deserved to be treated with respect. Only upon reading my parents' will and testament could I start to believe that I was not 'the problem'.

The lack of inclusiveness in my family of origin led to a permanent rift. Doctors said I had to 'cut off' from this family because they were 'toxic' to my health.

Fifteen years on, at age 74, I love being my best friend. Catching up on life with one's healthy self after decades with an eating disorder is an ongoing adventure. Recovery has involved learning healthy self-management skills to replace the harmful, defunct eating disorder gearbox for navigating life. I often feel like the youngest in my family of George, our children, and grandchildren. They all seem wiser than me, and I respect their caring guidance. They patiently encourage me to do new things. Small but meaningful things like watching my granddaughters taking their ponies over the jumps at the equestrian centre, eating at McDonald's (my granddaughters laugh at this once-a-year outing), going on weekend 'escapes' and holidays with children and grandchildren, and watching the grandchildren play competitive sports. I continue to push aside fear barriers and embrace new experiences. Rediscovering my authentic, healthy self is a continual, joyous process.

My diary today takes the form of a 'family diary'. (In 2024, the National Library of Australia acquired my lifetime diary collection, stating it would be a valuable resource for researchers studying eating disorders.) Like my life, today's diary is an open book. It preserves thoughts and feelings shared by all family members. My family with George harbours NO secrets. Our major family values are unconditional love, respect, trust, and transparency. The loving voice of my created family has helped to silence the eating disorder, and healing continues. My love of nature remains—a pocket-front garden in a small home by the sea brings as much joy in mature age (Lachlan's gracious term for 'growing old') as the bushland and the river in my childhood.

Another layer of family for me is the eating disorder field, where advocacy participation helps me feel accepted, respected, and purposeful. I liken attendance at an eating disorder conference to receiving an injection of wellness. My lifelong love of writing, which helped me to survive and heal from my eating disorder (doctors always encouraged me to 'keep working' as a journalist because writing provided a vital if slender thread of self-belief and worthiness in an otherwise illness-ravaged mind), continues. I love helping people tell their stories because everyone's story counts. I share this passion in my local community, my website, and by writing books like this. The answers to eating disorders, I believe, are hidden in the dark corners of our minds and through storytelling, we can help researchers find those answers.

My message is that whatever form our family takes, the generation of love, trust, hope, and connection is vital for self-healing and feeling 'okay'. Food has a role, too. Today, I eat food because I love it. Three meals and three snacks daily give me the energy to embrace being a grandmother, mother, friend, and writer. Most importantly, I feel at peace within.

Key themes in my story of overcoming anorexia are threaded through the family stories in *My Family is Back*. These themes include dealing with family relationships, managing unhelpful emotions, overcoming misunderstandings and isolation, encouraging inclusiveness and transparency, and improving communication, resilience, and connection with self and family.

What you will find in this book

An eating disorder affects the child and their family, too.

My Family is Back aims to educate and inform families and health professionals about eating disorders. Families don't cause eating disorders, but together with the treatment team, their role in the recovery process is paramount. The answers to an eating disorder are found in the family, and MFT allows families the opportunity to discover these answers with others going through a similar experience. If my family had had access to MFT when I was a child, we could have found a way through the eating disorder together instead of being torn apart.

Notwithstanding growing empirical evidence for MFT, real-life stories are often a more powerful means for learning than any amount of academic text. Families identify with stories that show that people who have been ill with an eating disorder, even for a long time, can get better.

The stories of families are powerful because their experiences connect with people who are struggling today and show that there is hope for a way out of this illness. Before the family stories, Chapter 1 explains what an eating disorder is, and Chapter 2 describes how and why MFT is helpful.

Understanding eating disorders

Eating disorders can be serious and life-threatening, but this book aims to show that the prospects for recovery, especially with early intervention, can be very positive. This chapter explores some of the processes that contribute to the development of anorexia nervosa, hopefully making this puzzling illness easier to understand

Eating disorders are not a new phenomenon. Medical accounts of eating disorder symptoms have been found as early as the seventeenth century, with full descriptions of anorexia nervosa as an illness appearing towards the end of the nineteenth century. There are different types of eating disorders, but the focus of this book is primarily on anorexia nervosa. Three central features define anorexia nervosa. First, there is a substantial restriction of food intake, leading to significant weight loss or, in the case of younger children, a lack of appropriate weight gain. Second, people with anorexia nervosa have an intense fear of gaining weight or becoming fat despite being at a significantly low weight. The third feature is a disturbance in how one's body weight or shape is experienced. This chapter also discusses the frequency of eating disorders and how eating disorders develop. Contributory factors include temperament, neurobiology, genetics, and cultural and social influences. The chapter also looks at the impact of an eating disorder on the family and how the family changes and becomes intertwined with the illness.

Understanding multi-family therapy

This chapter provides an overview of some of the research that provides empirical evidence for the key role that families play in the process of recovery from an eating disorder. We start by explaining two closely linked treatments, how they developed, and their aims.

The first story describes the development of what has become known as Maudsley family therapy for anorexia nervosa. Explanations are given about the beginning of treatment, engagement in treatment, the development of the therapeutic relationship, and early weight gain. This leads to discussing how families are helped to support the young person in managing the eating disorder and exploring issues of individual and family development.

The second story explains MFT, an increasingly popular intensive treatment model. This chapter also includes details of empirical evidence for family therapy and MFT for anorexia nervosa.

Gathering the stories of families

Families in the UK, the USA, and Canada share their stories in this book. Families who had completed the MFT programme were contacted about the plan to write *My Family is Back,* and interested families contacted June to discuss their inclusion.

The families selected for interview invitations had completed the MFT programme at least two years earlier, allowing time for reflection on the process and time to consider how MFT had enriched and changed lives.

The value of this approach is like taking a telephoto lens, looking from a distance, and saying, 'Give me the whole story'.

It allows the family members to put their MFT experience into the context of their life journey.

The story-gathering process involved candid interviews with family members in their homes, both with the child who developed the eating disorder and with their parents and siblings. Their stories, which are shared through pseudonyms to provide anonymity, form 'the voice' in this book.

How to tell if your child has an eating disorder

Julian and Ivan often get calls in their clinic from parents and loved ones who are worried about their child or adolescent. This can range from very serious food restriction and binge-purge behaviours to a more subtle change in food preferences and behaviours. Not all young people (or adults) who change their eating patterns have an eating disorder. Many people decide to change what they eat for health reasons in ways that are not damaging to them physically or psychologically. Changing daily habits to improve well-being can be a really great way for people to feel better about themselves. Having said that, Julian and Ivan know from decades of research that dieting behaviour and a drive towards a 'thin ideal' are both risk factors for developing an eating disorder. So when should you worry? This chapter outlines what an eating disorder is and is not, and how to respond if you are concerned.

Navigating the search for multi-family therapy

Given eating disorder-focused family therapy is now suggested in most international guidelines, it is more likely nowadays that eating disorder clinics and professionals are aware of it and offer it. MFT, on the other hand, can be harder to access. There are several reasons for this. The most common is that a service needs to be large enough to have multiple families currently receiving treatment to participate in the groups. For sole clinicians working in private practice, unless they are a large practice specialising in eating disorders, this may not be the case. Nevertheless, many services across Australia, New Zealand, Europe, the UK, the USA, Chile, and many other countries offer MFT. This chapter provides a global appraisal of where MFT can be accessed.

Section I

Understanding eating disorders and multi-family therapy

Chapter 1

Understanding eating disorders

Most people these days have come across eating disorders, whether through personal experience, through knowing someone suffering from an eating disorder or, probably most commonly, through the portrayal of eating disorders in the media. While the media has become more positive and better informed in recent years, there is still a great deal that is inaccurate and unnecessarily negative. Many of the stories people come across are accounts of individuals with a severe and enduring form of the illness whose lives and the lives of those close to them have been blighted. These accounts are all too real and highlight the devastating effects eating disorders can have on the individual, their family, and society as a whole.

This picture, however, is not the whole story. This book aims to show another, more hopeful aspect: that the prospects for recovery, particularly in the early stages of illness, can be very positive.

It has been known for some time that children and adolescents suffering from an eating disorder are most likely to recover if the illness is recognised early and if the family is mobilised as a critical resource to help in the process of recovery. Research reviews, as well as clinical guidelines in many countries, including the UK, the USA, Australia, Germany, and others, support the view that treatment with the strongest supporting evidence is eating disorders-focused family therapy (often referred to as Maudsley family therapy or family-based

DOI: 10.4324/9781003641070-3

treatment). We will describe the treatment approach in more detail later, but the central principle is that helping the family to rediscover its strengths and resilience and (re)activating its capacity for trust and care, enables the young person to accept the help from their parents to face the overwhelming fears of eating. Early changes in eating behaviours, in turn, promote hope and self-belief that the family can work together towards recovery.

A more recent extension of this treatment approach builds and further develops these ideas by bringing together groups of families who can share their experiences and support one another during this process. The stories of families taking part in multi-family therapy for anorexia nervosa in different treatment centres around the world are at the heart of this book.

What are eating disorders?

The increased attention to eating disorders in recent years could give the impression that they are a new phenomenon brought about by the ills of modern society. This is far from the case, however, with descriptions of anorexia nervosa dating back to the late 19th century (Gull, 1874; Lasègue, 1873) and medical accounts of apparently similar conditions found as early as the 17th and 18th centuries (Kagawa, 1768; Morton, 1694). Other forms of eating disorders, such as bulimia nervosa, binge eating disorder, or avoidant/restrictive food intake disorder (ARFID), have emerged more recently. However, their descriptions in the medical literature and inclusion in diagnostic manuals were generally preceded by other, much earlier accounts that, in hindsight, were probably descriptions of the same conditions. Thus, for instance, Gerald Russell, in his discussion of the history of bulimia nervosa (Russell, 2004), describes three cases from the late 19th century and the first half of the 20th century reported by Pierre Janet, Ludwig Binswanger and Moshe Wulff as possible cases of bulimia nervosa. So, eating disorders are not a new phenomenon, but their presentation has changed over the years.

Perhaps the most striking change over time is that the drive for thinness, central to our current understanding of eating disorders, does not feature in early accounts of anorexia nervosa (Russell, 1995). Until relatively recently, the same was true of accounts of eating disorders from non-Western countries (Lee, 2001; Nasser, 2003; Suematsu et al., 1985). This suggests that cultural factors have shaped the presentation of eating disorders even though they may not be their direct cause. The second major change is the considerable broadening of the definition of what constitutes an eating disorder, including those with a binge eating presentation (bulimia nervosa, binge/purge anorexia nervosa, and binge eating disorder) since the 1980s. The third key change is the growing recognition that eating disorders afflict a much more diverse population than was previously thought, whether in terms of age, gender, sexual orientation or gender identity, race, ethnicity, or social class. The evidence shows clearly that eating disorders do not discriminate and affect all people (Bryant-Waugh & Baudinet, 2025).

Our description of eating disorders will focus primarily on anorexia nervosa, as this is central to the theme of this book. We will briefly describe two of the other main eating disorder subgroups, bulimia nervosa and ARFID. A full description of all the eating disorder subcategories and their current formal diagnostic criteria can be found in Chapter 24.

Fundamental to all eating disorders is a core disturbance of eating behaviours that significantly impacts physical and psychological well-being, as well as psychosocial functioning. Other features vary between the eating disorder subgroups, and a significant number of individuals may move between these diagnoses over time.

Anorexia nervosa is probably the best known and, together with bulimia nervosa, is the most researched eating disorder. Three central features define anorexia nervosa. First, there is a substantial restriction of food intake leading to significant weight loss or, in the case of younger children, lack of appropriate weight gain. Second, people with anorexia nervosa have an intense fear of gaining weight or becoming fat despite being at a significantly low weight. The third feature is a disturbance in the way in which one's body weight or shape is experienced. There is an undue influence on the individual's self-evaluation or persistent lack of recognition of the seriousness of current low weight.

Some people suffering from anorexia nervosa also binge and/or use compensatory behaviours such as vomiting or laxatives, or exercise compulsively. Anorexia nervosa can vary considerably in its presentation. 'Atypical' (the word used in diagnostic manuals) presentations include individuals who are not underweight relative to norms based on age, sex, and height, even though they have lost a significant amount of weight. Like other individuals with anorexia nervosa, they have an intense preoccupation and fear of being fat and a body image disturbance that impacts their sense of self.

Anorexia nervosa has a profound impact on the individual, their family, and wider society. The effects are both psychological and physical, leading to significant impairment, reduced quality of life as well as high levels of distress in family and other social relationships (Herpertz-Dahlmann et al., 2015). Eating disorders can have a profound effect on physical well-being, resulting in acute medical difficulties that can be life-threatening and, in some cases, may require inpatient treatment. Anorexia nervosa has the highest mortality rate of any psychiatric illness (Miskovic-Wheatley et al., 2023) and, without effective treatment, may take on a persistent and enduring course with severe impacts on physical and psychological health and psychosocial functioning (Wonderlich et al., 2020).

Bulimia nervosa is primarily characterised by recurrent episodes of binge eating, which is defined as periods of eating very large amounts of food in a short period of time and a subjective sense of a loss of control. This is coupled with compensatory behaviours designed to control weight, most commonly vomiting, laxative use, and periods of food restriction. People diagnosed with bulimia nervosa have a weight within the normal range or are at a higher weight. As with anorexia nervosa, those with bulimia nervosa are troubled by a fear of gaining weight and an overvaluation of the role that body shape or weight has on their sense of self-worth.

Binge eating disorder and ARFID are newer diagnoses and were formally recognised only in the most recent edition of the *Diagnostic and Statistical Manual of Mental Disorders* (*DSM-5*) (American Psychiatric Association, 2013) and the World Health Organization's *International Classification of Diseases* (ICD)-11 (World Health Organization, 2019).

Binge eating disorder shares some of the same features with bulimia nervosa in that central to the diagnosis are episodes of binge eating, a sense of loss of control over eating, and marked distress and feelings of guilt and shame about the episodes of binge eating. Unlike in individuals with bulimia nervosa, the binge eating is not associated with the regular use of inappropriate compensatory behaviours such as self-induced vomiting, laxative misuse, or excessive exercise.

ARFID is a heterogeneous group of eating disorders that often occurs in younger children but is also found in all age groups. ARFID is diagnosed when someone is significantly restricting their overall amount of food and/or the range of foods, but (unlike in anorexia nervosa), this is not due to body image disturbance or fear of weight gain. The food restriction is at a level that leads to nutritional and/or psychosocial impairment. The eating disturbances in ARFID can result from extreme disinterest in food, extreme avoidance of food due to its sensory qualities, significant fear of the consequences of eating (e.g. choking), or a varying combination of these factors. Importantly, there must also be an absence of medical or psychiatric illness that might explain the food avoidance and lack of weight gain or failure to thrive.

How common are eating disorders?

Prevalence[1] rate estimates of eating disorders vary depending on the country and age range studied. A Global Burden of Disease study estimated that 55.5 million people were suffering from an eating disorder in 2019 (Santomauro et al., 2021). Lifetime prevalence of anorexia nervosa has been estimated to be as high as 4 per cent among women and 0.3 per cent among men (van Eeden et al., 2021). Anorexia nervosa occurs more frequently in women than in men. Until relatively recently, the literature commonly reported that eating disorders in men account for no more than 10 per cent of those afflicted by the illness. More recent studies show that these estimates may miss a significant proportion of male sufferers, with some studies suggesting that as many as a third of those with an eating disorder are male (Murray et al., 2017; Sweeting et al., 2015). There is also emerging evidence that among individuals who identify as transgender or gender diverse, the lifetime prevalence of eating disorders is high (above 4–5 per cent) (Coelho et al., 2019).

Bulimia nervosa has a similar prevalence to anorexia nervosa, with lifetime prevalence estimated at 3 per cent of women and 1 per cent of men (van Eeden et al., 2021). Given binge eating disorder and ARFID have only recently been included in diagnostic manuals, their prevalence is less well studied. For the years 2018–2020, the prevalence of binge eating disorder was estimated at up to 1.8 per cent in adult women and 0.7 per cent in adult men (Giel et al., 2022). For ARFID, a large population-based survey in Australia estimated the prevalence of ARFID at 0.3 per cent of the general population (Hay et al., 2017). A Swiss study of 1,444 children aged 8–13 found that 3.2 per cent reported features of ARFID (Kurz et al., 2015).

How do eating disorders develop?

Temperament, neurobiology, genetics

Eating disorders are far from fully understood. However, a growing body of literature about the range of predisposing and maintaining factors associated with eating disorders points to a complex interplay between neurobiological and psychological vulnerabilities, environmental factors (Frank, Shott et al., 2019), and the important role played by genetics and gene-environment interactions (Bulik et al., 2019).

Those who go on to develop anorexia nervosa tend to have temperamental and personality traits such as a tendency towards being anxious, having low tolerance of uncertainty, having a tendency towards perfectionism, possessing relatively inflexible thinking, and demonstrating strong attention to detail (Frank, Shott et al., 2019). Other personality or temperamental factors associated with anorexia nervosa include high sensitivity to social threats, low sensitivity to rewards, and high levels of harm avoidance (Kaye et al., 2013). Brain imaging studies of individuals who have developed anorexia nervosa indicate that the temperamental and personality predispositions are associated with differences in brain structures and brain mechanisms. Some of these appear to operate from the early stages of the development of the illness. Others may evolve or become stronger as a response to malnourishment and starvation.

There is also evidence that many of the temperamental predispositions, such as a tendency towards anxiety, low tolerance of uncertainty, or a tendency towards perfectionism, become stronger with being malnourished. Indeed, much of the behaviour and cognitions families may observe in their child who has developed anorexia nervosa are a direct consequence of starvation (Kalm & Semba, 2005).

How the neurobiological processes interact with cognitive experiences and emotions to shape the development of anorexia nervosa in a particular individual is complex and will, of course, vary in detail between individuals. The following is an example of a mechanism that has been suggested as a common process underpinning the development of anorexia nervosa (Frank, DeGuzman et al., 2019). The initial trigger of the process is weight loss, most often due to a conscious decision to eat more healthily, to get fit or thinner, or to feel better about oneself. Sometimes, the weight loss is not deliberate but due to, for example, a physical illness, a side effect of medication, or perhaps to wearing braces that make eating more difficult. While this initial weight loss or dieting is not the 'cause' of the eating disorder, it can trigger specific neurobiological responses that contribute to the development of the illness.

In general, food restriction and weight loss will lead to endocrine changes that signal the need to seek food and eat. In most individuals, this is accompanied by psychological changes that make lack of eating unpleasant, while the presence of food is rewarding and pleasurable. Those who develop anorexia nervosa often report a different response to food, which may be inherently less rewarding for them, whereas food restriction may have the effect of blunting levels of anxiety. The response to weight loss may reinforce food restriction psychologically in two ways that fit the temperamental predispositions.

First, the high harm avoidance trait will strengthen behaviours that reduce anxiety, and second, perfectionist traits will reinforce dieting behaviour through a sense of achievement of meeting the goal of successful dieting. However, this top-down conscious motivation not to eat comes into conflict with the biological feedback mechanism that signals the need to eat through changes in gut hormones and neurotransmitters. This conflict results in raised levels of anxiety, which may be experienced as a fear of losing control and further reinforces the conscious motivation not to eat. The continued weight loss leads to additional changes at the brain level that result in low mood and/or unpredictable mood swings. There are also increased difficulties in recognising one's own or others' emotions, leading to social isolation and feeling misunderstood.

As the illness progresses, the vicious cycle of trying to relieve the distress by purposefully avoiding food further drives the anxiety that may lead to angry outbursts which are followed by profound feelings of shame and guilt. The neurobiological drivers of the eating disorder and the effects of starvation can become all-pervasive, making the young person feel that nothing beyond their immediate experience exists and making it impossible to believe that anything can change. The progress of the illness and the ongoing effects of starvation continue to reinforce the persistent preoccupation with thoughts of food and body shape, distorted and overvalued perception of body size, and fear of losing control. For many, there is a sense of being taken over by the illness and a loss of sense of identity outside of the illness.

There are several important caveats. First, anorexia nervosa is not an inherited illness in the sense of a specific gene causing it. What is inherited is a vulnerability to develop the illness. There is no known single factor (genetic or environmental) that is necessary or sufficient to cause anorexia nervosa (Bulik et al., 2019). Second, the personality and temperamental traits that can lead to vulnerability are also potential strengths, and part of the process of recovering from anorexia nervosa is to help the person to (re)discover and make best use of their temperamental predispositions (Hower et al., 2021).

The role of culture and social factors in eating disorders

Neurobiology and genetics clearly have a powerful role in the development of eating disorders. However, important social and cultural factors are also at play at individual and societal levels. Some authors have historically emphasised the role of social factors in eating disorders to the extent of defining eating disorders as culture-bound syndromes or ethnic disorders (Gordon, 1990). This was based on the observed higher prevalence of anorexia nervosa in Western societies with greater representation in women of higher socio-economic status and the apparent rise in the incidence of anorexia nervosa in the second half of the 20th century, coinciding with changes in socially determined perceptions of ideal body size and thinness (Russell, 1995). More recent research has highlighted examples of the incidence of eating disorders rising in societies undergoing rapid cultural change and adopting a more Western-type lifestyle (Becker et al., 2011; Hoek et al., 2005; Pavlova et al., 2010).

It is tempting to conclude that social changes and an increasing pressure on women to be thin and conform to an idealised body shape in Western cultures have a key causal role in the development of an eating disorder. There are several reasons, however, why we need to consider in more complex ways the role that social and cultural factors play. First, the historical data and accounts of eating disorders in different cultures mentioned earlier, showing the variability in presentation over time and across cultures, do not support the notion that eating disorders are the product of Western societal pressure to be thin.

An intense fear of being fat is, of course, a key feature of current clinical accounts of most eating disorders and is typically central to how individual sufferers themselves describe what troubles them. However, this drive for thinness or fear of fatness was not part of early accounts of eating disorders and, even 20–30 years ago, seemed largely absent in description of eating disorders in non-Western countries (Lee, 2001; Nasser, 2003; Suematsu et al., 1985). This suggests that the notion of 'Westernisation' as an explanation for the rise in eating disorders is, at best, a gross oversimplification and that social and cultural factors may not necessarily be the cause of eating disorders but rather that they shape their presentation.

Perhaps the main point here concerns the importance of differentiating between the broader lessons about the role of culture drawn from research and how this applies to specific individuals and families. Unlike the researcher who strives for precision, clarity in classification, and generalisability, the clinician must be mindful of how a family's specific cultural and ethnic context shapes its experiences and how experiences of cultural change, migration, deprivation, or oppression might alter this. These elements provide the frame for understanding the uniqueness of the family's own understandings and beliefs and how they shape narratives of despair or hope.

Eating disorders and the family

Accounts of families of patients with anorexia nervosa go back to the earliest descriptions of the illness at the end of the 19th century. For instance, Lasègue (1873) emphasised the importance of considering the preoccupations of the patient's relatives and provided a detailed characterisation of family responses to the illness and interactions between the patients and their families (Vandereycken & Deth, 1990). This is perhaps the clearest early account of the family response to illness symptoms and behaviours, and the patient's response, in turn, to the family's emotional reaction, and how this can lead to fixed and difficult-to-change patterns of interaction in the family.

Notwithstanding Lasègue's perceptiveness of the bidirectional nature of these patterns and the way this trapped and disabled the family, he is more often cited for his recommendation to isolate the patient from the parents, a view shared by many of his contemporaries such as Gull (1874), who described parents as 'generally the worst attenders', or Charcot (1889), who viewed parents as 'particularly pernicious'.

The view of the family as dysfunctional is also found in the writings of influential psychodynamic authors (Bruch, 1973; Sours, 1980; Waller et al., 1940), who described the family context as part of the aetiology of anorexia nervosa. One of the most compelling accounts was Bruch's (1973) description of the impact of a mother's strong need to look after her child, leading her to anticipate and meet the child's needs before the infant could experience them herself. Bruch postulated that this form of care would result in a sense of overdependence and pervasive ineffectiveness in the child. Bruch believed that the exploration of the underlying family problems provided both part of the explanation of why someone developed an eating disorder as well as an element of what had to be resolved for treatment to be successful. Bruch was highly critical of the earlier psychodynamic sexual drive explanations, emphasising instead the role of early mother-infant attachment. Often overlooked, in many ways, was Bruch's most important contribution, stressing the importance of combining psychological intervention with restoring nutrition.

In the 1970s, the newly developing field of family therapy started applying the new family systems conceptualisations to eating disorders and actively involving families in the treatment of their child's illness (Minuchin et al., 1975; Selvini Palazzoli, 1974). These early family therapy models of anorexia nervosa (e.g. Minuchin and colleagues' notion of the 'Psychosomatic Family'—Minuchin et al., 1978) did not suggest (as is sometimes claimed) that the family is the cause of the eating disorder, but rather that a complex and evolving interaction between a vulnerability in the child and a particular type of family constellation together results in the development of an eating disorder.

Minuchin et al. (1975) argued that a specific type of family organisation and particular transactional style were closely related to the development and maintenance of the psychosomatic syndrome and that, in turn, the child's symptoms had a role in maintaining the stability of the family system. Treatment in this paradigm aimed to disrupt the putative link between the symptoms and the ongoing dysfunctional family transactions that maintained it. The weakness of Minuchin's model was that the empirical data did not support the notion that a specific family constellation or a specific type of family functioning could be linked with the development of anorexia nervosa (Dare et al., 1994; Eisler, 1993; 2005; Kog et al., 1989; Konstantellou et al., 2011). This approach added a focus on the here and now, an important shift in thinking that remains an integral part of current understandings of family-focused treatments.

Other family therapy authors went a step further, explicitly arguing that the notion of 'cause' is unhelpful (Hoffman, 1985). They posited that the key issue (regardless of how the problem developed) is that the family has become trapped in a pattern of trying to deal with the problem in ways that may become part of what maintains the problem (Haley, 1980).

This shift away from the view that families create the problem to an understanding that the family dynamics that clinicians observe when they meet the family are better understood as a response of the family trying to cope with a distressing, potentially life-threatening illness (Eisler, 2005), has been fundamental. We will describe later how this shift has led to a more collaborative approach to working with families, focusing on family strengths and resilience. Put simply, the family became a treatment resource rather than a problem in need of treatment.

The impact of an eating disorder on the family and family reorganisation around the illness

How families respond when faced with what are generally bewildering signs that their child is developing a potentially major illness with both serious psychological and physical symptoms will vary from family to family. How families adjust to the developing illness will vary depending on the nature of their pre-existing family relationships, their child's age and developmental stage, the characteristics of individual family members, and their broader social context. As the illness takes hold, however, and the distress of the individual with the eating disorder, as well as that of the family, increases, fairly predictable patterns will often emerge as the eating disorder becomes the central focus of family life (Cottee-Lane et al., 2004; Eisler, 2005).

Typically, there will be interactive cycles of parental and child anxiety and distress, sometimes splitting the parents. Frequently, feelings of guilt and blame will emerge, which may be overt or, in some families, more covert. These may be accompanied by critical or angry outbursts followed by feelings of remorse and further distress. Inevitably, families feel overwhelmed, helpless, and hopeless and have a sense of not being in control (Voriadaki et al., 2015).

It is important to recognise how the (completely understandable and appropriate) high levels of concern and anxiety and of feeling overwhelmed can have a disabling effect on the family. On one hand, it feeds into the parents' sense of helplessness. On the other hand, the raised levels of anxiety make it more difficult for the parents to mentalise (Ierardi et al., 2022), that is, put themselves in their child's shoes, resulting in the child feeling misunderstood and distrusting their parents. The resulting mistrust is likely to increase tension in the family and further raise levels of anxiety, creating a vicious circle. There are two further likely consequences of this evolving dynamic. First, how the family members interact becomes increasingly constrained, with everyone fearful of doing anything outside their narrow routine. Families often feel stuck, recognising that what they are doing is not working, but avoid changing their behaviour 'in case it makes things worse'. They may also express that time has reached a standstill (Cottee-Lane et al., 2004).

The second consequence is that important aspects of the usual way a family is organised or the ways in which they tend to interact become amplified. For instance, in many families, one parent has a closer relationship with the children than the other parent. This may change over time as the children grow older, and their needs change. Each parent will meet these needs in different ways. In the face of needing to deal with a life-threatening illness, the 'closer' parent may be drawn increasingly close, while the other parent may become less involved and more distant. These positions are likely to be perceived differently by individual family members. Thus, the more involved parent (often, but by no means always, the mother) may feel unsupported, but at the same time is reluctant to encourage her partner to get more involved as he 'does not understand' and could make things worse.

The less involved parent (e.g. the father) may feel that it would be better if the parents, together, took a more assertive stance at mealtimes. However, the father does not want to undermine his wife and perhaps stays away from mealtimes to avoid conflicts, unaware that his child sees this as him 'not caring'. In other families (more commonly where a young person presents with binge/purge symptoms and/or in families of older patients with a more protracted illness), there may be increased levels of negativity in the family relationships with high levels of criticism or hostility (Anastasiadou et al., 2014; Zabala et al., 2009).

In each family, the patterns that evolve around the eating difficulties will be specific to this family. Over time, the family pattern becomes more strongly intertwined with the illness, contributing to each family's perception that they are the problem.

Understandably, as the whole system of care becomes increasingly distressed, resources reduce, and the family becomes reorganised around the illness, with the eating disorder becoming ever more central to family life (Eisler, 2005). The illness shapes the relationships in the family, but its course is also shaped by how the family has changed. Any problems that may have been in the family before the illness are likely to be magnified. For example, suppose there are stresses or tension in the couple's relationship. In that case, these may become more visible, and it is easy to conclude that marriage is where the 'real' problem lies, and the eating problem somehow keeps the family together. In many instances, we observe only the normal family life-cycle adjustment process made more visible (to an outside observer and the family) by a life-threatening problem.

It is not unusual for parents whose children are at the point of growing up and leaving home to reflect on their relationship as a couple. It is a normal part of the family life-cycle transition. Imagine how different this is likely to feel when this occurs in the context of worries about a child developing a serious mental health problem. The parents may start questioning whether their relationship has 'caused' their child's problem, blaming themselves or each other. This is likely to increase the tension in the family and increase the distance between the couple. If marital discord clearly predates the onset of the eating disorder, the temptation to blame this for the eating disorder is greater but equally mistaken.

This brings us full circle to the earlier discussion about the role of neurobiology and genetic predispositions in the development of anorexia nervosa. It is normal to want to make sense of what is happening. We build a picture from what we experience, what we observe around us, what we have experienced in the past, and from confirmation (or lack of confirmation) of our expectation of what happens next. The 'neurobiology story' of anorexia nervosa illustrates that a lot of what determines what happens is outside of our consciousness. The way we make sense of things can become misleading. It is a bit like trying to complete a complicated jigsaw puzzle just by looking at the picture and taking no notice of the shape of individual pieces. Once we focus on a piece of the picture that 'looks right' (even though the pieces do not fit), we may start undoing other parts of the jigsaw to complete the picture.

In the family context, various narratives will evolve over time and may attach multiple meanings to the same events. When a family faces a difficult-to-understand problem, these narratives can quickly become disabling, and efforts to help may be experienced differently from how they were intended. For example, trying to help may be experienced as controlling, while backing off may feel like a lack of care.

Note

1 Prevalence is the number of cases present in a particular population, while incidence refers to the number of new cases that develop over a specified time (e.g. annual incidence)

References

American Psychiatric Association (APA). (2013). *The Diagnostic and Statistical Manual of Mental Disorders*, 5th Edition. Arlington: American Psychiatric Publishing.

Anastasiadou, D., Medina-Pradas, C., Sepulveda, A. R., & Treasure, J. (2014). A systematic review of family caregiving in eating disorders. *Eating Behaviors*, *15*(3), 464–477. https://doi.org/10.1016/j.eatbeh.2014.06.001

Becker, A. E., Fay, K. E., Agnew-Blais, J., Khan, A. N., Striegel-Moore, R. H., & Gilman, S. E. (2011). Social network media exposure and adolescent eating pathology in Fiji. *British Journal of Psychiatry*, *198*(1), 43–50. https://doi.org/10.1192/bjp.bp.110.078675

Bruch, H. (1973). *Eating disorders: Obesity, anorexia nervosa, and the person within.* New York: Basic Books.

Bryant-Waugh, R., & Baudinet, J. (2025, June). Feeding and eating disorders. In A. Thapar, D. Pineda, S. Cortese, C. Creswell, T. Ford, J. F. Leckman, & A. Stringaris (Eds.), *Rutter's child and adolescent psychiatry* (7th edition). London: Wiley-Blackwell.

Bulik, C. M., Flatt, R., Abbaspour, A., & Carroll, I. (2019). Reconceptualizing anorexia nervosa. *Psychiatry and Clinical Neurosciences*, *73*(9), 518–525. https://doi.org/10.1111/pcn.12857

Charcot, J. M. (1889). *Clinical lectures on the diseases of the nervous system*. London: New Sydenham Society.

Coelho, J. S., Suen, J., Clark, B. A., Marshall, S. K., Geller, J., & Lam, P.-Y. (2019). Eating disorder diagnoses and symptom presentation in transgender youth: A scoping review. *Current Psychiatry Reports*, *21*(11), 107. https://doi.org/10.1007/s11920-019-1097-x

Cottee-Lane, D., Pistrang, N., & Bryant-Waugh, R. (2004). Childhood onset anorexia nervosa: The experience of parents. *European Eating Disorders Review, 12*(3), 169–177. https://doi.org/10.1002/erv.560

Dare, C., Le Grange, D., Eisler, I., & Rutherford, J. (1994). Redefining the psychosomatic family. *International Journal of Eating Disorders,* 16, 211-225. https://doi.org/10.1002/1098-108x(1994 11)16:3<211::aid-eat2260160302>3.0.co;2-x

Eisler. I. (1993). Families, family therapy and psychosomatic illness. In S. Moorey & M. Hodes (Eds.) *Psychological Treatments in Human Disease and Illness.* London: Gaskill.

Eisler, I. (2005). The empirical and theoretical base of family therapy and multiple family day therapy for adolescent anorexia nervosa. *Journal of Family Therapy, 27*(2), 104–131. https://doi.org/10.1111/j.1467-6427.2005.00303.x

Frank, G. K. W., DeGuzman, M. C., & Shott, M. E. (2019). Motivation to eat and not to eat – The psycho-biological conflict in anorexia nervosa. *Physiology & Behavior, 206,* 185–190. https://doi.org/10.1016/j.physbeh.2019.04.007

Frank, G. K. W., Shott, M. E., & DeGuzman, M. C. (2019). The neurobiology of eating disorders. *Child and Adolescent Psychiatric Clinics of North America, 28*(4), 629–640. https://doi.org/10.1016/j.chc.2019.05.007

Giel, K. E., Bulik, C. M., Fernandez-Aranda, F., Hay, P., Keski-Rahkonen, A., Schag, K., Schmidt, U., & Zipfel, S. (2022). Binge eating disorder. *Nature Reviews Disease Primers, 8*(1), 16. https://doi.org/10.1038/s41572-022-00344-y

Gordon, R. A. (1990). *Anorexia and bulimia: Anatomy of a social epidemic.* Cambridge, Mass: Blackwell.

Gull, W. W. (1874). Anorexia nervosa (apepsia hysterica, anorexia hysterica). *Transactions of the Clinical Society of London, 7,* 22–22.

Haley, J. (1980). *Leaving home: The therapy of young disturbed people.* New York, NY: McGraw Hill.

Hay, P., Mitchison, D., Collado, A. E. L., González-Chica, D. A., Stocks, N., & Touyz, S. (2017). Burden and health-related quality of life of eating disorders, including Avoidant/Restrictive Food Intake Disorder (ARFID), in the Australian population. *Journal of Eating Disorders, 5*(1), 21. https://doi.org/10.1186/s40337-017-0149-z

Herpertz-Dahlmann, B., Dempfle, A., Konrad, K., Klasen, F., Ravens-Sieberer, U., & The BELLA study group. (2015). Eating disorder symptoms do not just disappear: The implications of adolescent eating-disordered behaviour for body weight and mental health in young adulthood. *European Child & Adolescent Psychiatry, 24*(6), 675–684. https://doi.org/10.1007/s00787-014-0610-3

Hoek, H. W., Van Harten, P. N., Hermans, K. M. E., Katzman, M. A., Matroos, G. E., & Susser, E. S. (2005). The incidence of anorexia nervosa on Curaçao. *American Journal of Psychiatry, 162*(4), 748–752. https://doi.org/10.1176/appi.ajp.162.4.748

Hoffman, L. (1985). Beyond power and control: Toward a "second order" family systems therapy. *Family Systems Medicine, 3*(4), 381–396. https://doi.org/10.1037/h0089674

Hower, H., Reilly, E. E., Wierenga, C. E., & Kaye, W. H. (2021). Last word: A call to view temperamental traits as dual vulnerabilities and strengths in anorexia nervosa. *Eating Disorders, 29*(2), 151–160. https://doi.org/10.1080/10640266.2021.1883882

Ierardi, E., Dascalu, A., Shai, D., Spencer, R., & Riva Crugnola, C. (2022). Parental embodied mentalizing: Associations with maternal depression, anxiety, verbal mentalizing, and maternal styles of interaction. *Journal of Affective Disorders, 311*, 472–478. https://doi.org/10.1016/j.jad.2022.05.105

Kagawa, S. (1768). In: Ippondo Koyo Igen, Publisher Unknown. Quoted in Nogami, Y., 1997. Eating disorders in Japan: A review of the literature. *Psychiatry and Clinical Neurosciences, 51*, 339–346.

Kalm, L. M., & Semba, R. D. (2005). They starved so that others be better fed: Remembering Ancel Keys and the Minnesota experiment. *The Journal of Nutrition, 135*(6), 1347–1352. https://doi.org/10.1093/jn/135.6.1347

Kaye, W. H., Wierenga, C. E., Bailer, U. F., Simmons, A. N., & Bischoff-Grethe, A. (2013). Nothing tastes as good as skinny feels: The neurobiology of anorexia nervosa. *Trends in Neurosciences, 36*(2), 110–120. https://doi.org/10.1016/j.tins.2013.01.003

Kog, E., & Vandereycken, W. (1989). Family interaction in eating disorder patients and normal controls. *International Journal of Eating Disorders, 8*(1), 11–23. https://doi.org/10.1002/1098-108X(199901)8:1<11::AID-EAT2260080103>3.0.CO;2-1

Konstantellou, A., Campbell, M., & Eisler, I. (2011). The family context: Cause, effect or resource? In J. Alexander & J. Treasure (Eds.), *A collaborative approach to eating disorders* (pp. 5–18). London, UK: Routledge.

Kurz, S., van Dyck, Z., Dremmel, D., Munsch, S., & Hilbert, A. (2015). Early-onset restrictive eating disturbances in primary school boys and girls. *European Child & Adolescent Psychiatry*, *24*(7), 779–785. https://doi.org/10.1007/s00787-014-0622-z

Lasègue, C. (1873). On hysterical anorexia. Medical times gazette, (6 September), 265-266; (27 September), 367–369 from the original French: Lasègue, C. (1873) De l'anorexie hysterique. *Archives Générale de Médicine*, *21*, 385–403.

Lee, S. (2001). Fat phobia in anorexia nervosa: Whose obsession is it. In M. Nasser, M. A. Katzman, & R. A. Gordon (Eds.), *Eating disorders and cultures in transition* (pp. 40–54). Hove, UK: Brunner and Routledge.

Minuchin, S. Baker, L., Rosman, B. L., Liebman, R., Milman, L., & Todd, T. C. (1975). A conceptual model of psychosomatic illness in children: Family organization and family therapy. *Archives of General Psychiatry*, *32*(8), 1031. https://doi.org/10.1001/archp syc.1975.01760260095008

Minuchin, S., Rosman, B., & Baker, L. (1978). *Psychosomatic families: Anorexia nervosa in context*. Cambridge, MA: Harvard University Press.

Miskovic-Wheatley, J., Bryant, E., Ong, S. H., Vatter, S., Le, A., National Eating Disorder Research Consortium, Aouad, P., Barakat, S., Boakes, R., Brennan, L., Bryant, E., Byrne, S., Caldwell, B., Calvert, S., Carroll, B., Castle, D., Caterson, I., Chelius, B., Chiem, L., … Maguire, S. (2023). Eating disorder outcomes: Findings from a rapid review of over a decade of research. *Journal of Eating Disorders*, *11*(1), 85. https://doi.org/10.1186/s40337-023-00801-3

Morton, R. (1694). *Phthisiologia: Or, a treatise of consumptions*. London, UK: Smith and Walford.

Murray, S. B., Nagata, J. M., Griffiths, S., Calzo, J. P., Brown, T. A., Mitchison, D., Blashill, A. J., & Mond, J. M. (2017). The enigma of male eating disorders: A critical review and synthesis. *Clinical Psychology Review*, *57*, 1–11. https://doi.org/10.1016/j.cpr.2017.08.001

Nasser, M. (2003). *Culture and weight consciousness*. London, UK: Routledge.

Pavlova, B., Uher, R., Dragomirecka, E., & Papezova, H. (2010). Trends in hospital admissions for eating disorders in a country undergoing a socio-cultural transition, the Czech Republic 1981–2005. *Social Psychiatry and Psychiatric Epidemiology, 45*(5), 541–550. https://doi.org/10.1007/s00127-009-0092-7

Russell, G. F. M. (1995). Anorexia nervosa through time. In G. Szmukler, C. Dare, & J. Treasure (Eds.), *Eating disorders: Theory, treatment and research* (pp. 5–17). Chichester, UK: Wiley.

Russell, G. F. M. (2004). Thoughts on the 25th anniversary of bulimia nervosa. *European Eating Disorders Review, 12*(3), 139–152. https://doi.org/10.1002/erv.575

Santomauro, D. F., Melen, S., Mitchison, D., Vos, T., Whiteford, H., & Ferrari, A. J. (2021). The hidden burden of eating disorders: An extension of estimates from the Global Burden of Disease Study 2019. *The Lancet Psychiatry, 8*(4), 320–328. https://doi.org/10.1016/S2215-0366(21)00040-7

Selvini Palazzoli, M. (1974). *Self-starvation: From the intrapsychic to the transpersonal approach to anorexia nervosa*. London, UK: Human Context Books.

Sours, J. A. (1980). *Starving to death in a sea of objects*. New York: Aronson.

Suematsu, H., Ishikawa, H., Kuboki, T., & Ito, T. (1985). Statistical studies on anorexia nervosa in Japan: Detailed clinical data on 1,011 patients. *Psychotherapy and Psychosomatics, 43*(2), 96–103.

Sweeting, H., Walker, L., MacLean, A., Patterson, C., & Hunt, K. (2015). Prevalence of eating disorders in males: A review of rates reported in academic research and UK mass media. *International Journal of Men's Health, 14*(2), 1–8.

van Eeden, A. E., van Hoeken, D., & Hoek, H. W. (2021). Incidence, prevalence and mortality of anorexia nervosa and bulimia nervosa. *Current Opinion in Psychiatry, 34*(6), 515–524. https://doi.org/10.1097/YCO.0000000000000739

Vandereycken, W., & Deth, R. V. (1990). A tribute to Lasègue's description of anorexia nervosa (1873), with completion of its English translation. *British Journal of Psychiatry, 157*(6), 902–908. https://doi.org/10.1192/bjp.157.6.902

Voriadaki, T., Simic, M., Espie, J., & Eisler, I. (2015). Intensive multi-family therapy for adolescent anorexia nervosa: Adolescents' and parents' day-to-day experiences. *Journal of Family Therapy*, *37*(1), 5–23. https://doi.org/10.1111/1467-6427.12067

Waller, J. V., Kaufman, R. M., & Deutsch, F. (1940). Anorexia nervosa: A psychosomatic entity. *Psychosomatic Medicine*, *2*(1), 3–16.

Wonderlich, S. A., Bulik, C. M., Schmidt, U., Steiger, H., & Hoek, H. W. (2020). Severe and enduring anorexia nervosa: Update and observations about the current clinical reality. *International Journal of Eating Disorders*, *53*(8), 1303–1312. https://doi.org/10.1002/eat.23283

World Health Organization. (2019). *ICD-11: International classification of diseases (11th revision)*. https://icd.who.int/

Zabala, M. J., Macdonald, P., & Treasure, J. (2009). Appraisal of caregiving burden, expressed emotion and psychological distress in families of people with eating disorders: A systematic review. *European Eating Disorders Review*, *17*(5), 338–349. https://doi.org/10.1002/erv.925

Chapter 2

Understanding multi-family therapy

Why families are key in overcoming anorexia nervosa

So far, we have described some of the processes that can contribute to or shape the development of anorexia nervosa. We hope this description will have helped to make this puzzling illness easier to understand. We have also tried to show how these processes impact the family in ways that often make the family feel helpless and unable to see a way forward. However, as we said in our introduction, the key aim of this book is to provide a more hopeful story, which demonstrates that with timely treatment, the prospects for recovery from anorexia nervosa are good and that families, far from being the source of the illness, have a key role in overcoming it.

We will start by providing an account of two closely linked family-oriented treatments, how they developed, and their aims. The first account is the development of what has become known as Maudsley family therapy for anorexia nervosa. The second, central to this book, is the closely related multi-family therapy for anorexia nervosa (MFT-AN). We will then summarise some major research findings that provide empirical evidence for our claims.

DOI: 10.4324/9781003641070-4

Family interventions for eating disorders

Development of the Maudsley approach

Maudsley family therapy for anorexia nervosa was developed in the early 1980s as part of a clinical research programme at the Maudsley Hospital/Institute of Psychiatry in London, evaluating family therapy for eating disorders through a series of clinical research trials. The treatment model used in these studies built on the previous family therapy approaches discussed in Chapter 1 but introduced a major conceptual shift. Earlier family therapy models for anorexia nervosa assumed that the disorder arose in the context of a specific type of family dynamics, such as Minuchin and colleagues' psychosomatic family' (Minuchin et al., 1978), in which the anorexic behaviours were seen as an expression of underlying interpersonal family conflicts. The treatment, therefore, was thought to work by modifying the problematic family interaction patterns. The theoretical accounts of these putative family dynamics were derived from clinical observations, but while compelling, the clinical accounts were not supported by empirical evidence (Eisler, 1995). This raised major questions about the nature of the process of change underpinning family therapy.

The key shift introduced by the Maudsley team was the notion that the family dynamics and patterns of family interaction observed by clinicians were largely the result of the way the family had changed in response to a potentially life-threatening illness (Eisler, 2005) rather than a family system that was expressing its 'dysfunction' through the anorexic behaviour of one of its members.

The central aim of the therapy, therefore, moved away from the notion of modifying a dysfunctional family system to viewing the family as a resource where parents were mobilised to help overcome the child's illness. While many of the interventions were superficially similar to those used in earlier models, their aim was fundamentally different. For example, encouraging parents to unite and work together was not primarily aimed at restoring normative family functioning but rather at helping the parents rediscover their sense of agency so they could more effectively support the process of recovery in their child. In the first instance, this requires a change in the child's eating behaviours to enable the restoration of nutrition and reverse the physical and psychological effects of starvation that had become part of the patterns which were maintaining the illness. This conceptual shift enabled a more collaborative, less blaming approach in keeping with other contemporaneous developments in family therapy (e.g. Hoffman, 1985).

Since the early Maudsley studies, the treatment has been further developed by several clinical research groups (Baudinet et al., 2022; Eisler et al., 2015; Gorrell et al., 2023). In this chapter, we use the term 'eating disorder-focused family therapy' (FT-ED) as a general description of a systemic family therapy approach with a specific focus on the eating disorder. Several manualised versions of FT-ED exist, including family-based treatment for anorexia nervosa (FBT-AN; Lock & Le Grange, 2012), family-based treatment for bulimia nervosa (FBT-BN; Le Grange & Lock, 2007), parent-focused therapy (PFT; Le Grange et al., 2016), Maudsley family therapy for bulimia nervosa (FT-BN; Baudinet & Simic, 2025; Stewart et al., 2015), and Maudsley family therapy for anorexia nervosa (FT-AN; Blessitt et al., 2020; Eisler et al., 2016). Most studies have focused on children and adolescents up to 18 years of age. However, FT-ED has also been piloted with young adults (Dimitropoulos et al., 2018; Dodge et al., 2024). There is considerable conceptual overlap between these versions of FT-ED, and they are all more similar than different (cf. Gorrell et al., 2023).

The treatments share the following key concepts (Simic & Eisler, 2019):

(a) focusing on engaging the family as a key resource to help and support the child in the process of recovery, coupled with a strong message that the family is not seen as the cause of the problem;

(b) expecting that the parents will take the lead in managing their child's eating in the early stages of treatment while emphasising the temporary nature of this role;

(c) changing eating behaviours, restoring nutrition, and emphasising early weight gain; and

(d) shifting the focus of therapy to adolescent and family developmental life cycle issues in the later stages of treatment.

Maudsley family therapy for anorexia nervosa[1]

Engagement in treatment and development of the therapeutic alliance

When the family comes to treatment, they generally feel overwhelmed by what has been happening. The parents feel helpless, and their child feels misunderstood and has stopped trusting the parents. In assessing the presenting problem, beginning with an accurate diagnosis and a detailed evaluation of medical risks, a key task is to engage the family and offer a new perspective that validates their experience and provides the possibility of change. The detailed assessment of the young person's physical condition and associated medical risks here serves a dual purpose. Besides ensuring medical safety, it helps to create a context for engaging the patient and their family and providing a safe base for treatment (Byng-Hall, 2008). Hearing from all family members about their perspectives on the problem, combined with the expertise of the team, is reassuring for the parents while often also helping the young person to feel more receptive to treatment, albeit sometimes only reluctantly at first.

Building a therapeutic relationship with a young person with anorexia nervosa has sometimes been described as challenging and can fluctuate over time. Early on, connections with the therapist may be tentative, and establishing trust may take time. The physical and psychological effects of starvation can impair insight, so patients may genuinely lack awareness of the extent of their fragility and the risks they are facing or be unwilling to openly admit they are unwell.

Parents may feel disheartened by their child's apparent lack of engagement, believing treatment will not work without it. They may also question their ability to provide effective support for their child's recovery in the absence of visible motivation to recover on their part. For this reason, the therapist pays as much attention to the engagement of the parents as to the patient. This does not mean that the patient is ignored. The therapist continues to look for opportunities to empathise with the patient's predicament and to express interest in understanding their perspective.

An important component of the early stage of treatment is psychoeducation provided by the therapist about the physical and psychological effects of starvation, the neurobiology and temperament underpinning the development and maintenance of anorexia nervosa or the prognostic importance of early weight gain and restoration of healthy nutrition. Psychoeducation is not just about providing information; it is also part of the process of engagement, reinforcing a sense of safety and changing the understanding of perplexing experiences and difficult behaviours. Young people, as well as their parents, will often readily engage in a conversation about neurobiology, temperament, or brain processes connected with the illness, identifying which ones apply to them or other family members.

During the assessment, the therapist will also explore how the illness has affected everyone in the family. This can lead to a conversation that labels the illness as separate from the person (often described as 'externalisation', White & Epston, 1990), which can help reduce feelings of guilt and blame. Externalising is used carefully and in collaboration with the patient and their family. Some young people dislike it, feeling dismissed or patronised, and it is important not to use language that objectifies or demonises the illness. However, where externalising the illness makes sense to the young person and their family, it can help the patient to allow their parent/s to help them eat as a joint endeavour in defiance of the illness.

A meal plan is offered to the parents as a guide to what the patient needs to eat to start the recovery process. While parents are supported in rebuilding their confidence in making judgements about what their child needs to eat, in the early stages, a meal plan can often give them some certainty and confidence they are feeding their child enough to begin recovering. The meal plan is not a fixed or permanent treatment tool. Its use is seen as temporary, with more flexibility expected as treatment progresses, eventually making the meal plan redundant.

Following the assessment, parents are provided with advice and the assurance of ongoing support to help them care for and feed their child at home. The patient may be seen two or three times in the first week, depending on the severity of their physical presentation. However, more typically, patients begin a process of weekly family sessions.

Helping the family to manage the eating disorder

While engaging the family is an ongoing process, the primary emphasis quickly shifts to identifying and developing parental skills to support their child in eating and gaining weight. The therapist weighs the young person at the start of each session, with the conversation partly dictated by the weight trajectory. Weighing continues through treatment until a collaborative decision is reached that weight should no longer be the focus. This usually happens once weight is within a healthy range and has been maintained for some time or, with a child still growing, the trajectory is consistently positive.

While exploration of family beliefs and relationships is ongoing, this phase of treatment is predominantly behavioural, skills-based, and practical. Therapists call on their experience of other families and recount what strategies other families have tried to support their children to eat. Families are encouraged to create a predictable mealtime structure that may provide some containment of the young person's anxiety, acknowledging that distress and worry are an unavoidable part of the process of recovery. The therapist explores the different roles parents can have that fit specific families and how parents can best support each other through the stressful time. When progress is slow, adding some separate sessions with parents and the young person can sometimes help open up new conversations (Simic et al., 2016).

Further and repeated psychoeducation is also needed throughout this process to help parents and patients understand why food, in the first instance, is their 'medicine'. The therapist cites research to support the development of family knowledge and motivation to keep going. For example, attention can be drawn to research that shows that early weight gain is predictive of good outcome (Le Grange et al., 2014), or to studies exploring the impact of starvation on physical and psychological function (Kalm & Semba, 2005).

Psychoeducation can encourage the continued efforts of parents and patients as symptoms and anxiety intensify as anorexic behaviours are challenged more consistently. Once the young person is consistently gaining weight and illness behaviours are reducing, the family is supported to move away from rigid adherence to a meal plan and fixed food choices. By this stage, the improved nutrition should begin to reverse some of the effects of starvation, such as improvements in mood, although eating disorder cognitions are likely to persist for some time.

Exploring issues of individual and family development

Once the young person is restoring weight consistently, three major shifts in treatment begin. First, there is a move away from the emphasis on behavioural change and a gradual increase in focusing on broader issues related to adolescent and family life-cycle development.

Second, the young person is encouraged to increase the level of responsibility they take in ensuring their continued recovery. Parents are encouraged to take a less central role in managing mealtimes while continuing to provide support and encouragement. Young people vary in the degree to which they welcome this relational shift. They might also miss the reassuring sense of certainty and predictability derived from rigidly following a meal plan, being regularly weighed, and having regular clinic appointments with the 'expert' therapist. For the family as a whole, this is a challenging phase when they need to develop flexibility and manage the uncertainty that increased independence necessarily evokes.

The third shift concerns the nature of the therapeutic relationship. The anxiety that the relational changes in the family inevitably evoke requires the therapist to consider carefully the timing and pacing of the process. The aim is to maintain progress while ensuring the hitherto dependent relationship of the family on the therapist also begins to change. The conversations with the family become increasingly open-ended and exploratory, with the therapist adopting a more non-expert position defined by curiosity rather than certainty (Sluzki, 2008). This changed therapeutic positioning is achieved through and maintained by the therapist's accrued knowledge and understanding of the family over the months of treatment in earlier phases. This provides a safe context for both the young person and the parents to increase their tolerance of uncertainty (Mason, 1993).

For some families, any emerging issues are readily perceived as reflecting the tensions that typically arise in families managing normal family life-cycle changes. For them, this process is managed over a relatively short period and ending treatment is achieved more readily. For others, individual or family difficulties will have been obscured by the illness and its treatment become more apparent. These issues are managed with the whole family, separately with the parental couple or parent, and/or individually with the patient.

This changing therapeutic positioning is happening continually throughout treatment. However, when moving towards the end of treatment, it is vital that an open, non-expert position increasingly dominates. This approach means families and individuals are more likely to feel equipped to manage without the therapist and treating team being deferred to for decision-making. If therapy has been helpful, the family may have already begun to increase their tolerance of uncertainty; the patient will often be more than ready to move on; and the parents will start to show they no longer need their therapist and the team to help them make decisions or to solve problems.

Ending treatment, discussion of future plans and discharge

Preparing to end treatment is not a distinct moment but is more a culmination of factors that are arrived at throughout the processes and conversations in therapy. It is when parents and young people reach a point where it is evident they know enough about the illness, about their strengths, about their vulnerabilities, and about one another that they also know that however safe and comfortable it might feel to continue attending a clinic, this is not likely to be helpful in the longer term. The end of the therapeutic relationship and connection with the multi-disciplinary team (MDT) often invokes mixed feelings. Reviewing the family journey through treatment highlights what the family have learned about themselves and each other, and how their relationships have been strengthened by what they have achieved through the treatment process (Wallis et al., 2017).

Any dilemmas about ending treatment will usually have arisen before, so the therapist can normalise most worries and support a narrative that recognises the family's achievements and strengths. Conversations will have developed over time that address worries about relapse, so when treatment is ending, the family is their own expert when 'relapse prevention', for example, is raised.

Ending treatment is also not the end of the recovery process. Young people commenting on their process of recovery emphasise that while the support they received and the rekindling of a sense of trust were major ingredients contributing to their recovery, taking back responsibility for their own progress is what ultimately allowed them to reclaim their life from the illness (Baudinet, Eisler, Konstantellou et al., 2024).

Multi-family therapy

In recent years, new intensive treatments have been developed to try and help those for whom outpatient care alone is insufficient. While FT-ED is helpful for most, some people need something more intensive or different to recover. Historically, these young people were often admitted to hospital or residential care. Inpatient admissions can be lengthy and costly, with mixed outcomes and often with frequent relapses (Gowers et al., 2000; Hay et al., 2019; Lay et al., 2002). Thankfully, this picture has improved somewhat, with recent studies showing some promise for inpatient admissions that include psychological treatment (Nadler et al., 2022; Quadflieg et al., 2023).

Nevertheless, being taken away from one's family, community, and social context is always challenging, and there is a need to try to help people in their social context find ways to move forward. Increasingly, data are showing that brief hospitalisation followed by outpatient treatment is most effective (Madden et al., 2015). Alternatively, intensive day programme treatment (also known as partial hospitalisation) (Baudinet et al., 2020; Simic et al., 2018) and other intensive family-focused outpatient treatments (e.g. Fink et al., 2017; Rockwell et al., 2011), where the young person attends a clinic several days per week but returns home in the evenings, have also shown promise (cf. Baudinet & Simic, 2021 for review). They have also been reported to reduce isolation and help families get 'unstuck' when things do not seem to be progressing in outpatient treatment (Colla et al., 2023; Gledhill et al., 2023).

Multi-family therapy (MFT) is one intensive treatment model that has become increasingly popular (Lemmens, 2023). It is a group-based intervention in which several families (usually between two and nine) work together towards recovery. The group usually works with a team of clinicians for several hours or full days of treatment (Cook-Darzens et al., 2018; Gelin et al., 2016; Scholz & Asen, 2001).

The earliest descriptions of MFT were for people struggling with schizophrenia (Laqueur et al., 1964; McFarlane, 2002), depression (Anderson et al., 1986; Lemmens et al., 2009), and substance misuse (Kaufman & Kaufmann, 1977). Nowadays, it is used around the world for people with a range of psychological and behavioural difficulties.

MFT, specifically for eating disorders, was first described in the literature in the 1980s. The earliest groups were for young adults with bulimia nervosa and anorexia nervosa (Slagerman & Yager, 1989; Wooley & Lewis, 1987). MFT for adolescents with anorexia nervosa (MFT-AN) was first developed in the 1990s by teams at Dresden University of Technology, Germany (Asen, 2002; Scholz & Asen, 2001), and the Maudsley Hospital, London, UK (Dare & Eisler, 2000). MFT-AN programmes use an intensive format where families meet for several full, consecutive days. Conceptually, the treatment builds on the same theoretical principles as FT-AN (Dare et al., 1990; Eisler, 2005; Eisler, Simic, Blessitt et al., 2016), but with the addition of the group context of sharing the experience with other families in an intensive day setting. The MFT-AN model developed at the Maudsley Hospital has been widely disseminated with adaptations made to fit the local health service context (see Chapter 25 for details). The 19 stories that are at the heart of this book come from families who took part in MFT-AN in three eating disorders centres in different parts of the world: in London, UK, the Maudsley Centre for Child and Adolescent Eating Disorders (MCCAED); in the USA, the University of California San Diego (UCSD) Eating Disorders Center; and in Toronto, Canada, the Hospital for Sick Children (SickKids).

At MCCAED, 10 days of MFT-AN were offered alongside FT-AN sessions over six to nine months (Simic & Eisler, 2012). This started with four consecutive days (each 10:00 a.m.–4:00 p.m.), followed by six single follow-up days (also 10:00 a.m.–4:00 p.m.) spread over six to nine months. This programme has been evaluated in a randomised controlled trial (RCT) (Eisler et al., 2016), and has been running for over two decades with great success. More recently, a five-day version has also been piloted with good feedback and outcomes (Baudinet, Eisler, Simic et al., 2021; Baudinet et al., 2023).

At UCSD, the model was modified to become a five-day stand-alone MFT-AN, called intensive family therapy (IFT), with each day starting at 9:30 a.m. and going until 4:00 p.m. An important modification at UCSD has been the inclusion of family contracts as described below. At SickKids, the MFT-AN programme, similar to that at MCCAED (up to 10 days over six to nine months) was added to their routine multimodal care (Gabel et al., 2014).

The overarching aims of MFT-AN are to support people to stay out of hospital and speed up the recovery process by offering early intensive help when families are feeling most in crisis. By bringing families together, MFT-AN allows people to learn from each other and share experiences from a wider range of people with lived experience of eating disorders, not just clinicians (Blessitt et al., 2020; Scholz & Asen, 2001). People have described this approach as helping them to feel less isolated and less stigmatised (Dawson et al., 2018; Simic & Eisler, 2015). MFT is often described as a 'hot house' learning environment in which participants feel safe to express emotions, share their personal experiences. and try out new behaviours with the support of a team of people around them (Asen & Scholz, 2010).

MFT-AN is also unique because it includes a range of different types of activities. The group does not sit around talking for the whole time. They make things, problem-solve in smaller groups, eat together with the support of the clinicians, role-play, and do creative tasks using art materials. Alongside the structured activities, there are important informal interactions between families as well as with staff during breaks which add to the richness of the experience. All this helps people to learn in new ways—by listening, doing, observing, and practising (Baudinet, Eisler, Roddy et al., 2024; Baudinet et al., 2023). There is also a lot more time to discuss not just food and eating but all other things that are going on in the young person's and their family's life.

For a sense of the kinds of themes covered across MFT-AN, see the Table 2.1.

Each MFT-AN day is usually scheduled between 10:00 a.m. and 4:00 p.m., providing an intensive experience and covering a lot of content. Each MFT day generally consists of three therapeutic activities, three clinician-supported meals (morning snack, lunch, afternoon snack), and a closing activity.

MFT-AN is different from other therapies in that it is mainly activity based. Some activities involve the whole group working together; others are conducted in separate groups. These smaller groups can vary, and include working together with others in a similar family role (e.g. mothers, fathers, siblings, and young people). Some tasks are given to individual families

Table 2.1 Example themes and activities for all MFT days*

MFT Day	Theme	Activity 1 – opening (10:00 a.m.–11:00 a.m.)	Activity 2 (11:30 a.m.–1:00 p.m.)	Activity 3 (2:00 p.m.–3:00 p.m.)	Activity 4 – closing (3:30 p.m.–4:00 p.m.)
Day 1	Engagement/ Understanding the illness	Photo cards	**Parents**: Preparations for first MFT lunch **Young people**: Portraits of AN	Feedback on portraits of AN	One thing to take home from the day / ball pattern exercise / mindfulness
Day 2	Managing mealtimes	Sunday lunch	Mealtime role reversal role play + Foster family	Feedback on Foster families (fishbowl)	Pebble and balloon
Day 3	Impact of illness on the family and family strengths	Family sculpt	**Young people**: Make treasures **Parents**: Food discussion and check-in **Siblings**: Own experience of the illness in family	Family crest	Traps and treasures

Day 4	Looking forward	Timelines	Feedback from timelines	Toolboxes	Photocards / Note to future self
Day 5 (FU1)	*Managing conflict and relationships*	Headlines	De-escalation clocks	Brain scans	Mindfulness—e.g. dealing with difficult emotions
Day 6 (FU2)	*Flexibility and relationships*	Speed dating	**Parents:** Meal planning **Young people and siblings:** Care tags	Internalised other or Anorexia press conference	Reflection
Day 7 (FU3)	*Managing uncertainty*	Tolerating uncertainty	Speed problem solving	Motivation see-saws	Reflection / Loving-kindness meditation
Day 8 (FU4)	*Adolescence and independence*	Life circles	Parents as experts in adolescents (What's old is new and what's new is old)	Life rivers	Independent eating plan

(Continued)

Table 2.1 (Continued)

MFT Day	Theme	Activity 1 – opening (10:00 a.m.–11:00 a.m.)	Activity 2 (11:30 a.m.–1:00 p.m.)	Activity 3 (2:00 p.m.–3:00 p.m.)	Activity 4 – closing (3:30 p.m.–4:00 p.m.)
Day 9 (FU5)	Reconnecting with the life cycle	Spaghetti towers	Where do we stand?	Trip down memory lane	Setting up the activity run by families on final day
Day 10 (FU6)	Endings	Photo cards	Recovery recipes	The tables have turned	Final Post-it task

* Multi-Family Therapy for Anorexia Nervosa: A Treatment Manual (1st ed.) by Simic, M., Baudinet, J., Blessitt, E., Wallis, A., & Eisler, I. 2021 © by Routledge. Reproduced by permission of Taylor & Francis Group. This is a guide only. The MFT-AN model is flexible, so while there will be some activities that are much better suited to early or late in treatment, there is always flexibility to change things to meet the needs of the group. See Simic, et al. (2021) for details on each activity.

to work on, or a young person joins with parents from other families ('foster' family groups), or there can be larger mixed groups with individuals from different families joining to work on a task. Every task is followed by feedback and reflections with the whole MFT-AN group.

The activities themselves are also varied—some are based in group discussion, others are largely non-verbal, and others invite people to create things (e.g. drawings, sculptures) or problem-solve tasks and come up with practical lists. While all the activities have a serious focus, many are conducted in a playful manner with humour and laughter, allowing new perceptions to emerge and perhaps difficult things to be spoken about in a safe and containing way. All the activities commonly used are outlined in the various manuals (see e.g., Hill et al., 2022; Simic et al., 2021). To bring some of them to life, we have described a few key activities below.

Portraits of anorexia nervosa

This exercise is completed by the young people and provides an opportunity for them to get to know one another and to talk about their experiences of the illness. It is usually completed on day 1 of MFT-AN. Each young person creates something that communicates to others what it is like to struggle with anorexia nervosa. They can draw, mould clay, or generate an object using craft materials provided. Very often, the 'portraits' generated powerfully express feelings of isolation, of being torn between the illness and the healthier parts of themselves, guilt, shame, and difficulties with intrusive or obsessive thoughts about food and their bodies.

Families often remember this activity as a moment where they were able to understand something new about what it is like to experience anorexia nervosa. Frequently, even those young people who struggle to acknowledge that they are ill with anorexia nervosa will actively participate in this task and produce a 'portrait' every bit as agonising and evocative as the other 'portraits'.

Mealtime role reversal

The mealtime role activity, usually done on day 2 of MFT-AN, is an opportunity for a parent and child to swap roles and role-play an imaginary meal. The young person with anorexia nervosa role-plays one of their parents, and the parent role-plays the young person with anorexia nervosa. Partway through the role play, a staff member also steps in as anorexia, standing or crouching behind the parent role-playing the young person, and verbalises in a loud whisper some common anorexic thoughts, such as, 'don't eat it, your mother just wants to make you fat'.

This activity is done as a whole group together and helps parents to understand the competing motivations when their child is faced with eating. The young people are also given insight into the concerns and challenges the parents face when trying to support them. When the young person is able to role-play strategies to support eating (which is almost always the case), it can highlight to parents that they notice parents' attempts to help them. The way in which families engage in this task can be quite varied. Some play it very seriously, others are playful, exaggerating the roles to the point of caricature. Either way, the activity is a powerful way of helping families put themselves in the shoes of others and open up new ways of understanding their struggles.

Family sculpt

The family sculpt exercise often happens on day 3 of MFT-AN. It is mostly a non-verbal task in which a member of the group (usually a young person), makes a 'sculpture' of their family using other members of the audience to represent the family members. The 'sculptor' positions these volunteers within the circle of MFT-AN participants in a way that represents relationships, communications, or emotions in the family at three different time points.

They start by making a sculpture that expresses how things felt to them before the illness entered their lives. Once this is established, they then reposition people to a new position that represents how things felt when the illness was at its worst (which might be the present). At this point, the MFT-AN clinician also adds in a staff member to represent 'anorexia', which the young person positions within the family sculpture. Lastly, they reposition everyone to express how they would like things to feel in the future when anorexia is less present in their lives.

At each time point, the 'sculptor' is encouraged to consider how close or distant people are, their posture and other body language, the directions they are all facing, and their facial expressions. Those taking part remain silent throughout the exercise, with the focus being on the visual representation of how things have been in the family and how they have changed over time due to the illness. The family sculpt is often a very powerful experience both for those in the sculpt and for those observing, with frequent comments on how it has brought home the impact that anorexia has had on the whole family.

Timelines

The timelines activity is commonly used across many MFT models. The task involves families working together to think ahead over a six- to 12-month period. The family draws three timelines: 1) predictable events that will happen for the family, such as birthdays, anniversaries, work or school events (e.g. exams), and planned holidays or visits from people; 2) what life will look like if things continue towards recovery; and 3) what things will be like if there is no progress.

The task aims to help families think carefully about the steps needed to stay focused on recovery and planning what each

family member can do to ensure they are continuing to progress. It helps families also to plan upcoming events and think
realistically about what they might be like and what supports
they need to put in place to help them go as well as possible. For
example, if a parent has a big birthday in the coming months,
on the recovery line, the family can plan for eating out and can
think through how to manage that (e.g. knowing the restaurant
in advance, thinking about who is ordering the food etc.). One
of the common effects of living with anorexia nervosa is that
the family becomes very here-and-now focused as if 'frozen
in time', and this task helps open conversations with a broader
time horizon.

Contracting

In some MFT-AN programmes (e.g. at the University of
California San Diego Eating Disorders Center), the intensive
MFT week includes writing (and signing) family contracts for
recovery. This is a way of summarising and consolidating all
the learning from the MFT intensive week and making commitments to the next steps in a really practical way. This is done
within families and collaboratively (e.g. young people as a
group helping each other to think what they want to include for
themselves in their contract) so that everyone agrees on how to
manage the weeks and months ahead. As you will read in some
of the stories in this book, this can be highly useful to ensure
learning is not lost and everyone in the family has a clear way
forward when things feel difficult.

Multi-family meals

Within most MFT-AN models, supported meals are a core part
of each day. Typically, three meals are supported in a group
format: morning snack, lunch, and afternoon snack. Families
usually eat together at a table with one or two other families.

Staff are available to check in around food types, amounts, and support if the young person is struggling to finish. Tea, coffee, fruit, and biscuits are also often available to supplement any missing food as needed.

While anxiety-provoking, the mealtimes offer a unique opportunity for families to practise meals they will have at home with additional support and to try out new foods. There are numerous opportunities for families to observe how others manage mealtimes and learn practical tips from each other. Staff also provide support, reflections, and containment if emotions are running unhelpfully high.

There is also opportunity in some programmes to eat with others in the group who are not your family members. On the second day of the Maudsley MFT programme, young people eat with one or two parents, each from a different family, as a way of modelling distraction and to practise eating in different situations. All of this helps prepare the young person and parents for life outside the group and to begin to challenge any rigidity there may be around mealtimes. Structured feedback may include parents observing the young people discussing as a group what they have found helpful or unhelpful during mealtimes.

Empirical evidence

Family therapy and multi-family therapy for anorexia nervosa

The treatment of adolescent anorexia nervosa has attracted a significant amount of family therapy research, with 15 published randomised control trials showing eating disorders-focused family therapy (FT-ED) leads to improved outcomes. These outcomes are largely maintained at follow-up of up to five years (Jewell et al., 2016; NICE, 2017). FT-ED has been shown to result in better weight outcomes compared to individual therapy (Austin et al., 2025; Jewell et al., 2016).

Clinical guidelines across different countries (e.g. the UK, the USA, Spain, France, Netherlands, Australia, Germany) align on key recommendations for adolescents with anorexia nervosa:

1) outpatient therapy should be the first line treatment;
2) hospitalisation should be considered only for those who have not responded to outpatient care or who are at high medical risk;
3) FT-ED should be the first line psychological treatment; and
4) treatment should be provided by a specialist professional and/or clinicians with substantial experience in the treatment of eating disorders (Hilbert et al., 2017).

While the research provides a reasonably consistent picture of the effectiveness of FT-ED for children and adolescents, there are important caveats. These include a lack of consensus in the field regarding how good outcome is defined (Murray et al., 2018). There is large variability between studies in illness severity at baseline or methodological limitations, such as small sample sizes, insufficient blinding of research assessments, or lack of replication by independent researchers (Fisher et al., 2019). Finally, as is often the case in treatment trials, study samples may fail to reflect the diversity of real-world populations. For example, groups such as ethnic minorities, males, and transgender individuals remain underrepresented due to overly narrow study inclusion criteria, the process of recruitment, or simply because many clinical services for eating disorders are unrepresentative of the population at large (Marques et al., 2011; Rasmussen et al., 2023; Regan et al., 2017; Sweeting et al., 2015). For all these reasons, a degree of caution is required in the interpretation of the research findings.

Compared to FT-ED, the evidence base for MFT-ED is smaller. However, a number of small case series and one larger randomised control trial have suggested that MFT-AN helps young people with anorexia nervosa gain weight, reduce other eating disorder symptoms, reduce feelings of isolation, and improve family well-being (Baudinet & Eisler, 2024; Baudinet, Eisler, Dawson et al., 2021).

The largest MFT-AN study is an randomised controlled trial conducted in the UK that compared the outcomes following MFT-AN and/or FT-AN for 169 adolescents and their families (Eisler, Simic, Blessitt et al., 2016). A higher proportion of young people receiving MFT-AN compared to FT-AN achieved weight recovery maintained at six months follow-up (Eisler, Simic, Blessitt et al., 2016). While this is encouraging, it is important to note that, as per the model, those randomised to the MFT-AN arm of the study also received single-family FT-AN sessions on an as-needed basis. Interestingly, the number of FT-AN sessions was similar for participants in both arms of the study, meaning those receiving MFT-AN essentially received the multi-family groups as an addition to standard FT-AN. This complicates conclusions about whether improved outcomes are due to MFT itself or increased treatment intensity. Despite these uncertainties, MFT is a treatment that enhances outcomes and shows promise.

There is one further caveat to interpreting the research results. While randomised control trials provide the most robust evidence about the comparative efficacy of treatments, they do not always fully capture the complexity of everyday clinical practice (the study of which are usually called 'effectiveness' trials). In real-world settings, treatments can be more flexible and better tailored to the specific needs of individual patients and their families. This may include combining therapies, adjusting intensity, or treatment duration. Decisions about these variations can sometimes seem somewhat arbitrary. Ideally, they should take into account the best available research evidence, including randomised control trial findings and other relevant evidence, as well as clinical judgements and patient and family preferences and needs (Sackett et al., 1996). However, the delivery of treatments in everyday practice has its own pitfalls, and treatments may be less effective than in the context of a carefully controlled research setting, for example, because of subjective biases, insufficient training of staff, or lack of ongoing quality supervision.

To address this question, we report the findings from a recent naturalistic study conducted at the MCCAED service in London.

The study presents the treatment outcomes of 357 consecutive referrals referred to MCCAED (of whom 290 had a diagnosis of anorexia nervosa or atypical anorexia nervosa) (Simic et al., 2022), and a four- to seven-year follow-up of the same group (Stewart et al., 2022). MCCAED has a catchment area covering a population of 2.2 million in south-east London and the sample is, therefore, representative of an urban and suburban help-seeking population. We will focus on the findings relating to the 290 patients with anorexia nervosa, as this is most directly relevant to this book.

Most young people with anorexia nervosa (97 per cent) received FT-AN as the main treatment, with a third also attending MFT-AN and over half also receiving some individual therapy. Most were treated purely as outpatients, though 26 per cent required additional, more intensive day treatment, or inpatient care.

The median length of treatment for the whole group (11 months) was similar to most randomised control trials but much more variable. A quarter were seen for six months or less, a third for up to one year, and the rest for more than a year. Treatment was significantly longer for those whose outpatient therapy had to be enhanced by the more intensive treatments (median 16 months). Outcome at the end of treatment using a simple classification based on clinical symptoms[2] (weight, resumption of periods, bingeing, or vomiting) compares well with outcomes in the more rigorous randomised control trial studies. Among outpatient-only cases, 80 per cent had a good or intermediate outcome, while this dropped to 67 per cent for those needing more intensive care.

Comparable randomised control trials report outcomes ranging from 65 per cent to 80 per cent.

In the earlier described randomised control trial of MFT-AN (Eisler, Simic, Hodsoll et al., 2016), 58 per cent of participants receiving only FT-AN achieved good/intermediate outcomes, compared to 76 per cent of those who also participated in MFT-AN. These findings highlight the potential benefits of adding MFT-AN to standard FT-AN.

The long-term outcome at four to seven years provides a mixed picture. At the time of the follow-up, very few (6.7 per cent) reported having an eating disorder. However, approximately a third had required some additional help for the eating disorder since the time of discharge from MCCAED. Of this third, 20 per cent was for prolonged outpatient treatment and/or hospital admission. Other mental health problems were more common (54 per cent at some point during the follow-up period), and nearly a third had needed substantial treatment for other problems, most commonly anxiety or depression.

The most encouraging finding was that at follow-up, the great majority reported that any remaining eating disorder difficulties did not interfere with their lives at all, or only in a minor way, with only 10 per cent reporting significant interference. The picture was slightly less positive for other mental health problems, but again, only 15 per cent reported significant interference. When asked about their general and social well-being, most said they were generally well or had at most minor concerns, with 14 per cent reporting some significant social well-being concerns and 11 per cent some significant general well-being concerns.

It would be a mistake to downplay the fact that for a proportion of those who have experienced an eating disorder, problems will continue and, for some, to a very significant degree. Nevertheless, what is clear is that with good treatment, particularly if provided early on in the illness, the long-term prognosis is positive.

Notes

1   The account of the treatment in this chapter is adapted from the detailed description of FT-AN in the *Maudsley Service Manual for Child and Adolescent Eating Disorders* (Eisler et al., 2016).
2   *Good outcome:* Weight above 85 per cent median body mass index (mBMI), regular periods, and no bulimic symptoms. *Intermediate outcome:* Weight above 85 per cent mBMI, no periods, and/or occasional bulimic symptoms (less than weekly). *Poor outcome:* Weight below 85 per cent mBMI or bulimic symptoms of once a week or more (Russell et al., 1987).

References

Anderson, C. M., Griffin, S., Rossi, A., Pagonis, I., Holder, D. P., & Treiber, R. (1986). A comparative study of the impact of education vs. process groups for families of patients with affective disorders. *Family Process, 25*(2), 185–205. https://doi.org/10.1111/j.1545-5300.1986.00185.x

Asen, E. (2002). Multiple family therapy: An overview. *Journal of Family Therapy, 24*(1), 3–16. https://doi.org/10.1111/1467-6427.00197

Asen, E., & Scholz, M. (2010). *Multi-family therapy: Concepts and techniques.* London/New York: Routledge.

Austin, A., Anderson, A. G., Lee, J., Vander Steen, H., Savard, C., Bergmann, C., Singh, M., Devoe, D., Gorrell, S. D., Patten, S., Le Grange D., & Dimitropoulos, G. (2025). Efficacy of eating disorder focused family therapy for adolescents with anorexia nervosa: a systematic review and meta-analysis. *International Journal of Eating Disorders, 58*(1), 3–36. https://doi.org/10.1002/eat.24252

Baudinet, J., & Eisler, I. (2024). Multi-family therapy for eating disorders across the lifespan. *Current Psychiatry Reports.* https://doi.org/10.1007/s11920-024-01504-5

Baudinet, J., Eisler, I., Dawson, L., Simic, M., & Schmidt, U. (2021). Multi-family therapy for eating disorders: A systematic scoping review of the quantitative and qualitative findings. *International Journal of Eating Disorders, 54*(12), 2095–2120. https://doi.org/DOI: 10.1002/EAT.23616

Baudinet, J., Eisler, I., Konstantellou, A., Hunt, T., Kassamali, F., McLaughlin, N., Simic, M., & Schmidt, U. (2023). Perceived change mechanisms in multi-family therapy for anorexia nervosa: A qualitative follow-up study of adolescent and parent experiences. *European Eating Disorders Review*, *31*(6), 822–836. https://doi.org/10.1002/erv.3006

Baudinet, J., Eisler, I., Konstantellou, A., Simic, M., & Schmidt, U. (2024). How young people perceive change to occur in family therapy for anorexia nervosa: A qualitative study. *Journal of Eating Disorders*, *12*(1), 11. https://doi.org/10.1186/s40337-024-00971-8

Baudinet, J., Eisler, I., Roddy, M., Turner, J., Simic, M., & Schmidt, U. (2024). Clinician perspectives on how change occurs in multi-family therapy for adolescent anorexia nervosa: A qualitative study. *Journal of Eating Disorders*, *12*(1), 103. https://doi.org/10.1186/s40337-024-01064-2

Baudinet, J., & Simic, M. (2021). Adolescent eating disorder day programme treatment models and outcomes: A systematic scoping review. *Frontiers in Psychiatry*, *12*, 539. https://doi.org/10.3389/fpsyt.2021.652604

Baudinet, J., & Simic, M. (2025). *Integrated family therapy for adolescent bulimia nervosa: A treatment manual*. London, UK: Routledge.

Baudinet, J., Simic, M., & Eisler, I. (2022). From treatment models to manuals: maudsley single- and multi-family therapy for adolescent eating disorders. In M. Mariotti, G. Saba, & P. Stratton (Eds.), *Systemic approaches to manuals* (pp. 349–372). Cham, Switzerland: Springer. https://doi.org/10.1007/978-3-030-73640-8

Baudinet, J., Simic, M., Griffiths, H., Donnelly, C., Stewart, C., & Goddard, E. (2020). Targeting maladaptive overcontrol with radically open dialectical behaviour therapy in a day programme for adolescents with restrictive eating disorders: An uncontrolled case series. *Journal of Eating Disorders*, *8*(1), 68. https://doi.org/10.1186/s40337-020-00338-9

Blessitt, E., Baudinet, J., Simic, M., & Eisler, I. (2020). Eating disorders in children, adolescents, and young adults. In *The handbook of systemic family therapy* (pp. 397–427). Hoboken, NJ: John Wiley & Sons. https://doi.org/10.1002/9781119438519.ch49

Byng-Hall, J. (2008). The crucial roles of attachment in family therapy. *Journal of Family Therapy*, *30*(2), 129–146. https://doi.org/10.1111/j.1467-6427.2008.00422.x

Colla, A., Baudinet, J., Cavenagh, P., Senra, H., & Goddard, E. (2023). Change processes during intensive day programme treatment for adolescent anorexia nervosa: A dyadic interview analysis of adolescent and parent views. *Frontiers in Psychology, 14.* https://doi.org/10.3389/fpsyg.2023.1226605

Cook-Darzens, S., Gelin, Z., & Hendrick, S. (2018). Evidence base for multiple family therapy (MFT) in non-psychiatric conditions and problems: A review (part 2): Evidence base for non-psychiatric MFT. *Journal of Family Therapy, 40*(3), 326–343. https://doi.org/10.1111/1467-6427.12177

Dare, C., & Eisler, I. (2000). A multi-family group day treatment programme for adolescent eating disorder. *European Eating Disorders Review, 8*(1), 4–18. https://doi.org/10.1002/(SICI)1099-0968(200002)8:1<4::AID-ERV330>3.0.CO;2-P

Dare, C., Eisler, I., Russell, G. F. M., & Szmukler, G. I. (1990). The clinical and theoretical impact of a controlled trial of family therapy in anorexia nervosa. *Journal of Marital and Family Therapy, 16*(1), 39–57. https://doi.org/10.1111/j.1752-0606.1990.tb00044.x

Dawson, L., Baudinet, J., Tay, E., & Wallis, A. (2018). Creating community—The introduction of multi-family therapy for eating disorders in Australia. *Australian and New Zealand Journal of Family Therapy, 39*(3), 283–293. https://doi.org/10.1002/anzf.1324

Dimitropoulos, G., Landers, A. L., Freeman, V., Novick, J., Garber, A., & Grange, D. L. (2018). Open trial of family-based treatment of anorexia nervosa for transition age youth. *Journal of the Canadian Academy of Child and Adolescent Psychiatry, 27*(1), 50–61.

Dodge, E., Baudinet, J., Austin, A., Eisler, I., Le Grange, D., & Dimitropoulos, G. (2024). Family therapy for emerging adults with anorexia nervosa: Expert opinion on evidence, practice considerations, and future directions. *European Eating Disorders Review,* 1–11. https://doi.org/10.1002/erv.3129

Eisler, I. (1995). Family models of eating disorders. In G. I. Szmukler, C. Dare, & J. Treasure (Eds.), *Handbook of Eating disorders: Theory, Treatment and Research.* (pp. 155–176). Oxford, England: John Wiley & Sons..

Eisler, I. (2005). The empirical and theoretical base of family therapy and multiple family day therapy for adolescent anorexia nervosa. *Journal of Family Therapy, 27*(2), 104–131. https://doi.org/10.1111/j.1467-6427.2005.00303.x

Eisler, I., Simic, M., Blessitt, E., Dodge, L., & MCCAED Team. (2016). *Maudsley service manual for child and adolescent eating disorders.* https://mccaed.slam.nhs.uk/wp-content/uploads/2019/11/Maudsley-Service-Manual-for-Child-and-Adolescent-Eating-Disorders-July-2016.pdf

Eisler, I., Simic, M., Hodsoll, J., Asen, E., Berelowitz, M., Connan, F., Ellis, G., Hugo, P., Schmidt, U., Treasure, J., Yi, I., & Landau, S. (2016). A pragmatic randomised multi-centre trial of multifamily and single family therapy for adolescent anorexia nervosa. *BMC Psychiatry, 16*(1), 422. https://doi.org/10.1186/s12888-016-1129-6

Eisler, I., Wallis, A., & Dodge, L. (2015). What's new is old and what's old is new. In K. L. Loeb, D. Le Grange, & J. Lock (Eds.), *Family Therapy for Adolescent Eating and Weight Disorders* (pp. 6–41). New York: Imprint Routledge.

Fink, K., Rhodes, P., Miskovic-Wheatley, J., Wallis, A., Touyz, S., Baudinet, J., & Madden, S. (2017). Exploring the effects of a family admissions program for adolescents with anorexia nervosa. *Journal of Eating Disorders, 5*(1), 51. https://doi.org/10.1186/s40337-017-0181-z

Fisher, C. A., Skocic, S., Rutherford, K. A., & Hetrick, S. E. (2019). Family therapy approaches for anorexia nervosa. *Cochrane Database of Systematic Reviews*, Issue 5. https://doi.org/10.1002/14651858.CD004780.pub4

Gabel, K., Pinhas, L., Eisler, I., Katzman, D., & Heinmaa, M. (2014). The effect of multiple family therapy on weight gain in adolescents with anorexia nervosa: Pilot data. *Journal of the Canadian Academy of Child and Adolescent Psychiatry, 23*(3), 4.

Gelin, Z., Cook-Darzens, S., Simon, Y., & Hendrick, S. (2016). Two models of multiple family therapy in the treatment of adolescent anorexia nervosa: A systematic review. *Eating and Weight Disorders: 21*(1), 19–30. https://doi.org/10.1007/s40519-015-0207-y

Gledhill, L. J., MacInnes, D., Chan, S. C., Drewery, C., Watson, C., & Baudinet, J. (2023). What is day hospital treatment for anorexia nervosa really like? A reflexive thematic analysis of feedback from young people. *Journal of Eating Disorders, 11*(1), 223. https://doi.org/10.1186/s40337-023-00949-y

Gorrell, S., Simic, M., & Le Grange, D. (2023). Toward the Integration of Family therapy and family-based treatment for eating disorders.

In P. Robinson, T. Wade, B. Herpertz-Dahlmann, F. Fernandez-Aranda, J. Treasure, & S. Wonderlich (Eds.), *Eating disorders: An international comprehensive view* (pp. 1–17). Cham, Switzerland: Springer Nature . https://doi.org/10.1007/978-3-030-97416-9_59-1

Gowers, S. G., An, J. W., Shore, A., Hossain, F., & Elvins, R. (2000). Impact of hospitalisation on the outcome of adolescent anorexia nervosa. *British Journal of Psychiatry, 176*(2), 138–141. https://doi.org/10.1192/bjp.176.2.138

Hay, P. J., Touyz, S., Claudino, A. M., Lujic, S., Smith, C. A., & Madden, S. (2019). Inpatient versus outpatient care, partial hospitalisation and waiting list for people with eating disorders. *Cochrane Database of Systematic Reviews, 2019*(1), CD010827. https://doi.org/10.1002/14651858.CD010827.pub2

Hilbert, A., Hoek, H. W., & Schmidt, R. (2017). Evidence-based clinical guidelines for eating disorders: International comparison. *Current Opinion in Psychiatry, 30*(6), 423–437. https://doi.org/10.1097/YCO.0000000000000360

Hill, L. L., Knatz Peck, S., & Wierenga, C. E. (2022). *Temperament based therapy with support for anorexia nervosa: A novel treatment.* Cambridge, UK: Cambridge University Press. https://doi.org/10.1017/9781009032063

Hoffman, L. (1985). Beyond power and control: Toward a "second order" family systems therapy. *Family Systems Medicine, 3*(4), 381–396. https://doi.org/10.1037/h0089674

Jewell, T., Blessitt, E., Stewart, C., Simic, M., & Eisler, I. (2016). Family therapy for child and adolescent eating disorders: A critical review. *Family Process, 55*(3), 577–594. https://doi.org/10.1111/famp.12242

Kalm, L. M., & Semba, R. D. (2005). They starved so that others be better fed: Remembering Ancel Keys and the Minnesota experiment. *The Journal of Nutrition, 135*(6), 1347–1352. https://doi.org/10.1093/jn/135.6.1347

Kaufman, E., & Kaufmann, P. (1977). Multiple family therapy: A new direction in the treatment of drug abusers. *The American Journal of Drug and Alcohol Abuse, 4*(4), 467–478. https://doi.org/10.3109/00952997709007004

Laqueur, H. P., Laburt, H. A., & Morong, E. (1964). Multiple family therapy. *Current Psychiatric Therapies, 4*, 150–154.

Lay, B., Jennen-Steinmetz, C., Reinhard, I., & Schmidt, M. H. (2002). Characteristics of inpatient weight gain in adolescent anorexia nervosa: Relation to speed of relapse and re-admission. *European Eating Disorders Review*, *10*(1), 22–40. https://doi.org/10.1002/erv.432

Le Grange, D., Accurso, E. C., Lock, J., Agras, S., & Bryson, S. W. (2014). Early weight gain predicts outcome in two treatments for adolescent anorexia nervosa: Early weight gain for adolescent anorexia nervosa. *International Journal of Eating Disorders*, *47*(2), 124–129. https://doi.org/10.1002/eat.22221

Le Grange, D., Hughes, E. K., Court, A., Yeo, M., Crosby, R. D., & Sawyer, S. M. (2016). Randomized clinical trial of parent-focused treatment and family-based treatment for adolescent anorexia nervosa. *Journal of the American Academy of Child & Adolescent Psychiatry*, *55*(8), 683–692. https://doi.org/10.1016/j.jaac.2016.05.007

Le Grange, D., & Lock, J. (2007). *Treating bulimia in adolescents: A family-based approach* (1st Edition). New York: Guilford Press.

Lemmens, G. (2023). Multifamily therapy – Spreading across the world. *Journal of Family Therapy*, *45*(1), 1–3. https://doi.org/10.1111/1467-6427.12425

Lemmens, G. M. D., Eisler, I., Buysse, A., Heene, E., & Demyttenaere, K. (2009). The effects on mood of adjunctive single-family and multi-family group therapy in the treatment of hospitalized patients with major depression a 15-month follow-up study. *Psychotherapy and Psychosomatics*, *78*(2), 98–105. https://doi.org/10.1159/000201935

Lock, J., & Le Grange, D. (2012). *Treatment manual for anorexia nervosa: A family-based approach* (2nd Edition). New York: Guilford Press.

Madden, S., Miskovic-Wheatley, J., Wallis, A., Kohn, M., Lock, J., Le Grange, D., Jo, B., Clarke, S., Rhodes, P., Hay, P., & Touyz, S. (2015). A randomized controlled trial of in-patient treatment for anorexia nervosa in medically unstable adolescents. *Psychological Medicine*, *45*(2), 415–427. https://doi.org/10.1017/S0033291714001573

Marques, L., Alegria, M., Becker, A. E., Chen, C., Fang, A., Chosak, A., & Diniz, J. B. (2011). Comparative prevalence, correlates of impairment, and service utilization for eating disorders across US ethnic groups: Implications for reducing ethnic disparities in health care access for eating disorders. *International Journal of Eating Disorders*, *44*(5), 412–420. https://doi.org/10.1002/eat.20787

Mason, B. (1993). Towards positions of safe uncertainty. *Human Systems: The Journal of Systemic Consultation & Management*, *4*, 189–200.

McFarlane, W. R. (2002). *Multifamily groups in the treatment of severe psychiatric disorders.* New York & London: Guilford Press.

Minuchin, S., Rosman, B., & Baker, L. (1978). *Psychosomatic families: Anorexia nervosa in context.* Cambridge, MA: Harvard University Press.

Murray, S. B., Loeb, K. L., & Le Grange, D. (2018). Treatment outcome reporting in anorexia nervosa: Time for a paradigm shift? *Journal of Eating Disorders*, *6*(1), 10. https://doi.org/10.1186/s40 337-018-0195-1

Nadler, J., Correll, C. U., Le Grange, D., Accurso, E. C., & Haas, V. (2022). The impact of inpatient multimodal treatment or family-based treatment on six-month weight outcomes in youth with anorexia nervosa: A naturalistic, cross-continental comparison. *Nutrients*, *14*(7), 1396. https://doi.org/10.3390/nu14071396

National Institute for Health and Care Excellence (NICE). (2017). *Eating disorders (NICE Guideline ng69).* Retrieved from: www. nice.org.uk/guidance/ng69

Quadflieg, N., Naab, S., Schlegl, S., Bauman, T., & Voderholzer, U. (2023). Inpatient treatment outcome in a large sample of adolescents with anorexia nervosa. *Nutrients*, *15*(19), 4247. https://doi. org/10.3390/nu15194247

Rasmussen, S. M., Dalgaard, M. K., Roloff, M., Pinholt, M., Skrubbeltrang, C., Clausen, L., & Kjaersdam Telléus, G. (2023). Eating disorder symptomatology among transgender individuals: A systematic review and meta-analysis. *Journal of Eating Disorders*, *11*(1), 84. https://doi.org/10.1186/s40337-023-00806-y

Regan, P., Cachelin, F. M., & Minnick, A. M. (2017). Initial treatment seeking from professional health care providers for eating disorders: A review and synthesis of potential barriers to and facilitators of "first contact". *International Journal of Eating Disorders*, *50*(3), 190–209. https://doi.org/10.1002/eat.22683

Rockwell, R. E., Boutelle, K., Trunko, M. E., Jacobs, M. J., & Kaye, W. H. (2011). An innovative short-term, intensive, family-based treatment for adolescent anorexia nervosa: Case series: Anorexia nervosa family therapy. *European Eating Disorders Review, 19*(4), 362–367. https://doi.org/10.1002/erv.1094

Russell, G. F. M., Szmukler, G. I., Dare, C., & Eisler, I. (1987). An evaluation of family therapy in anorexia and bulimia nervosa. *Archives of General Psychiatry, 44,* 1047–1056. https://doi.org/10.1001/archpsyc.1987.01800240021004

Sackett, D. L., Rosenberg, W. M. C., Gray, J. A. M., Haynes, R. B., & Richardson, W. S. (1996). Evidence based medicine: What it is and what it isn't. *BMJ, 312*(7023), 71–72. https://doi.org/10.1136/bmj.312.7023.71

Scholz, M., & Asen, E. (2001). Multiple family therapy with eating disordered adolescents: Concepts and preliminary results. *European Eating Disorders Review, 9*(1), 33–42. https://doi.org/10.1002/erv.364

Simic, M., Anderson, L. K., Berner, L. A., Knatz Peck, S., Hunt, K., Kaye, W., & Eisler, I. (2016). When family therapy isn't enough: New treatment directions for highly anxious and dysregulated adolescents with anorexia nervosa. In S. B. Murray, L. K. Anderson, & L. Cohn (Eds.), *Innovations in Family Therapy for Eating Disorders* (pp. 139–158). New York: Routledge. https://doi.org/10.4324/9781315626086-22

Simic, M., Baudinet, J., Blessitt, E., Wallis, A., & Eisler, I. (2021). *Multi-family therapy for anorexia nervosa: A treatment manual.* London, UK: Routledge. https://doi.org/10.4324/9781003038764

Simic, M., & Eisler, I. (2012). Family and multifamily therapy. In R. E. Fox, & K. P. Goss (Eds.) Eating and its Disorders (pp. 260–279). Oxford: Wiley-Blackwell. https://doi.org/10.1002/9781118328910.ch18

Simic, M., & Eisler, I. (2015). Multi-family therapy. In K. L. Loeb, D. Le Grange, & J. Lock (Eds.), *Family therapy for adolescent eating and weight disorders* (pp. 110–138). New York and London: Routledge.

Simic, M., & Eisler, I. (2019). Maudsley family therapy for eating disorders. In Lebow, Jay, A. Chambers, & D. C. Bruenlin (Eds.),

Encyclopedia of couple and family therapy. Cham, Switzerland: Springer.

Simic, M., Stewart, C. S., Eisler, I., Baudinet, J., Hunt, K., O'Brien, J., & McDermott, B. (2018). Intensive treatment program (ITP): A case series service evaluation of the effectiveness of day patient treatment for adolescents with a restrictive eating disorder. *International Journal of Eating Disorders, 51*(11), 1261–1269. https://doi.org/ 10.1002/eat.22959

Simic, M., Stewart, C. S., Konstantellou, A., Eisler, I., & Baudinet, J. (2022). From efficacy to effectiveness: Child and adolescent eating disorder treatments in the real world (part 1) – Treatment course and outcomes. *Journal of Eating Disorders, 10*(1), 27. https://doi.org/ DOI: 10.1186/s40337-022-00553-6

Slagerman, M., & Yager, J. (1989). Multiple family group treatment for eating disorders: A short term program. *Psychiatric Medicine, 7*(4), 269–283.

Sluzki, C. E. (2008). 'The ancient cult of madame': When therapists trade curiosity for certainty. *Journal of Family Therapy, 30*(2), 117–128. https://doi.org/10.1111/j.1467-6427.2008.00421.x

Stewart, C. S., Baudinet, J., Munuve, A., Bell, A., Konstantellou, A., Eisler, I., & Simic, M. (2022). From efficacy to effectiveness: Child and adolescent eating disorder treatments in the real world (Part 2): 7-year follow-up. *Journal of Eating Disorders, 10*(1), 14. https:// doi.org/10.1186/s40337-022-00535-8

Stewart, C., Voulgari, S., Eisler, I., Hunt, K., & Simic, M. (2015). Multi-family therapy for bulimia nervosa in adolescence. *Eating Disorders: The Journal of Treatment & Prevention, 23*(4), 345–355. https://doi.org/10.1080/10640266.2015.1044348

Sweeting, H., Walker, L., MacLean, A., Patterson, C., & Hunt, K. (2015). Prevalence of eating disorders in males: A review of rates reported in academic research and UK mass media. *International Journal of Men's Health, 14*(2), 1–8.

Wallis, A., Rhodes, P., Dawson, L., Miskovic-Wheatley, J., Madden, S., & Touyz, S. (2017). Relational containment: Exploring the effect of family-based treatment for anorexia on familial relationships. *Journal of Eating Disorders, 5*(1), 27. https://doi.org/10.1186/s40 337-017-0156-0

White, M., & Epston, D. (1990). *Narrative means to therapeutic ends*. New York: W. W. Norton.

Wooley, S. C., & Lewis, K. G. (1987). Multi-family therapy within an intensive treatment program for bulimia. In J. Elka Harkaway (Ed.), *Eating disorders* (pp. 12–24). Rockville: Aspen Publishers.

Our stories

Families with experience
of multi-family therapy

Chapter 3

Introduction

In this section, you will meet families who, with immense courage, share their experience of multi-family therapy (MFT) in recovering from anorexia nervosa. The families generously share their stories because they know that anorexia nervosa can impact any family, anywhere. They offer empathy, hope, and inspiration to others experiencing this illness today. Their message is clear and strong: early intervention with evidence-based MFT provides the skills and knowledge to assist recovery.

Here, you will enter the homes where the families have become caught up in the emotional upheavals that can occur when anorexia nervosa develops. Read about how the parents, with remarkable resilience, describe behavioural changes, when and where they accessed help with MFT, and what skills they learned. Accompany the families as they strive to understand and manage the stressors of helping a child reconnect with their healthy self.

Together with their parents, children with experience of anorexia nervosa and MFT candidly share their stories. These stories describe the difficulties of living with and recovering from an illness that develops, uninvited, in the mind. For every child, the impact of the illness and the outcome of MFT differs; each family has unique dynamics and pathways. Ultimately, however, each child emerges from the experience with a greater understanding of family and self.

DOI: 10.4324/9781003641070-6

Home is where the hard work of recovery takes place. The families, whose names are represented by pseudonyms, hope the stories of their experience will encourage and give hope to families who have a child with the illness today. The parents and children tell June, 'We feel safe sharing our story with you because "you have been there, too"'.

Accompany June as she meets these ordinary yet extraordinary families. In Chapter 23, Ivan and Julian reflect on these stories and highlight some of the key points that make these accounts so powerful.

Chapter 4

The importance of being treated with respect

REBEKAH

Being treated as a person instead of a patient meant a lot to Rebekah, 13, when she developed anorexia and began multi-family therapy (MFT). Rebekah says, 'When with these professionals, I calmed down, and they drew me out of that fearful state. What helped was the wealth of their knowledge and the fact that they were experts. Knowledge appeals to me. I like to know the facts. I don't want an adapted-for-kids version of the truth. So, what appealed to me was the level of expertise, and I felt these people knew what they were talking about, and they were actually talking to me. They were listening to me. They were more interested in what made me tick and what kind of person I was before I became ill. I was treated like a capable individual. In previous treatment, I did not feel this'.

Rebekah attended MFT sessions with her parents, brother, and sister. This is the family's story:

The mother

Snow was falling as we departed home very early on a four-hour drive to the hospital's eating disorder unit to be assessed for MFT. Rebekah was an inpatient in our local hospital, and we had obtained permission to take her out for the day; she had a nasal gastric tube because her weight was so low. She had developed anorexia in September, and now it was almost Christmas.

DOI: 10.4324/9781003641070-7

Immediately, at the city-based hospital, we noticed a difference with the health professionals. The MFT team spoke directly to Rebekah while we were in the room, and they sounded like they were striking a deal, like, 'We will go so far, and you need to go so far and meet us in the middle'—this approach was important to give Rebekah a feeling of some sense of control. They spoke to her rather than to us, the parents, like, *'Rebekah, we can do this for you; what will you put on the table for us?'*

This technique of patient participation appealed to Rebekah. She was very much of the idea that the MFT people were the best people dealing with anorexia. Rebekah likes to feel she is getting the best. She is academic and likes to aim for the top; she wants to go to a top university, and she believes that the team at the city-based hospital is the best. To get her there, we kind of beefed it up, suggesting that to be referred to and offered a place in MFT was a privilege. The alternative was a residential unit, which none of us wanted. Something amazing changed in Rebekah's attitude during that assessment session, and we went home with Rebekah feeling she could trust the MFT team. We began MFT about five weeks later, at the end of January.

Four years later, I don't remember specific sessions during MFT, but I do remember thinking that other ordinary people also have this illness in their family. I felt relieved to think our family was not alone.

Often, families were together for the sessions—one time, the mother in one family had to be with the dad in another family and encourage a child from neither parent to eat a meal. This was challenging and helped us understand and analyse the dynamics between the three people involved. It also helped us look from outside the box—a fresh perspective.

The dad I paired with was not as insistent on the child eating as my husband, Pete, was with Rebekah. This dad's approach made me think. I work with young children and know the importance of message consistency, and now I could see this applied also with Rebekah, especially at mealtimes. Should

Pete be a bit less insistent and forceful, I wondered. The process made us consider if we had the best way or if we should try another way.

At home, I was more of a peacekeeper, and Pete was more of a confrontationist. I would tiptoe around the food and say, 'If you won't eat this, will you eat that?' or 'If you won't eat this now, will you eat it at half past four?' Pete would say more directly, 'You need to eat it now'. This meal activity helped me realise that Pete and I had been playing off against each other, and we needed to get more in tune with saying the same thing.

I also learned that there was more than one solution. There was a myriad of them. MFT was not like we sat in front of a PowerPoint presentation and learnt that if we do this, this, and this, our daughter will recover. It was more of a shared journey. There was no handbook called 'This is What Works'.

The MFT team encouraged us to keep the everyday parts of our lives normal. They were instrumental in getting Rebekah back to school in February and March, and even called the school to say she needed to resume everyday life. I think the school had gotten scared about how Rebekah presented when she was developing anorexia and how she was not eating. I supposed she was considered a 'health and safety' risk; they had kept ringing me at work, expressing concern until we agreed to keep her home. Getting her back to school was a relief, as her being home had caused me to stop work. For a time, the illness had completely taken over our lives.

The MFT team was forthright in explaining the anorexia nervosa and its effect on the mind and body. They told Rebekah facts, like the brain of an adolescent is more malleable to change in recovering from anorexia, and the prognosis was far better the younger you were. I'm sure Rebekah believed them because she believed they were the best, but she would not have believed me. The team was confident, too, about prescribing medication for a 13-year-old. Initially, I was not confident about this, but because I also implicitly trusted the MFT team, I trusted this was part of what would help Rebekah turn a corner, which she did.

Seemingly, small steps meant a lot. The day Rebekah stopped the compulsion to write down every calorie and every raisin consumed—well, I didn't think at the time such small steps were milestone days, but they were, looking back.

We still had arguments around food—there were good and bad days, but gradually more good days. Incidents of extreme anxiety, like when Rebekah gets a 'B' instead of an 'A' in exams, still occur but have become less and less. These are normal things any child must do, but they are heightened in Rebekah's situation. She has a yardstick now—she knows the worst she ever felt was when she had anorexia. She has that dark place to avoid. I think this is helpful when she feels herself slipping, to think, *'Well, I'll do what it takes because I'm determined never to slip that far again'*.

The MFT team was always calm and matter-of-fact, which was important for Rebekah to be a functioning person. One time, paper clips were placed on the floor, and mothers were asked to direct their daughters to walk blindfolded across the room, avoiding the paper clips. This exercise helped me to realise I needed to guide Rebekah and take control of her anorexia for her.

Primarily, MFT normalised the illness, stopped us from feeling like we were fighting it on our own, and gave us some authoritative, confident approaches and a range of tools to try new strategies.

The father

With the MFT team, we suddenly found ourselves with professionals who knew where we were and understood what this illness was about.

Until that point, the professionals we met had patients with a range of issues, so eating disorders were only a tiny part of what they did, and almost every time we met somebody, it was a new experience. At the eating disorder unit, even on the assessment visit, we felt the team knew what to do and gave us great confidence in the way they approached and understood where we were and in the way they described for us to go forward.

The MFT team was frank and scarcely optimistic, which was quite frightening. It was scary because we felt we were with the experts, and this was fairly obvious because we would say something, and they would write it down, and we would be wondering, *'Have we said the right thing or the wrong thing?'* And they would nod all the time as though they understood. There was none of this with the people we had talked to before. Now, we felt listened to, which was an enormous difference in manner and approach.

The MFT staff was professional yet sympathetic and supportive. In assessing Rebekah's condition, they seemed to be seeking a solution from a theoretical viewpoint. The doctor did not rate our chance of success highly, describing Rebekah's illness as dominating. Unless something happened to change her determination, trying to change that by persuasion alone would be like hitting a brick wall.

At that point, we had not met other families in our group and didn't know what was coming up. What we did know, however, was that now we felt we were being taken seriously. One issue with Rebekah was that she got ill very quickly—she had been diagnosed only in September and was on a drip by the middle of October. She had got to the stage where she restricted everything but water. All this had happened within six weeks.

On the first day of MFT, we had a chance to meet and talk with people who had completed the previous course. At that point, I started to wonder if we were getting anywhere; my hope was in the professionals rather than the activities, which seemed trivial and more like relationship icebreakers and builders.

But meeting the other families was interesting. They were not at all like we expected. We began to feel like we fit in a mould we hadn't realised existed. Anorexia is a divisive illness, but we now knew we weren't alone, and there was an element of feeling that we were in it together.

We noticed the divisive effects of the illness more in other families than in our own. Particularly, we saw how the sufferer would divide the parents and set them against each other, or argue one thing to one parent and another to the other. The divisiveness of the cajoling and creating was easier to see in people other than our own because we were somewhat blinkered to our own situation.

Certainly, at home with Rebekah, we had found ourselves blaming each other all the time, and we could see this in the other families. The attitude of one parent to the sufferer would be one of sympathy, and the other parent's attitude would be one of antipathy—the blame went to them: 'It is not their fault; it is your fault' and 'Why haven't you done this, or said that?'

We developed strategies based on observing these other families. Our long drives every day gave us, as a family, time to reflect. For example, we would say, 'Did you notice how these different people interact?' Claire and I began trying to find a truce whereby, rather than jumping on each other, we would agree with each other.

My behavioural traits were entirely like those of the rhino, and Claire's were like those of the kangaroo; in many other ways, we complemented each other. But in this particular situation, to help Rebekah, we had to devise a plan for working together. We also created a strategy for referring to the illness in the third person. We called it 'Ana' and had conversations where we would say, 'Ana is doing this' or 'Ana is doing that'.

We easily related to that concept because Rebekah previously had obsessive compulsive disorder (OCD), and we had talked about Oscar to identify the behaviours as belonging to that illness. Now, to get Rebekah back from anorexia, we needed to do all we could to discourage Ana.

At mealtimes, many things we had been doing had tended to incite the illness behaviours, and we took a while to learn new skills. This was the most horrendous period of our life. For instance, as the rhino, I would blame Claire-the-kangaroo for Rebekah not eating this, that, or the other. After MFT, instead of looking for blame, we began to look for opportunities to apply our new strategies. We were learning a lot about ourselves and each other.

As a result of Rebekah's illness and MFT, I have learnt to look at things from others' perspectives as well as my own. I have also learnt that while the traditional role model for a man is that he must be strong and hard, it is also appropriate to be vulnerable and soft and to allow your emotions and the things that hurt to show.

Was this difficult for me to do? No, because there was no option. We were at the stage where I would do almost literally anything to help save our daughter.

The illness is so devious that you learn to become devious as well. We would slip in an extra spoon of sugar or cream to help Rebekah gain weight; we would do anything to try and add extra calories. Little things became deeply serious—like the extreme scenario of weighing food to the exact gram. Take raisins, for instance. Are there six raisins in five grams, or is it seven, depending on which you choose?

When Rebekah developed anorexia, we initially kept to ourselves about it, but when we became desperate, we became very open, very quickly. We are church people and, you know, we are British, so we are reserved and don't usually share our feelings openly, that sort of thing. However, we consciously decided not to hide and pretend everything was okay. We could see that the illness was isolating us, and so we shared within our church environment, with people with whom we worked, and with people who needed to know at our children's schools. On the whole, we were immensely supported, but this illness is difficult for others to understand. We went to a faith meal at church, where everyone brought a chair. This was the first time Rebekah was eating in public, and she was about to sit down with a plate of food when somebody said well-meaningly, 'Oh, you look like you have a plateful there', and of course, Rebekah wanted to go home immediately.

Rebekah, one of the younger girls at MFT, turned a corner during the year-long MFT process and continued making progress. The MFT gave us markers, and sometimes we would look forward to that next therapy visit because we felt we were completely stuck, and the only hope on the horizon was that next meeting; other times, we would think we were not ready to go back for the next therapy session because we had not advanced or progressed. Sometimes, we were desperate for it, and sometimes, we wished the next session was further away to allow time to make forward strides.

We went to every session, but returning for the next session became increasingly difficult because seeing the other families reminded us very much of where we had been.

Recovery is not a smooth road. One evening during Rebekah's recovery process, we had an absolutely horrendous row when Rebekah basically threw her food at her sister, and she was self-harming and pulling her hair out. Arguments escalated, and I did not respond well. Rebekah threatened to call the police. I handed her the phone and said, *'By all means, ring them up'*, and she did. She didn't speak to the police, she put the phone down, but the police sent somebody around to check everything was all right. This happened during the 12 months of MFT, and Claire shared our experience at our next family therapy session. This was not a pleasurable experience, and we also had to tell my family and people at church because we wanted to be transparent. This experience fuelled our antipathy of the illness and our passion to go forward, and enabled us to empathise better, and understand and support others who experience traumatic circumstances.

How you handle your struggle defines who you are, and for Claire and I, through Rebekah's illness, our faith became more important to us. We prayed together more as a family and with our extended family because we did not know what else to do at various points.

Anorexia feels evil because it is so destructive; it is palpable. MFT gave us focus; it gave us confidence that we were doing the right things; it helped us to understand that this illness always presents as conflict, and the solution for us was to focus on working together. Importantly, we learnt ways to do this without conflict, because conflict does not achieve anything.

The confidence we had in the MFT professionals was immense. Learning by seeing the illness active in other families enabled us to learn lessons we could not see in our own situation because the mirror was not there. Seeing the illness affecting other people helped us to see ourselves in a different light. Seeing them making mistakes or handling a situation made us think, *'How would I handle this situation?'* and this becomes, *'How will I handle my situation?'*

The siblings

Lucy was 11, and James was eight when Rebekah developed anorexia nervosa at 13. Lucy and James were 15 and 12 when interviewed together:

Lucy: Travelling a long way to attend the MFT in the city was challenging because we had to miss school, and friends asked, 'Why are you going there?' Mum wrote letters to the important people at school who had to know, but like, friends asked questions, and I didn't know what to say. When we got to do the MFT, it was quite intense; we were shown many images, like PowerPoint presentations, that were upsetting and shocking. I remember thinking that Rebekah was getting like the images they were showing, and this was very worrying; it put the seriousness of her illness more into perspective.

I had heard some stuff about eating disorders, usually in the form of jokes, and it was hard to get my head around that this illness was not a choice thing. I learnt that Rebekah did not choose to be ill, and it had gotten to the point where she no longer had a choice. We had a siblings' session—just us and someone else's brother and someone else's sister. We drew pictures about how we felt and about anorexia. We referred to anorexia as Ana rather than say, 'Rebekah is this', or 'Rebekah is refusing to eat'. This kind of brought it apart—like we began to understand that the illness was not Rebekah.

James: Walking into the hospital, I felt intense and upset about what had happened with Rebekah and to our family over the past several months. At the same time, I felt happy and hopeful the problems would disappear soon now that we were getting help. In the long run, I knew we would be okay, but right then, when it was happening, we did not know what to do. Most of the time, while Rebekah was in conflict with Dad over not eating, Lucy and I would sit alone. We didn't know how to help.

Lucy: One activity we did at MFT, everybody did it, was where we got somebody to play the person with the anorexia. Someone was the anorexia voice, and somebody was the parent, trying to get them to eat, like re-enacting it in a way that showed the anorexia was the bully that was preventing the person from eating. The message I got from this was very forceful—it helped me understand why Rebekah could not eat. It helped me see that her anorexia was separate, and if we could get rid of it, she might be able to do the eating on her own.

James: I remember a 'daughter's swap' when the adults tried their techniques with other people's children to help them eat their lunch. A child from another family sat at our table, and Mum and Dad tried to encourage this girl to eat. This was a really good exercise as it showed the different ways parents can help their children eat. We were sitting at the table, too.

Lucy: The girl at our table didn't want to eat—just like Rebekah. It was more challenging because if the child is not your own, you don't want to yell at them or get cross. It is not your child to fight with. It was really difficult, but it showed that everybody was struggling. We were in this room full of people, all in similar situations, learning that anorexia could be dealt with.

James: MFT helped our family connect. It enabled us to help Rebekah by scaring off the illness. When we got home, the arguments decreased as she gradually stopped weighing her food and had family meals again.

Lucy: Rebekah had missed a lot of school and gradually returned, and when she started to join us in having a snack when we got home from school, this was like 'normal'. We tried to help distract the illness as much as possible, like watching movies and playing games. I am not saying this illness was a good thing, but helping Rebekah recover has brought our family very close; we had to work together to get rid of it, and that is what has brought us closer together and made our family stronger. We will be stronger for anything else that happens. I go to my friends' homes, and they don't sit with their families much, but our family tries to be together for meals.

James and I are close as brother and sister. Sometimes, Rebekah and I can go shopping together and do makeovers; other times, we argue, but this is what families do.

The patient

Rebekah developed anorexia nervosa at age 13 and attended MFT at the same age. When she was interviewed at 17, she was applying to Oxford:

I went to our family assessment at the city hospital's eating disorder unit feeling pessimistic, doom and gloom. I must have seen, by this point, 10 psychologists, three or four psychiatrists, numerous doctors and nurses, none of whom struck a chord. I thought this MFT team would be the same.

On the first day, when we met the team, I felt exposed and ashamed. I had a nasal gastric tube (NGT) inserted and, being out of the hospital environment for the day, felt quite paranoid. Walking from the car, along a tiny bit of street that's not even really public, into the hospital, I felt self-conscious and apprehensive and was shutting myself off to what was going on around me. My parents were talking to me, and I was in my own little world and not hearing them. I was expecting the MFT people, although not aggressive, to confront and speak harshly to me, as others did. I could not have been more wrong.

When with these professionals, I calmed down, and they drew me out of that fearful state. What helped was the wealth of their knowledge and the fact that they were experts. Knowledge appeals to me. I like to know the facts. I don't like to be told a watered-down version of the truth. I don't want an adapted-for-kids version of the truth. I've always been the child who annoys the parents, wanting to know exactly about the meaning of life and all these big questions. So, what appealed to me was the level of expertise, and I felt these people knew what they were talking about, and they were actually talking to me. They were listening to me. In previous treatment, I did not feel this.

With the MFT team, I felt I was in the right hands. The staff treated me as a person instead of a patient. They were more interested in what made me tick and what kind of person I was before I became ill. Previously, as a patient, I had felt like a battery kind of chicken that was progressively fattened up. With MFT, the professionals had a more holistic approach and treated me more on equal terms. They weren't patronising like other health professionals—especially those who would ask, 'Why have you chosen to do this to yourself?' The MFT staff treated me like a capable individual.

When we began the week of MFT, I felt less apprehensive than on the assessment day. I knew the professionals we were dealing with and that the situation was different to before. The unknown type of factor was minimised. I was nervous about meeting the other families, though, because I wasn't feeling much of a people person in those days. I also was in a better place from a health perspective. I was still severely underweight but had managed to get off the NGT and had a BMI of about 15. Not ideal, but not dying. So I could think more clearly and was not tired all the time. I suppose I felt more of a social anxiety, like, *'What do I do in this situation with new people?'* We were all wondering this on the first day.

MFT helped me realise that other people have this illness and to understand and reflect on my own problems better. It was good for me to see people at different stages of the illness as well—some girls were a lot worse than me and [there were] girls who were better than me, and I began to understand that this is a progression and, at whatever stage, it is possible to reach a better place.

I felt the MFT team did not have an ulterior motive. In previous treatment, the motive seemed to be, *'Hurry up and eat; we are kind of bored of this whole game'*, the undercurrent being that I had brought this illness on myself. I felt none of this with the MFT team; I found the team's acceptance of me when not at my best to be quite profound, as I had a very hard time accepting myself when I was ill. For the MFT team to care in this way was reassuring. Their attitude helped me to respect myself for the first time.

One thing that really struck a chord was the role-play thing where one person was the voice of 'Ana', and another person was the sufferer, which illustrated the effect of constantly hearing a barrage of negativity and that the voice of anorexia is separate from the voice that is you. From this, I learnt that my voice can be more powerful, and I don't have to submit to the negativity because it is not me doing it. Before, I had experienced much self-hatred when told by health professionals that I was doing it and I had to stop.

Learning I was not doing this to myself was refreshing, helpful, and quite shocking. Now, I was able to start building up my self-defence. At first, I would recognise a thought as being an anorexia thought but still act on it; but even recognising that thought was a huge step because I had been in complete denial. I still refused to believe I was ill on certain days, but I suppose that was a defensive strategy that was not the best.

Learning to live with the negative energy was a big step for me. I have had OCD since childhood, and the anxiety of not obeying the anorexia thought was sometimes overwhelming to the point where I would have panic attacks, lose control, or be angry. Learning to live with that kind of negative energy that tells you to give in, to be able to prolong your response to where you can make a more rational decision, to follow the thought or delay, was good for me. MFT was helping me learn strategies to do this in a productive way.

The MFT team helped me to learn the delaying tactic. For instance, washing my hands was the initial thing. Anxiety can spiral within a 10-second time frame, so now, instead of responding to this urge, I would go and read a book and make sure I read at least a chapter. This would take five to 10 minutes, therefore delaying the illness thought by a considerable amount of time. This would progress to longer things, like I would read two chapters or three chapters. Eventually, I would get to the stage where the thought had minimised, not disappeared, but reached the stage where I did not want to act on it.

Eventually, by doing other things, I could manage to not even give in to the little ripple. I could acknowledge the thought was there but know that it was part of the illness, and while still feeling very anxious, I would know I didn't have to respond to it.

I reached the stage at MFT where, as long as my food was weighed and meticulously prepared, I would eat it as quickly as possible. I rationalised that eating quickly and getting it over with would make it less bad.

I would feel mortified afterwards, though. I would feel I had been binge eating when I had been eating a normal meal, or not even what a normal person would eat at that stage, because I was not on normal portions; the aim was to get my weight up gradually. So, I had to slow my eating and become more aware of the process and how to feel, rather than wolfing it down without tasting it and feeling horrendous afterwards. By slowing the process, I would not feel so knotted with anxiety. That took a lot of time to achieve.

All the while, my food intake was steadily increased, and I had to get my head around that while trying to mindfully manage my eating. All my meals were organised with military precision. It struck me, eventually, how impractical it was to spend so much time planning, taking two hours to prepare a meal to the point where I was satisfied everything was right. Then, however long it took to eat the meal—something other people did without thinking about it.

I found a method of counting helpful to counter mealtime anxiety. I would calmly count to 20 in my head for each bite. I would try to do this in a clinical and numerical way because this would help me feel more detached from the anxiety and to be aware of how the food tasted. I would get a rhythm going, which helped, and further along the process, I would have someone sit and talk to me while I was eating.

The MFT provided a meal plan, which I had to check and approve. My judgement would not count, but I felt my approval was important, so I could feel I had a say and had to familiarise myself with it. The counting strategy came soon after this.

After MFT, I chose to wipe the slate clean and attend a new college—none of the people there knew about my illness, and I found it easier to find a kindred spirit and developed a few close friendships rather than a lot of friends. Eating in front of other students remained the most challenging thing. For a long time, I ate breakfast and the evening meal but no lunch. I was in a pattern of eating two meals a day, and to eat lunch at school took a lot of practice and trial and error.

The main thing MFT did for me was to increase my awareness and level of empathy for people in similar situations, as well as my perspective that things could get better because, for a long time, I had refused to believe that they could.

The human touch that MFT entailed was helpful, and the approach didn't feel clinical or contrived. However, to say the treatment was easy or to look at it through rose-tinted spectacles would be wrong. Some anxiety was associated with the programme from a social perspective—for instance, I felt distressed because one girl was more ill than me. I don't think her presence set me back, but coping was an upsetting and difficult process. On the regular follow-up trips back to MFT throughout the year, I sometimes felt judged because I was doing better than other girls.

The illness caused me to over-analyse other people's appearances. Regarding one thin girl, I suppose the anorexia part of me was saying, *'Look at her; you want to be like her'*, and the part of my brain that was me was appalled looking at this girl and was saying, *'She is not really even a person anymore because she is so ill'*. The girl's personality had kind of died. She would refuse to eat and always be hunched over and crying and screaming and would not speak. I found that distressing because I was once that girl.

Chapter 5

Everyone in the family has a role in recovery

NATALIE

MFT helped our family to be a cohesive unit. That's empowering and unifying as well. Each family member was made to explore their role in the family. This was hard for everybody and could have been damaging—like, if one of us had found it too hard and said, 'I'm not doing this anymore', recovery would have fallen in a heap. The MFT aim seemed to be to isolate the illness part of me, break this ball and chain that was keeping me the way I was not meant to be, stopping me from moving, from growing, or exploring the wonderful other things I could do. The treatment was quite successful at this.

Natalie, age 24, eight years after MFT

The patient

When diagnosed with anorexia, my family and I were quickly referred to the nearest eating disorder unit offering multi-family therapy (MFT). I kicked my heels, but comparatively, I was happier on the first day of MFT than the other girls. Only one other girl was well enough to talk coherently; the other three were very sick. Two girls were hospitalised, so they had formed a relationship outside the therapy, which skewed the dynamic of our group. Having inpatients as well as outpatients was a challenge.

Some of the activities have stuck with me. One time, we were placed in separate groups, parents and siblings in one group and

DOI: 10.4324/9781003641070-8

girls with the illness in another, and we drew a size representation of ourselves on a piece of paper against the wall. Then,
we stood next to our drawing, and they took a pen and drew
our body outline. So, we had these two representations—one
was real because we were aware that a pencil was being drawn
closely around our body outline, and the other was what we
imagined ourselves to be. This was disturbingly powerful. The
illness brain is so powerful that you can convince yourself you
are a certain size when you are not. The disparity between my
two drawings was shocking. That helped me a lot. I still find it
helpful to have a perspective that is not only grounded in my
own reality but other people's realities.

The meal times at MFT were difficult because this was
the whole point really—getting better in order to have this
healthy relationship with food, this concept, this ideal, but it is
really about a relationship with yourself; this is what I learnt.
Mealtimes were a struggle, and luckily, I was not as thin as the
other girls or hospitalised, so I had a little freedom. I remember
contrasting this with the other girls who were hospitalised and
the screaming that went on before meals. I felt empathetic
towards those girls.

I understood how hard it was for them but was completely
detached at the same time. Their behaviour was not triggering
for me. There was an interesting dynamic between the five of
us. One girl was keen to get better; I was a bit apathetic and
couldn't give a shit; another girl was only 12; and then there
were the two girls out of hospital who goaded each other on. If
one didn't eat, the other wouldn't, and if one had eaten and the
other refused, all hell broke loose.

For me, eating with another family was not hard. I was
already complying and working on regaining weight, not to the
point of being better, but sufficiently to want to get it over with.

There was a freedom-like exercise, like what would you be
doing if you didn't have to do all these things because you are
this way. This was patronising to the sick girls because they

were already doing what they wanted, and that was not to eat. We made charts of what we would like to do, normal things like going out with friends. This had to do with pre-adolescent/ young adulthood independence, which helped us be aware of what we were missing out on.

This involved splitting, like, the anorexia-dominated you from the real you, and that bothered me and rubbed me up the wrong way completely. Such a separation seemed like creating a scapegoat, stigmatised in a way, and I didn't find this helpful. I don't think there is a complete block or separation. I mean, it's like trying to separate your brain from your body—one can't survive without the other. I understand this is a method of talking about something and dealing with it, but I found it quite false.

The scientific explanations were more interesting. Like, the effect on the brain of not eating, and also the social explanations. We did a lot of social activities, like on the first night, there was a projection of a series of mannequins, which portrayed the changes through the ages; there was a comparison of culture, as well, like in some cultures, it is considered ideal to be big and meaty and juicy and round, and that's not the case in our present culture, especially in mainstream fashion. I found that putting this in context was helpful.

People love to wonder how things that happened in the past are affecting them in the present and may affect them in the future. We didn't do much of that. But we had intensive therapy sessions where that question was asked a lot. 'So tell me about you' 'Tell me about your day', and so you go through your day, and they pick up on things, and you start to self-question, and this becomes integral to this process. I found this helpful.

We went to monthly sessions after the initial week; the second last monthly session was on my 17th birthday, and we had a chocolate cake. The girls and I were, like, able to pretend to eat some of the cake. It was a big celebration. I was feeling pretty happy and positive by then. Also, seasonally speaking, we started MFT in November and finished in like, June, with winter in between. Everyone suffers and feels particularly shit in dark and cold weather. When spring and summer come along, spirits are on a natural arc, and mine were, too.

My most important support came from family, and this was due to the family being made aware that this illness affects everybody. Dad was particularly good. My sister Sarah, who was 13, kind of kept out of my way, and my brother Sam, who was closest in age, was a friend. There was a knock-on effect in that I worried deeply about Sarah developing an eating disorder, especially when I was feeling lost after therapy ended and trying to deal with it by myself. Anorexia is not contagious, but it does affect everyone around you.

MFT helped our family to be a cohesive unit. That's empowering and unifying as well. Each family member was made to explore their role in the family. This was hard for everybody and could have been damaging—like, if one of us had found it too hard and said, *'I'm not doing this anymore'*, recovery would have fallen in a heap.

The MFT aim seemed to be to isolate the illness part of me, break this ball and chain that was keeping me the way I was not meant to be, stopping me from moving, from growing or exploring the wonderful other things I could do. The treatment was quite successful at this. It made me quite defensive, too—the process of separating this Anorexic Natalie from this wonderful, great, sparkly Natalie—that was really hard, that separation. I couldn't see that I had lost my sparkle! I thought I was great as I was. We constantly look at the world through filters, from different ways, say, depending on whether we are a psychologist or a carpenter, and anorexia was my filter. I saw it as part of my identity, and perhaps that was the issue for me.

The illness itself and the therapy made me aware of an unrealised potential and capability. The therapy is different in a positive way because it is life-affirming. When you realise you can do anything, including kill yourself, you also realise you have this massive potential for survival.

MFT also shows the importance of having healthy human relationships as well as healthy relationships with self. As a result of the therapy, I was able to make friends with different people who showed me a different way of living. This was as important and instrumental as the therapy: friends who accepted me for who I was, supported me, pulled me out of the shit, and looked out for me. I wasn't grateful then, but I am very grateful now.

Eight years after the therapy, I see it as an achievement. I have had no relapses since the therapy, although, at times, I have been made aware of a tendency to go that way. If things are getting tough, I am aware I may go that way, that is, if I start restricting food intake, and am always finding new ways to cope. It is a funny contradiction, as pointed out in the therapy— you look like you are very controlled from someone else's perspective, but you are out of control. My major network of support remains family and friends, stemming from the time of my illness.

I wasn't aware of it then, but during my MFT year, Dad cooked up a deal with the publican in the nice pub around the corner, several streets from our home. The deal was that I could work in the pub on Sundays, provided I ate half a pizza for lunch. They paid a pretty good rate, cash in hand, for a 16-year-old and fed me lunch as part of the deal. I thought, *'Oh, they are feeding me lunch; I can't do my normal thing, be weird, and refuse to eat it, and guess I'll have to get as skinny a pizza as I can'*, and I'd ask for 'half a thin pizza with no cheese' and perhaps have peppers on it. But the pizza was served with cheese, and I had to eat it, sitting with the manager. I had no idea that Dad was behind this. I tried to keep the pizza portion as small as possible, but yes, I ate it. Now I can see that the publican was an important part of my support team. I go to that same pub today and can eat two pizzas.

The best thing about MFT was that I was doing it with my family. The siblings' support was different from that of my parents' and equally vital. I trusted them. Sarah was silent, non-judgemental, just going along with things; I am sure she was very worried but did not show it. Her mere presence provided strong support. Sam, 14 at the time I was sick, was safe company, and he understood. He is family-orientated and compassionate and would do weird things with me, like, if I needed to walk in the middle of the night or after a meal, he would walk with me. If I were exhibiting that kind of weird anorexic behaviour, Sam would make it kind of normal, make it okay. He would eat his meal with me, and he helped me learn that I had to get through it. He would sit there until I finished my meal.

The worst of the illness was in the two months following the family therapy week. I went to the other extreme and became a compulsive overeater. To me, it was extreme. I went to a party, and this thing in my head had just broken, almost; it was like going from one extreme to the other. I polished off 92 sausage rolls—in one night. I was so full I could hardly walk. I was really, like, about to be sick. The sausage rolls seemed stuck in my oesophagus; my stomach was so full. I remember going home and feeling so sad about this, and the next day, promising myself not to eat anything at all. I can't stand sausage rolls any more.

My body seemed to go from famine to feast on a very physical level. It was like something clicked in my brain and sparked a fear of starving. I did some sickening things. I went to another party, being socially active at this point. Being a party girl was almost like an escape, almost. It was like a form of freedom, even though part of me couldn't fully communicate at that point. I went to this poor girl's house, opened her pantry cupboard and ate everything inside but could not swallow. I carried a little plastic bag around so I could chew the food and spit it into the bag. I did this for about four hours. People were saying,

'What's the problem with you?' This behaviour continued for months.

Part of the reason for family members walking with me after meals was to counter this binge-eating thing. I was still having regular therapy sessions and was able to tell the therapist, 'I have lost control'. I was never able to purge or vomit, but the bingeing made me feel really sad and sometimes like, I felt paralysed by sadness and couldn't do anything; other times, I would walk for hours. Walking was good for me; it was like psycho-geography in that I walked through my thoughts and was directly influenced by my environment. I could do that as far as my legs would go.

Mum and Dad gave me a bicycle for my 17th birthday, which coincided with completing MFT, and the sense of freedom was astonishing. Riding the bike helped me feel independent, and this was important. I cycled 3000 km in Europe this past summer with a friend for fun. What was amazing was how much food I needed to eat for fuel. We rode 100 to 120km a day.

My sense of self is in a really good place. I have learnt an incredible amount as a consequence of this illness about what it means to be alive. I'm very self-aware and am conscious not only of myself but also of how my actions affect other people. I maintain my recovery had a lot to do with being distracted from the illness, with my mind being diverted to other things. A few people came into my life and have stayed in my life. They were welcome, pleasant, and joyous distractions. Not necessarily rise-above-the-eating-disorder thoughts but being put into situations where there was no place for those illness thoughts. To be with friends and keep up with them, I needed to eat.

The MFT broke some kind of ice in our family, like we were forced to communicate with each other in a very honest way, and eight years later, this still stands. I mean, we were already a close family, but during the illness, I was lying to my parents, not communicating, and starving myself to death.

At 24, I'm not thinking long term, but I want to finish my degree, be nice to people, and have fun. I would like to work in travelling. I work in a pub now.

The mother

When we went to the first meeting of MFT, I felt relieved to see who was in this group—we had a psychiatrist, a medical doctor, and a psychologist. We had everybody together, so everybody knew what they were doing. No contradictory messages were coming from different people. That's what I thought was so brilliant. And meeting other families was a great relief.

The group exercises were great, but it was the continuous support that made the difference. We knew that at the end of the week together, there would still be somebody there—not only for our child but also for us. As family members, we were allowed to call and say, 'Please help', if the need arose.

The continued support was useful because the first two months after the MFT four-day session were hard. I took two weeks off work, and Dave rearranged his shift patterns. Natalie would run away, destroy furniture, and kick holes in walls. Behave badly.

We went on a family holiday with my brother, and Natalie managed to destroy part of the house. My brother was furious, saying, 'What the hell is she doing?' Physically, my husband and I had to constrain Natalie and put her in the back of the car because she was going so wild and out of control. Being able to talk to our MFT therapist about moments like this was helpful. My husband would take the heat out of these situations. I could get in a bit of a tizz, but Dave was very good, considering he had no previous experience with mental health problems.

Within the MFT group, it was not about being compared with other families but saying, 'Oh yes, this has happened to my child, and this is how hard it is', so we could see we were on a parallel.

Being in a group helped us clearly see that we could not handle this illness alone. For example, we all did the timeline together. You might wonder what the point of this is, but others are doing it, so you do it, too. Eating meals together helped normalise it as much as possible for the young people, for whom it was obviously not normal.

I remember the body dysmorphia session, where the children drew a picture of what they thought they looked like, and then the mothers drew around their body shape to reveal actually what they were. I was shocked when I saw Natalie without clothes on, and I think she was shocked, too. She was so thin and so scared. Until then, I hadn't realised how terrified she was.

Much of the MFT focus was on structure around eating, and this was very helpful to both the young person and us—for we could now say, 'This food is what your medical doctor says you must have', 'You know, it is the equivalent of having an antibiotic every four hours'. We could say, 'That's what the medical expert says, and you've got to do it'. We could absolve blame, really, from parents being seen as the enforcers. This worked better in a group of people from our point of view and also from the young person's point of view because they could see that everyone was expected to eat. It wasn't just 'them' on their own; it was everyone, and this is how they all were being treated. If they didn't do this, well, hospital was not an attractive option.

Public holidays were the trickiest times. At our first Christmas, shortly after starting MFT, Natalie did very well on Christmas Day; the next day, she refused to eat. She had done what was expected and, overcome by fear, said, 'I am not eating again, ever'. We had to wait a week to see our therapist and get Natalie back on track. It would have been good, on the day after Christmas, to have had someone on the other end of the phone giving reassurance and saying, *'All right, it does not matter for this day; we know it is difficult for you, it is a normal experience at this time of the year, and go back onto the plan, tomorrow. Just give her one day off'.*

Natalie needed to understand that she was not taking her medicine, that is, the food, and needed to get back on track quickly. As it was, we lost a week. It felt much longer than a week. We can't expect people to work during public holiday time, but having a prior preparation plan, knowing this might happen, would be good. To hear something like, *'Don't panic too much; the young person is drinking water, and they will live. They don't even have to have a bit of lemon in it'*. This would have been helpful.

Initially, meal and snack times were about precision. Natalie would tell us the time and ask, 'Where is my snack?' We had to be exactly on time and provide exactly what was on the list, like at 11:00 a.m., 1:30 p.m., 3:30 p.m., and the other meal, tea at 5:00 p.m. Otherwise, she would become panic-stricken. Dave was the primary carer, and he would say, 'We will go for a walk after you eat this'. This was very useful. They went on a gentle sort of stroll around the neighbourhood, not a power walk.

Natalie was adventurous, to say the least, and had a really hard time because she drank a lot and smoked weed and stuff like that. We would lock the house at night, but she would shinny two floors down the drainpipe, and that drainpipe is not strong or sturdy. She would escape out the window from her bedroom at the top of the house, go down the drainpipe, and jump over the back fence. So even though we had locked the doors, we would discover she had disappeared. We just had to carry on.

Other times, she would perch up on the beams in the top of our house and refuse to come down all day to avoid mealtimes. This was within the MFT time. It was hard work coping with these dangerous and reckless behaviours, which went on for about a year. Reckless, reckless, reckless. I began to worry that the drugs and alcohol were taking the place of the anorexia. Fortunately, Natalie was being monitored closely with weekly psychotherapy sessions at the Maudsley. Without that support,

I think that period of her life could have had dire consequences. We weren't involved in the psychotherapy sessions; we just had to be there for her at home, really.

Between us, Dave and I provided 24-hour care. I think the experience of helping Natalie recover from anorexia has been very positive for our family in that our five children have all grown into nice, kind, mature people who have compassion for those of their friends who have mental health problems. They can cope with mental health problems and don't judge or avoid people because of such illness. They are there for them, along with their illness, and they like them as people.

The detrimental side of coping with Natalie's illness was that I did not have time to show interest in what the two siblings, Sam and Sarah, closest in age to Natalie, were doing. They managed to scrabble along taking care of themselves. Still, as for pushing them forward and supporting them academically, like into university and college, I lost that bit of momentum for them. They had to manage themselves, basically. I only had time to think, *'They are going to school, so that's good'*.

Sarah, especially, I think her needs were overlooked. She could see big problems were going on with her older sister and, therefore, did not pipe up about her own concerns. She went through a tough time at school but is in a better place now. The impact on school results was the negative side of this illness. I mean, siblings needed to be involved in the family therapy, but maybe it could include instruction on how to support the siblings through this period when time is taken up with caring for the sick child.

They had a separate meeting for siblings during the four days, but a session to enable a parent-sibling conversation would have been helpful, too. The siblings aren't ill, but the illness has a long-term impact on the family dynamics. To hear from the siblings voice their concerns would be useful—like, *'Is my sister so ill that she is going to die?'* and for parents to say, *'She is very ill, but no, she is not going to die, because we are doing this'*. The siblings needed to know the illness was serious, but they also needed reassurance.

Before this illness, we were a busy family, with Natalie, the eldest of five, and both parents working. The siblings have always been close, and they like each other and look out for each other.

MFT worked incredibly well by involving the parents in the treatment process, involving them in interactions with professionals and other parents; it provided structures and medical support, which was always in the background if necessary as an intervention of the last resort.

We learnt about the level of anxiety faced by our children and learnt how to negotiate with them when they were still very ill, about what they could get away with and what they couldn't. An example was Dave saying, 'Okay, we will go out for a walk after you have eaten', in a calming, managed tone of voice. Dave was more negotiable and hands-on with Natalie and did the emotional negotiation.

He was also inventive in outsmarting the anorexia. A job he organised in the pub gave Natalie some independence and freedom. What didn't work was Dave's attempt to put extra butter in the mashed potato and baked beans. I said, 'You can't do that because the young person is trusting you'. 'She is trusting you to deliver what you say you are going to deliver'. We didn't argue about it; I just commented that I didn't think that was the right approach.

Sometimes, Natalie locked herself in the bathroom for 12 hours. I didn't know until we went to the therapy that such behaviour was due to the illness. We learnt that '*This isn't the person, this is the illness'*, and our role was to help the young person. To disengage the behaviours of the illness from our child was very helpful. To solve the bathroom problem, we took door handles and locks off, and took the locks off all doors in the house, except for the front door.

Sometimes, I threw my hands in the air, called our therapist, went to see her, cried and cried, and went home feeling better and more able to cope. This didn't happen often in the 12 months, but to do this was very helpful.

The sibling (Sarah)

Age 18

I thought MFT would be fun, and I was glad to miss maths at school, but when I was told that Natalie's illness could be fatal and that people die from this illness, this was frightening and confronting. I found there was a lot of ignorance about the disease, and you don't know what it is like until you or a family member go through it. This was very stressful. When I returned to school, I burst into tears.

Mum and Dad told my form teacher, and she came to me and said, 'Alright, dear, would you like to go and see a counsellor?' I was like, 'I'm not ill', but it was, like, a knock-on effect. I was in Year Eight, and family was my main support. This intense period lasted 18 months.

The worst time was when we were going to MFT, and Natalie was most ill—until this point, her illness was more in the shadows—and now we knew how serious it was and seeing other children with the illness as well. Suddenly, this illness was something that had to be confronted and dealt with.

It was good to see parents of other children at the MFT because Mum and Dad were, like, pulling their hair out, and now they knew they were not crazy, and other parents were going through the same thing. It was good to talk to some siblings as well, being able to relate to someone in the same position as me.

MFT was instrumental in Natalie getting better because everyone in the family was affected, but we didn't know what to do, and now we each had a role. Like, before we went to these sessions, I had no idea. I knew that Natalie was ill because she obviously was not eating much, but I did not know how serious an eating disorder was

MFT is important for siblings because taking care of a child with anorexia is a distracting time for the parents, helping their child get better. My brother Sam, who was closest to Natalie in age, was her biggest sibling support. I didn't really have someone to share support with. Like, I was not ill. I am the middle child, two older and two quite a few years younger—the younger children were too little to understand and didn't go to therapy week.

I learnt that things might get better or worse, and I just had to stick it out. I learnt that when things look really grim, *you can't let up*. The way a sibling copes is in many ways up to them, in their own family. Being quite academic, I focused on my schoolwork. This helped me cope.

Having siblings around Natalie was relaxing for her; our parents sometimes shouted, and things would get stressful. With siblings, the relationship was a lot calmer. Mealtimes were challenging, but we all pulled together. I was never involved in trying to get Natalie to eat her meals. I never said, 'You've got to eat that'. That was not my role.

MFT was helpful to see that not just our family was having a tough time with anorexia, that we were not alone, and that life would improve. It didn't matter that Natalie's siblings were overlooked at times because we weren't ill.

• See Chapter 6, where Natalie's dad, Dave, shares his story.

When dad is the primary carer

DAVE

I had to treat this carer role like a real job. Saving a life is a big job. One time, Natalie caught me putting butter in the baked beans because sometimes she would eat beans on toast, and I had to quickly say, 'No, no, these aren't your beans; these are for the other children'. If I knew of a family struggling today, worrying their child has an eating disorder, I would share my experience and recommend MFT. I'm sure more people than me think that if only you will take medicine for this illness, you will get better. There's more to it than that. I've learnt a lot. Like, when we first saw a GP when Natalie was 15, the GP said, 'Well, Natalie, at least you haven't lost your boobs yet'. I thought the GP was trying to be helpful and bright, but Natalie has since explained that was the wrong thing to say because it reinforced her thought that she was fat.

– Dave, primary carer for daughter Natalie

The father

I was sceptical about family therapy. I had an attitude like, *if you are ill, you take medicine, and you get better*. I had no idea what to expect when I turned up for multi-family therapy (MFT). I had not encountered mental illness before. I felt shocked when the doctor said Natalie had anorexia. I was not in denial; I didn't have a clue. When told about the illness, I felt scared, even though we got onto it early.

DOI: 10.4324/9781003641070-9

The time lapse between getting a diagnosis and starting MFT was only about one week. We were lucky. The eating disorder unit was based at the hospital up the road, and the session was beginning. Other families had to drive for hours every day or find accommodation locally. So, getting there was a piece of cake compared with the practical problems facing other families.

At the introductory evening, well, I got another shock, learning there is an awful lot more to an eating disorder than just wanting to be thin. The disease took over our lives, and my wife Heather had to be at home, or I had to be at home for every meal. Fortunately, I worked shifts, so the disruption to Heather's professional career was minimised. On the days I could not be at home, she had to be there and take the afternoon work.

One dad said that he felt utterly useless and powerless. I felt like a punching bag often, but I did not mind. I was also a boulder. I learnt that we had to get Natalie fed, and the more she ate, the less of a grip the anorexia would have on her. It seemed to help to have small amounts regularly. A friend who had experience said anorexia was like an abusive boyfriend who would rather kill you than let you go. So, I knew we had to be regimented and not give in to the illness. Natalie would eat and want to go for a walk, to walk off the calories, and that was fine; it became part of the deal: *you eat, we walk.*

Anorexia is a devious disease. To help Natalie recover, we had to be devious, too. My primary role was helping her to eat and getting others to help. At school, one teacher kept an eye on her at lunchtime.

I had to treat this carer role like a real job. Saving a life is a big job. One time, Natalie caught me putting butter in the baked beans because sometimes she would eat beans on toast, and I had to quickly say, 'No, no, these aren't your beans; these are for the other children'. I had to put on another tin of beans for Natalie. That was a bugger. Getting her to eat, well, I just had to be patient and try and look at it from Natalie's point of view. For her, every mouthful was horrendous.

Some things she did were horrifying and disgusting, and, as Natalie says, things got worse before they got better.

Natalie mentions that her brother Sam would go walking with her. Well, I worked at night, and Heather was notorious for leaving our back door unlocked, so I would nick out from work and come home at 2:00 a.m. just to make sure the house was secure. We had finished our week of MFT when one night, coming home, I passed someone as I was getting near home and thought, *'He looks like Sam'*. I guessed Natalie had gone to a night spot about a mile and a half from home, and Sam was going after her to make sure she was safe. I turned the car around, belting up the road, and a cat ran out in front of me. I screeched to a halt.

The cat wasn't trapped under the wheels but had been kind of run over. It was still alive. So what had happened was that Natalie and Sam had gone off wandering, and I went after them because I wanted to tell them I could not cope with doing night shifts and chasing after them. I also wanted to get across to Natalie that there was a consequence to every act. The consequence of her action of going out at 2:00 a.m., even though I knew that her act was compulsive, she was driven—she didn't just wake up and fancy a walk—a consequence of all that was me running over a cat.

Anyway, the two children got in the car, and I was very angry. I regretted being so angry but couldn't help it. I was upset over the cat but did not want to get sacked from my job. I could put up with some intrusion, but I needed a job. I said, 'Natalie, there is a consequence. We have a dead cat'. Thankfully, we found the cat was not dead and had scarpered, and I hope it lived happily ever after.

What came out of this was how supportive Sam was—Natalie would wake him up and say, 'I want to go for a walk'. Every time, he would get up and walk with her to ensure she was safe. And I thought, *'Okay, this illness is a pile of poo; it's really negative'*, but *'Sam's care and support for his sister is something positive'*.

I can't say I noticed a particular day when things got better; it was more about noticing gradually less tension about eating. We had to reorganise our work routine totally—the disease takes over every aspect of family life.

Heather and I were united in our efforts to get Natalie to eat. There was no point in telling her, 'Right, girl, you are going to eat'. We had to cajole and encourage her.

There was no 'one person' responsible for Natalie's recovery, with the exception perhaps of Natalie herself. Helping her get over this illness encompassed a lot of people, both family and friends and community. One night during the MFT year, Natalie got drunk, and Heather and I had to walk 50 metres or more down the street to pick her up. She refused to come home, so we carried her. Heather was holding her under her armpits, and I was carrying her legs. I remember I almost said this but kept my gob shut, *'God, she weighs a ton!'* You think things like this, but you have to check yourself to avoid sparking the eating disorder trigger in case it goes off again. Even in that drunken state, Natalie would have been aware enough to take a comment on board.

As for MFT, I have gone from being sceptical to thinking it is wonderful and that the people who run it are very clever in getting kids to eat, survive, and live. That's really clever. The different activities they have, the awareness of it, they tell you the truth, but even then, you haven't a clue about what you are going into. Every night during the four-day session, we went home feeling depressed and deflated. I found this hard to cope with. It's eight years ago and a bit of a blur, but I remember feeling this way.

One night, when Heather and I arrived home from a particularly depressing session, a man with a disability was waiting for us and abused Heather in the street over a car parking issue, and Heather became hysterical. I got her in the house and went back to see him. I said, 'Look, you have done something really awful, and we are having a difficult time right now; our daughter is in therapy', and he said, 'Your daughter is in fucking therapy, what's she in fucking therapy for?' The only thing that stopped me from punching him—and I am not violent; I don't hit people—was the thought that *'if I punch him now, I will be arrested and have to go to Court; he will turn up in a suit'*. I could see the headline, *'Disabled Man Punched by Angry Neighbour'*. That was one aspect of it, but the real restraint on the strong urge to punch him right then was the thought that *'If I am arrested, I will miss the MFT session tomorrow, and it is more important to go to the session than deal with this idiot'*. I later had a word with the police, who had a word with him, eventually. Under normal circumstances, Heather would have said to that man: *'Get lost'*.

At MFT, I didn't get so much out of seeing other dads, but I did realise how much easier it was for my family than some others; the illness put such a strain on the relationship of one other couple that they broke up—there would have been other reasons too, but the illness didn't help. The parents of another child had already split up.

If I knew of a family struggling today, worrying their child has an eating disorder, I would share my experience and recommend MFT. I'm sure more people than me think that *if only you will take medicine for this illness, you will get better*. There's more to it than that. I've learnt a lot. Like, when we first saw a general practitioner (GP) when Natalie was 15, the GP said, 'Well Natalie, at least you haven't lost your boobs yet'. I thought the GP was trying to be helpful and bright, but Natalie has since explained that was the wrong thing to say because it reinforced her thought that she was fat.

The best result from MFT for my family was that Natalie began to eat. Eight years later, she can sit around the table and talk about her illness, which says a lot about family therapy.

When we finished our therapy, we were invited to return and share our story with others in new MFT groups set up out of London, which I thought was quite a compliment.

- See Chapter 5, where Dave's daughter Natalie and other family members share their stories.

Chapter 7

A tale of anorexia, two mothers, and friendship

LISA and HARRIET

Imagination and humour shine through in a friendship, giving two mothers strength and resilience to confront anorexia nervosa and save their daughters. The mothers find that connecting with someone outside their family with whom to share their turmoil 'in the moment' is crucial to coping—especially when anorexia is bent on hijacking the heart of their family home, the kitchen. Through reciprocal support, the two women protect each other's sanity from what they call 'the dreadful witch', hold their families together, and steer their daughters towards recovery.

The friendship between Lisa and Harriet began when each was feeling deeply alone with what was happening to her family. The openness and honesty of each mother helped foster trust and confidence in their reciprocal disclosures.

They met when one comforted the other in a break between sessions during the multi-family therapy (MFT) week. Words were hardly necessary. Just being there was enough. They instantly understood each other. Outside the MFT group, the two women agreed to share phone numbers and began texting 'live' moments as difficulties unfolded.

Now, each mother had someone 'out there' with whom to share and hear internal dialogue; she no longer felt alone. Texts became longer, prompting the sharing of email addresses for more reflective communications. Text messaging, however, remained important for the 'in the moment' release of

DOI: 10.4324/9781003641070-10

emotion—somewhere to safely direct fear and frustration, anger and despair, rather than bring them 'to the table'. This outlet helped to avoid the paralysing anxiety of (in their words) *doing something that might make things worse.*

Lisa and Harriet developed friendships among all the parents in their group, but they 'clicked' with each other especially. As the MFT year progressed, they exchanged emails in tandem with texts to offload emotions, ideas, thoughts and reflections, and empathy; offer alternative perspectives; and occasionally challenge each other. They shared the impact of the illness not only on their daughters but also on siblings, relationships, friendships, and extended family.

Their story illustrates that anorexia nervosa affects every member of the family and the importance of 'being there' for each other. Through reciprocal support, the two women protected each other's sanity from what they called 'the dreadful witch', held their families together, and steered their daughters towards recovery.

Harriet and Lisa said that without their friendship, the outcome for their daughters, themselves, and their families could have been very different.

The two friends went away together for a weekend meditation retreat sometime after the group sessions had finished. This was when they realised that while they had shared their deepest emotions, family difficulties, and their darkest moments, they actually knew little of each other's backstory, the normal likes and dislikes of everyday life, their careers and their experiences before anorexia entered their homes and their lives.

Harriet and Lisa's friendship had evolved in reverse of the usual pattern of friendship. During that weekend away, they spoke of their early lives, pregnancy experiences and other friendship-girly things. The women went on to cherish their enduring friendship on all levels.

Text and email excerpts from their MFT years, over a two-year period, illustrate how friendship helped in caring for their children in the 'treatment centre', the family home:

From: Lisa
Sent: 25 September 16:45
Subject: RE: hi

For moments of dire emotional turmoil, email is a lifeline and one we should both use.

One question I have about the girls is how to regain normal eating habits once their weight increases a bit.

Lydia will eat what she eats without too much of a fuss but just won't (or can't) open her mind to anything else, and I don't know whether to leave it to the fullness of time or insist week by week on one new food.

Each time, the transitions are accompanied by weeping and extra slow eating occasions, BUT after a few days, the new pattern is established and seems to work. So, should I be doing this across foods or be grateful for what she has? Please make me feel better...

Xxxx

From: Harriet
Sent: 25 September 18:13
Subject: RE: hi

I agree the immediacy of texting is a lifeline and a vital distraction from the awfulness of the illness, so let's keep it up.

I'm really surprised to hear you talk about introducing new foods each week; it hadn't occurred to me, and it seems like such a good idea. It's just so wearing pushing the boundaries of their limitations that I tend to opt for an easy life when she is cooperating. Cassandra eats most things I cook provided they don't contain added fat—olive oil in cooking is acceptable—but we have slipped into acquiescing to her 'no butter in potatoes and no cheese' stipulations, which has wiped lasagne and varied baked dishes off the menu. She eats only brown pasta, which, alongside the cheese ban, makes pasta dishes so unappetising I just don't bother.

It's difficult to know how much to push things, especially when they are so much better than they were. The nurse seems to favour the march forward fearlessly approach, but my sanity requires the challenge, progress and plateau approach so I can relax in between.

From: Lisa
Sent: 01 October 10:40
Subject: Re: musings

My dear Vesuvius,

About the next therapy visit:

I know we worry about how the therapists perceive our daughters (and ourselves), but let's face it: we don't smell, we can talk in sensible (well, nearly sensible) sentences, we don't hit or bully our children, and our children don't throw things, scream, swear or defecate anywhere but the loo. A friend says we are soooooooo great for even attending sessions (most people don't), for trying to help our kids through being there (most families reject a problem), and for being prepared to take some of the responsibility for what has gone wrong (even though this is misguided) that we shouldn't worry about the rest. I am also quaking in my shoes, but we must try not to give ourselves such a hard time.

From: Harriet
Sent: October 07, 3:52 PM
Subject: hi

Hi Lisa,

I just thought I'd share my shit day. Things have been going so well, but anorexia has been particularly agitated today and confronting it has revived those old feelings that any action I may take will make things worse....

Cassandra had slept in, and her morning snack was still untouched at 1pm. Lunch was on the horizon, so I started to get agitated and reminded her to take it. Twenty minutes later, I prompted her again, and she was very angry and tearful.

I felt really annoyed as she knew she must have this mid-morning snack. So, I confronted her on it, how I'm not prepared to go backwards and the consequences of further weight loss (I have fought to keep her in jazz dance class and PE, but these will be the first to go); how awful it is living with anorexia.... Sadly, her perception is that I'm saying how awful she is to live with, and nothing will budge that perception.

All this firmness and confrontation leaves me in a regretful mess. Cassandra has since gone to meet her friend in town (something I would otherwise welcome; she doesn't do it enough) and left with hardly a goodbye.

I hope you don't mind me sharing; writing seems to have helped defuse it.

Harriet x

From: Lisa
Sent: 07 October 18:02
Subject: Re: hi

Oh god, what a day! The first thing to do is say every combination of swear words you can think of and repeat them. My favourite combination is #### wank bollocks, then again louder, #### wank bollocks! Right, that's over, now for some thoughts:

1. I agree that fitting all the bits in when the day starts late is a BIG problem ... I THINK my conclusion, providing this

occurs on only one day a week and involves only one snack OR breakfast, I might overlook it because the benefits of sleep to their bodies is more important.

2. I always find that anorexia is also worse when Lydia is tired—like PMT or anything; we are much less resilient when we are worn out. So rather than just being an ordinary moody teenager, she becomes a moody anorexic teenager...

3. Lastly, it is good if Cassandra goes out—this means she has the spirit to fight, and I always find it helps Lydia to have some time out with friends. They change their mindset and when they come home again, they are usually feeling brighter.

That's my thoughts. Probably rubbish, but at least you know that I have days like you, and nothing is a simple answer, but at least you and I try and try and try again to help our girly girls.

xxxxxxxxxxxxxxx

From: Lisa
Sent: 08 October 13:15
Subject: Re: hi

I am about to look up secure units for mothers of children with anorexia—if there isn't one, it is definitely a business opportunity xxxxx tee hee.

I am glad raspberries are no longer available anywhere. As a preferred fruit option, they got so expensive, and the new choices of mangoes and peaches are marginally more affordable. The best win, though, is Lydia's new fad on spiced stewed apple—with cinnamon sticks and cloves. Now on BOGOF (buy one, get one free) at the local fresh food market—yippee!

From: Harriet
Sent: October 08, 12:50 PM
Subject: RE: hi

My current angst is the stress of ensuring acceptable foods are in the house. For instance, I suddenly realise there's only one banana left, and Cassandra should eat a banana with her breakfast. She would be happy to skip it but if she skips it because the banana monitor has failed to keep supplies topped up, her weight loss will be my fault, agh.

So, my life has reduced to feeling anxious about bananas. I develop irrational anxiety if Adrian approaches the bananas. I think, *damn, that means I'll run out earlier than I thought, I'll have to go back to the shops sooner to replenish them*; then I think, *why shouldn't he have a banana? He pays for them*, so I keep my mouth shut and feel stressed about the bananas running out. I have tried overbuying, but no one likes to eat bananas when they go speckledy; basically, I'm going bananas about bananas!

When will this madness end? Answers on a postcard, please, to the secure unit for mothers of children with anorexia.

See you tomorrow.

Harriet

From: Harriet
Sent: October 29, 7:07 PM
Subject: hi

I disappeared down a black hole last week and am tentatively stepping out.

The positives:

Cassandra has put weight back on after losing the previous week.

The paediatrician was positive about Cassandra's progress ....

Cassandra has been generally a pleasure to be with and very helpful ….

Cassandra has been expressing her feelings more openly ….

The negatives:

I have gained weight.

Cassandra is experiencing problems with her recently 'ortho-dontically' rearranged teeth.

Cassandra is having difficulty remembering things and with her schoolwork.

I am experiencing memory loss! I assume it's stress, but I can't rule out senility.

I absolutely must stop spending money I don't have.

How can we look as if we are eating less without arousing the dragon?

Harriet ###

From: Lisa
Sent: 30 October 00:00
Subject: Re: hi

Hi Harriet

You and I gaining weight is tricky. I spent about two hours today trying to think how I could diet successfully without causing ructions. I feel so FULL and yearn for a week when I don't have to eat anything sensible and can cut down big time. I have been eating meals because I think I must, and then I scoff chocolate, cakes, and crisps for comfort. This is getting serious as every-thing feels tight around the middle, and I am sure I am starting to look (more) like a whale.

xxxxxxxxxxxxxxxxxxxxxxx

From: Harriet
Sent: December 09, 6:04 PM
Subject: treading a path despite never knowing if it's the right way......

Are we nearly there? Shall I drive all the professionals mad by repeatedly asking this question? It's potluck, it seems, whether we reach our destination, and there are no clues to tell us we are on the right road.

Consequently, I do not know whether I have taken the right turn in confronting Cassandra this afternoon about the compulsive exercise she feels she must do to feel her life is worth living. In confronting her, I precipitated a huge emotional meltdown and catharsis. My heart aches to see my baby (I visualise the baby she was—the unspoilt potential, her perfect doll-like face, and the days when I had the power to protect her from pain). Seeing her sobbing in the fetal position and having nothing to offer except my presence and my contact breaks my heart. I feel like a giant sponge that has soaked it all up to carry for her, and I feel totally helpless.

In becoming this sponge, there is a limit to what else I can absorb. I feel there isn't enough time in the day to do all I need to do. My car is playing up, and I should book it into the garage, but I need it for shopping and work. I want to see the general practitioner (GP) about skin rashes. I feel overwhelmed at work, and I feel like letting go of everything so I can focus on my family and myself. If I must go head-to-head with anorexia, I need to be there to catch the fallout.

I feel on the verge of totally unravelling, dropping all the balls I'm juggling, and wanting to have responsibilities taken away; I have enough on my plate fighting the beast. This feels like the 'pre-admission to the secure unit' state. Am I nearly there—yes, I am, very close to insanity. I could be so productive with those paper chains...

Thinking of you xxxxxxxxxxxxxxx

From: Lisa
Sent: 09 December 23:22
**Subject: Re: treading a path despite never knowing if it's
the right way**

Oh Harriet, oh Harriet, oh Harriet.

Your fight is in full force, and I want to be behind you, covering
you in gangster fashion and keeping you safe from the bullets,
the batons and the knives.

On one level, it sounds like the demons driving Cassandra are
getting ever stronger. However, (and this is a BIG HOWEVER)
I wonder if this may be a different manifestation of what we
have seen with Lydia—that maybe this behaviour has actually
always been there since the anorexia came to visit. Now, rather
than remaining undetected/undetectable, Cassandra is doing it
in a way that a) lets you know it is going on, b) makes you confront it, and c) by so doing, you add weight and commitment to
her fight.

Being confrontational, really strict and uncompromising may
help her because, in turn, she has no choice but to fight back—
against the anorexia. If you choose to ignore or be kind and
loving, Cassandra must battle it alone. This might be claptrap,
but I am increasingly convinced the best way is to leave the
girls in no doubt about the rules, what is expected, and what
is not acceptable, which gives them more strength. Cassandra
standing on her own, trying to be strict with anorexia, is awful
for her. Knowing you are prepared to be strict, too, makes
Cassandra feel she is doing the right thing.

This sounds a long way from where you and I started—being
committed to small steps and wanting to beat this thing, holding our girls' hands rather than being their enemy. However, we
have shown the girls we are willing to do anything to help them
win the battle (let's count the hoops we have jumped through so

far), and the only difference now is that maybe through a better understanding, we are starting to support them in a slightly different way.

I often refer to two things, one of which 'T' (a *friend going through a similar experience*) said and the second the psychiatrist said. 'T' made rules: not allowing her daughter in the kitchen, not buying anything she asked for, and not negotiating once a meal was on its way. The psychiatrist said that we are great at communicating but that while this has stood us in good stead for coping with this challenge and means we have good relationships that will endure—it isn't necessarily what we need right now. What we need now are nerves of steel and steady grit to listen and support but not waver. These two things make me think we must stop thinking what we are doing is 'mean' and instead think of it as what is needed to help us give the girls more strength in their battle.

The parallel with Lydia isn't in exercise but in the hiding incidents and pulling away from friends. I am more convinced these things have come to light because she can't cope with them alone, so she makes sure that she is found out in a weird way. The finding out is dreadful; I collapse and then emerge, determined to be stronger. This gives her no option but to comply; I become her 'bad cop' for anorexia, and she does better.

Returning to your situation … I AM HERE for you. We are not perfect and don't really know what we are doing in this battle. But we are trying our damnedest, and I know this will be enough for our daughters. They just need to know for long enough that we are on their side, and one day, that knowledge will save them. Because I know it for myself, I know it for you.

Trust yourself as I trust you.

xxxxxxx

From: Harriet
Sent: December 10, 1:48 PM
Subject: RE: treading a path despite never knowing if it's the right way......

Thank you, comrade. Reading your email has been akin to being refuelled—energy, courage, determination, and renewed belief have poured into my empty cup. Your themes seem remarkably similar to my thought processes. I, too, am beginning to realise that Cassandra finds it hardest when left to cope alone— sometimes inevitable with my other commitments. Anorexia is like a bully whose voice is stronger when I'm not around to challenge it and defend her. When Cassandra goes up to her room to 'work', the voice bullies her into exercising instead, with threats of feeling so awful she will want to die if not. The exercise seems like an escape from facing up to these feelings, and I'm now wondering whether the answer is to go with her to this place and face it together. What could happen? Nothing could happen while I was there, hence my desperate need to cut back on other demands to keep me totally available. Perhaps she is scared of feeling suicidal (hell, I am), but perhaps if she stays in this awful place and I hold her hand, the storm will pass. Anxiety levels cannot stay in the air indefinitely; they have to come down, and then she can see that she has faced the worst.

I have felt concerned about the demons getting stronger, though we have spoken before about how this may be a sign the illness is becoming more threatened. I would definitely say that Cassandra's main anorexic behaviour at the moment is excessive exercise. She eats (within limitations) more normally in terms of amount, and the eating time has reduced, though she is always last to finish. Your idea of a secure unit for mothers and daughters is inspired. To have day-to-day support and face the demons with our child is far preferable to handing over to some 'Miss Hardbroom-esque' nurses who may fall into the persecuting role—as so many people do.

xxxxxxxxxx

From: Lisa
Sent: 16 January 10:42
Subject: The New Year—a new you!

Dear Harriet

Travelling tips

* Don't go water skiing, even in the Caribbean—skiing is okay but followed by exposure (no resistance to cold)
* Remember to take all the basics—custard powder, bran flakes, Special K bars, rye bread (a devil of a job to buy on an island)
* Choose only friends who will eat regularly and sensibly—avoids the battles of 'why have I got to eat lunch when no one else is' (ignoring the fact that everyone else has been stuffing cakes and biscuits all morning AFTER pancakes with bacon and maple syrup)
* Be prepared to pay for expensive meals in restaurants, even when less than half is eaten each time

Christmas survival guide

* Agree on food beforehand and portion size (yippee got it right!)
* Allow the child with anorexia to choose who to sit next to/ near and who to avoid (yippee, did this too!)
* Try to choose those with smaller appetites to be at that part of the table (to reduce the contrast of meal sizes)
* Invite small children/babies to act as a distraction (good, managed this too)

I hope we can meet in town next week for coffee, cake, a cinema or anything.

Much love

L

From: Lisa
Sent: 03 March 14:00
Subject: follow on from the text...

Classic decisions the TOMATA have to make (Tribe of Mothers of Teenagers with Anorexia):

- Do I wake her from a lie-in for breakfast or leave her to sleep (food versus healing/restorative slumber)?
- Do I choose meals I know will be eaten with less fuss rather than focus on the long-term plan of increasing flexibility and introducing higher-calorie meals?
- Do I insist on eating meals as a family—and potentially spoiling/introducing stress to everyone else's mealtime—in the interests of keeping Lydia integrated within family life or 'give in' to the demands of anorexia to eat at different times and to eat different foods but in so doing, reducing stress and anxiety?
- How far do we accommodate different meals and different foods, and does this condone anorexia rather than challenge it?

Much love

Lx

From: Harriet
Sent: 29 March 14:45
Subject: Can we ever say the right thing?

A: The answer is that we frequently say the right thing, but it is taken in through the ears, twisted and distorted by anorexia who resides right there—in the ear canal—and is fed through to the brain as an attack (anorexia classifies as an attack on anything that represents a bid to connect and build a relationship with the real and reasonable human being inside).

So, how do we cope with these distortions, misunderstandings, and attacks? My first answer is that it hurts, and I don't have a solution. But then I think, hang on. We have been coping for some time like this, reeling and recovering and trying again and again to connect. We have the emotional bruises to show, and if we falter, we must remember this evidence—we have survived so far and can continue to do so.

The good fight is honing our skills; we are not as naïve as we were; each new assault and reflection equips us further. Anorexia's attacks may at times knock us off our feet, but ultimately—as we are warriors of love, and such warriors are made of solid gold—we recover and strengthen. The harder we are hit, the harder we come back in defence.

One day, we will be invincible, and anorexia will shrink and scuttle away, never to return. Keep beating the drums, for that time is advancing...put your ear to the ground, and you will hear it...Dum ditty dum ditty dum dum dum...it is getting louder and louder.

I love your analogies and can especially relate to the one about the tandem. We have to carry our daughters over a long distance before they recover enough strength to do some of the pedalling themselves, and when they can, it may only be in short bursts until they build up their strength and confidence. They might pedal one day and be completely unable to pedal the next; some days, there will be a steep hill for us to climb and at others, we may be on the flat, so we must keep going until the day we can freewheel down the hill, and they can begin to cycle alone. I wish all this pedalling would improve my own fitness and return my weight to 'okay' on the BMI charts, but analogies have their limitations.

Xxx

From: Lisa
Sent: 08 July 22:42
Subject: fingers crossed

Lydia has just walked past, and I find myself thinking that a) she almost has shape in her calves b) her shoulders don't look so spiky and c) her spine isn't showing so much.

Of course, writing it down makes me fear (oh god, so much) that it is more of an illusion, but perhaps I'm not dreaming it, and perhaps the slow, slow approach is working.

This goes alongside an observation that more food is being eaten—quantity-wise—and Lydia's appetite seems to be return-ing. Last night, she actually ate seconds of potato, and tonight, her plate was full with a big piece of tuna (I bought a 210g piece just to see if I could get away with it), and although she left a thin slice on the chopping board, she ate the rest. She also ate three pieces of potato and a good dish of rice pudding. Another good thing was that (unbeknown to me) we had run out of Alpen bars, and spontaneously, she said yesterday that to make up for her snack, she ate a small pot of home-made granola from the coffee shop, which was oats, nuts and grains baked with honey. I would have been quite sceptical, but along with the other signs, I almost believe her!

Speak soon, my friend.

Xxxxxxx

From: Harriet
Sent: 09 July 00:05
Subject: fingers crossed—drumming on drums, dum ditty dum ditty dum dum dum

A few rays of sunshine from here. Cassandra texted me at work today to announce she was at the climbing centre. 'Avec qui?' was my curious reply. 'R a friend from School' came the reply.

'A friend from SCHOOL?' resounded around my head, a far cry from 'no f***ing friends'.

Love to you xxxxxx

This has been the story of the enduring friendship of two mothers….

Chapter 8

A job in a cheese shop provides a lesson in recovery

LYDIA

Healing can occur in unexpected places and in surprising ways. After multi-family therapy (MFT), Lydia's parents persuaded her to defer leaving home to start university for a year. This decision was hard for both the parents and Lydia to accept. But then Lydia was offered a job in a nearby cheese shop, and lessons unfolded, revealing that help and influence can come from surprising places.

The mother

We accepted Lydia wanted and needed to 'do' something with her gap year before starting university, and she set about finding work. She got a job in a science lab near my mother's home and began to work, staying for four days with her grandma and three days at home. Very quickly, it became clear this was leaving too much room for the 'dreaded witch' to grow in power. Despite her grandmother's efforts to care for her, Lydia lost weight and needed to come home for a sharper eye on her eating.

We didn't like the monitoring and watching we had to do, but we were prepared to wage the battle. This was too difficult for my mother—she couldn't treat a 17-year-old granddaughter like a young child. The weeping over meals was gone, but the limits on what Lydia would eat and wouldn't eat were in full

DOI: 10.4324/9781003641070-11

force; weighing portions was critical to avoid battles of 'this is too much' or 'that's not enough', and eating was still taking a long time. We felt that expecting someone outside our immediate family to undertake such supervision was not fair—not to mention the waste, as I am sure Lydia was throwing away the lunches that her grandmother had carefully and lovingly made for her.

So, Lydia returned home, resumed job hunting, and, along with working as a waitress in a café that remains a favourite haunt for our family, got an interview in a specialist cheese shop. This seemed an odd choice, although Lydia had always loved special foods, and the shop's professionalism appealed to her. I was intrigued because I knew that, working in such an environment, Lydia would be expected to get to know the cheese and … inevitably, must EAT it.

At this stage, Lydia was eating hardly any dairy food, and cheese had been off her 'acceptable' list for months. I mentioned this before her first interview, but she brushed my thoughts aside with her favourite phrase, 'I'll be fine'.

So began a momentously important phase. From the first day, Lydia loved the cheese shop, the street community around it, the people she worked with, the customers, and her growing knowledge and understanding of the cheese industry. She began to come out of herself and lose the sad, sad face of loneliness; she began to smile and relate to the world again. She was making new friends and developing a new persona. And, against all odds, she started eating cheese with a passion—savouring and tasting each piece, getting to know it, and understanding how it changes and develops during its life.

We were mystified at how this could happen when many other constrictions remained. During the following year, I frequently wanted to go into the shop and kiss everyone who worked there, to thank them for taking Lydia in, for not asking questions, and for bringing her back from an isolated place. But

I knew I couldn't do this—this was her space and sanctuary, and I had to keep my gratitude to myself.

When I asked Lydia about the cheese shop interview, where she was indeed asked to taste and comment on varieties of cheese and the difficulty she must have faced in eating it, she said, in effect, 'There was no choice. If I wanted the job, I knew I had to eat, and so I did'.

The anorexia somehow let her eat because her employers expected it and took for granted that she would do so. Week after week, Lydia would go to work, eat cheese, come home, and return to a more limited range of food. Then she began to bring cheese home for us to sample, too—and none of us ever looked back. Furthermore, Lydia believed—and believes to this day—that the cheese shop never saw her as ill and that if she told them she had an eating disorder, they would have laughed because, in the shop, she WASN'T influenced by anorexia thoughts; she was totally Lydia.

Throughout her university studies, Lydia regularly returned to work at the shop and remained close to the team. Only once, after final exams and some 'emotional bumps', when she had lost weight due to the pressure, was any comment made. On seeing her, one of the bosses said, 'For goodness sake, what have you done to yourself?' Followed shortly by 'Come on, we'll soon get you sorted'.

Far from taking this negatively, Lydia appreciated the straight, no-frills approach—and the fact that her employer cared enough to react and respond to her hurt. Within weeks, she was again safely back on the road to health.

This whole phase made me realise how unexpected events can help shape the future and that help and influence can come from unexpected places. We were groping our way forward, taking slow steps, but by being open to this opportunity and for Lydia to feel what it was like to WANT to do something again, she got hold of herself. The focus on being a cheese shop employee took the focus off 'the witch'. For Lydia, this must have been such a relief even for those few hours. I am eternally grateful.

The daughter (Lydia)

The cheese shop was and remains one of the safest places for me. I started work there in November of the year. I got ill and worked all through my gap year, during summers and Christmases throughout uni, and I even went back the first Christmas during the holidays from my real job.

When I applied and started the job, I knew it was laughable to many, but even on my first shift, when trying to impress, I knew I had to make a choice about how it was going to be.

In the beginning, I made a few safeguards about what cheeses I liked and didn't like—soft and blue seemed scarier, so I initially stuck to hard and goat cheeses, which I decided were less calorific. Although the anorexia was still strong in my head, in the shop, I felt like I was treated and could be totally my 'Lydia self'.

I could talk to the customers and my friends about the products, enjoy getting swept up in what I was doing, and stop worrying about what I was eating.

I also began to see that, somehow, the cheese I was eating as part of my job wasn't having a real effect at my weigh-in each week. Working at the cheese shop was like stepping into a happy, safe place and escaping. While inside, I could lose the anorexia, but as soon as I stepped out, it would be back. I avoided being at home for supper those evenings, and if I was, I found eating really hard.

Not only did eating the cheese help my recovery massively, but it also created a chance for me to be accepted as myself and as a valued friend and member of a team. This was really special to me. When my health went downhill, and I started to lose weight again, I went back to work in the cheese shop quite a lot, and again, it really helped. I worried I would resent the shop for making me ultimately gain weight, but actually, I saw cheese and the shop as a different category from everything else. This was because it was healing in a different way—more for my mind and soul than physically. The fact that it was healing to have confidence in my 'Lydia self' helped to overcome my other fears.

• See Chapter 7, to read about the special friendship between Lydia's mother, Lisa, and another mother, Harriet.

Chapter 9

Reshaping daughter–mother dynamics

MATHILDA

Mathilda was almost 18 when she developed anorexia. 'We could walk to the MFT sessions', says her mother. 'That was convenient, but so what? We still had to deal with the eating disorder. When I became a mother, and Mathilda is the eldest of two, I thought that if I tried hard, I could succeed in motherhood. What was shattering for me was that this seemed to be going badly. In going along to MFT sessions, my big fear was, "I am barely coping with my own daughter; how will I cope with hearing the stories of others?" It was so painful to see Mathilda so ill, so screwed up'. So began a journey that would challenge the dynamics between mother and daughter.

The mother

Initially, everything was looking good. Mathilda got loads better quickly and went travelling and off to university. But within months, she got sick and took a year to recover. So, she had two major illness episodes. In hindsight, the multi-family therapy (MFT) was very effective. Still, some root causes, or deep-seated family stuff that I think contributed to Mathilda developing anorexia, only came to light in the therapy after her relapse. We have a history of mental illness in our family but not eating disorders, and I didn't notice Mathilda having problems, like

DOI: 10.4324/9781003641070-12

anxiety, before her illness developed. She ate well and was well adjusted, strong-willed, and the most determined person I know.

It was when we went shopping for a ball gown for her that I saw her body and was shocked. Her boyfriend helped us get her to see a general practitioner (GP). She went alone because she was almost 18. The GP made a referral, and we received an appointment quickly. This was important because when Mathilda turned 18, she would need to go to adult services.

We were desperate to enrol in the MFT programme so we could participate in the therapy, and we got a referral quickly.

I knew little about anorexia and did not want to know how long term it would be. As Mathilda had got ill over three or four months, I hoped she could get well within a few months. The MFT staff were kind, but I felt shattered to learn recovery could take longer. It was all so sudden.

Mathilda had just finished her exams; she got 297 out of 300 in one paper. Before she got ill, she had been planning a gap year before going to university. The MFT people told her, 'Well, you have got your gap year to get better, and you will be able to start university on time'. To hear that was shocking.

To their credit, the MFT team did not force us to confront the possibility that Mathilda might not start university on time. I could not have coped with it. Getting through one day was enough. To be told she could have this illness for ten years, or her whole life, that would have been too shattering. My childhood affects my response here—my family had moved a lot, 14 homes by the time I was 18, and each move was going to be 'and we will live happily ever after', but we never did, and I needed a lot of therapy to come to terms with my childhood experience.

When I became a mother, and Mathilda was my firstborn, I thought if I tried hard, I could make a success of motherhood. What was shattering for me was that this seemed to be going badly. In going along to MFT sessions, my big fear was *I am barely coping with my own daughter; how will I cope with hearing the stories of others?* It was so painful to see Mathilda so ill, so screwed up. However, the MFT therapists were gentle and were saying that she could recover in her gap year.

We began attending the clinic in June, and the MFT started in November. Mathilda had taken to eating incredibly slowly, and I do not exaggerate; her meals would take 13 to 14 hours daily. We would start at 8:00 a.m., breakfast would hopefully be finished by 11:45 a.m., and then we would start lunch. She could not eat without one of us beside her, talking her through every mouthful. A bowl of cereal that anyone else would eat in ten minutes, would take her four hours.

My first impressions on our first day of MFT were that we were in a mixed group regarding background and education. The children with anorexia were all girls, and the way they ate differed for each of them. I'm a joiner-inner and enjoyed participating in the exercises. The process was not scary to me. What was frightening was hearing other people's stories. I suppose the correct answer is that I discovered I was not the only one; I was not alone, and there were others like me. The truth is, it made no difference to me. Because my vocation involves caring for others, I had to be very conscious that I was not at MFT to care for or rescue others; I was there as a patient.

They got us to make a collage with people, so when it was Mathilda's turn, she had to choose other people in the group, not me, to represent our family members and physically portray them at the moment. Mathilda was curled up in a ball; I was crouched over her, desperately trying to provide comfort; and her dad was standing behind me, looking distraught; and her brother was a bit separate. This is how she portrayed us. We were asked how we each felt about this, and then we were asked to describe how we would like things to look in a year. Mathilda had a very hopeful outlook. She had us all standing firm; we were all touching each other, and she was looking forward to the future. So, this was all quite positive.

The other activity particularly useful for Mathilda was drawing a timeline, which stated, 'Where you are now and where you plan to be in a year?' This was the catalyst for Mathilda. Straightaway, she pointed to a date 12 months ahead and said, 'That's when I go to university', and 'This is where I am now'. Suddenly, she could see that to get to university, she needed to start working on recovery right now. Her weight had been slowly increasing, and her bloods were improving, but she was still taking hours to eat. This was the final day of MFT, and on that day, she said, 'I've got to start eating'.

We thought if she could eat a meal in three hours, this would be an improvement, but she said, 'No, I am going to do it all; I am going to eat in half an hour. Tonight'. And she did.

She came home and ate the meal in 30 minutes—I had to spoon-feed her. She was having panic attacks but persevered. That one exercise helped her see that *'I've got to change now',* and she did. That was two weeks before Christmas, and Mathilda ate Christmas dinner with us on Christmas Day. We weighed everything, but she ate a normal festive meal within a normal time. The MFT was absolutely a turning point.

In another activity, the parents were split into pairs, not couples, and put in different groups. The young people had drawn up a list of questions—anything they liked—that they were allowed to ask the adults in private. Mathilda's questions were all about growing up. In one sense, in anorexia, she was literally trying to shrink down to nothing. Sitting at the dining table for 13 hours a day, in many ways, she was being like a toddler. So, she went around the table and asked the adults about this. Somehow, this helped me as a parent to see this perspective. They encouraged us, then, to personalise anorexia and talk about the illness as 'Anorexia says', and 'Anorexia does this', and we now call it 'the Bitch'.

MFT was the turning point for us. We had endured 14 weeks of this ridiculously long, 13-hour-a-day meal schedule, and now it stopped.

For me, MFT was all about Mathilda getting better. From that Christmas, she got loads better over the next six months, well enough to travel in China and Tibet—challenging destinations when meals are essential. She went on the Trans-Siberian Railway with her boyfriend. She had a good first year at university, and all was well.

Then, at the end of the first year, she stopped taking her medication and went to East Africa on a volunteer project, building playgrounds, which was physically demanding, digging ditches, sleeping on a concrete floor with six other girls and, in hindsight—*why didn't we see this?*—too difficult food-wise. There was no variety of food, no control. Within six weeks, she crashed. She finished the playground project and flew home, aware she was slipping but unable to stop the slip. How silly were we not to see the risks in such a trip—but she looked well, had coped well in China and was bubbly and enthusiastic about this humanitarian playground project. She came home, went to the GP, and spiralled downwards with eating disorder and depression.

Mathilda returned to university at the start of the second year. When I visited two weeks later, her mental state was such that I feared she would suicide. She was 20 by this time. To cut a long story short, she was admitted to a private mental health hospital as an inpatient for three months.

My daughter became unreachable, but eventually, we found day therapy, which helped with the hard stuff of the family dynamics. I felt I needed to acknowledge my failings as a parent and the damage I had inadvertently caused Mathilda. My behaviour was due to the way I was brought up, but the result of this sharing was helpful, and Mathilda came along in leaps and bounds. We have had ups and downs, but the bottom line is that she is okay.

Her weight and what she eats are stable. Her thoughts, the mental stuff, can be challenging at times, but she is incredibly determined and says, 'I'm never going to let another relapse happen. It's too hellish'.

Personally, out of Mathilda's illness, I have had to confront my own childhood stuff to provide what I call *'happy ever after'* for my children's lives. There has been a lot of self-growth for me as a result of dealing with these issues. Although MFT did not quite reach all parts of healing our family dynamics, it was an absolute lifesaver and a turnaround for Mathilda at that point.

The daughter (Mathilda)

The biggest thing I got out of the MFT was overcoming the fear of eating meals and snacks. At the start, I was eating really, really slowly. I couldn't even admit the possibility that I might eat fast. Never mind actually doing it. Then, several days later, we did this timeline and *'whoah'*, I realised I had to start eating fast and soon, or I would not start university on time. We were in a small room, standing around a table, and were told to draw a timeline on paper. Looking at my drawing, I suddenly could see that I would not get to university if I did not get my act together. The time caught up with my illness between June and November had gone in a flash, and the coming months would probably do the same. Unless I began eating fast, there was no way I would start university on time.

I had many rules about all kinds of foods. But now the dominant thought became, *'If I don't do something, I will not get to university'*.

I said, 'I think I need to eat fast', and Mum and Dad (who both came to all MFT sessions) and my therapist were like, 'Oh yes? How can we help you?' They suggested that I allow an hour, then 55 minutes, and gradually reduce the amount of eating time, but that sounded tedious, and I said, 'I would rather just do it'.

We went home, and Mum cooked dinner, and it was pretty tense. I'm sure Mum and Dad were wondering, *'What will she do? What is going to happen?'* And I thought, *'Am I going to do this? This is so scary'.* I thought, *'I don't even know how to chop a sausage into a reasonable size'.* So, Mum had to feed me. And I did it. My time taken to eat the evening meal was reduced from five or six hours to a normal time.

Mum took that week off work because I was worried that if I didn't eat for five hours a day, well, what would I do with all my free time? So Mum and I did normal, everyday things, like go to the cinema, and I saw my boyfriend again. I realised how abnormal my eating pattern had been. For the first time, I could see that it was pretty weird—that for 14 weeks of my life, I had consumed 14 hours a day in eating.

So now I could get out of the house more, and this broadened my horizons. To keep the momentum going, every week, I made a list of goals I needed to achieve in order to go to university. Some things were tiny, like *'Have a cheese sandwich one day this week'* and *'Drink a smoothie'* on another day. I would discuss the list with my therapist, and Mum and Dad knew about it, too. I would pick when I would do which challenge, which gave me a sense of control, and I could see myself getting better. I started to get more energy and time for things I used to do, like babysitting. I began earning a bit of money. That's what MFT did for me.

My eating disorder was extremely focused on food. Looking back, it is weird that I took hours to eat every meal. I had in mind that if I was going to eat, I had to savour it, so instead of wolfing it down, I had to make the most of every mouthful.

I was living at home at the time, and it must have been hard for my mother to support me so much and help my brother with his homework. I felt really bad about that.

Dad helped at mealtime; he would talk about South African politics, and I enjoyed that. Such conversations were an effective distraction while I was eating. I had a rigid routine about eating; it crept up suddenly. I always had to have my legs crossed, sit in the same chair at the kitchen table, and always have the meat and other foods served a certain way. And there were many things, like drinking calories, mixing, and counting carbs and proteins, which took ages.

My whole life was centred on eating. Eating quickly was too scary to contemplate. If I ate slowly, this was all I could do. After a meal, I might have had time to shower before starting the next meal. To maintain my weight, I had to eat all my waking hours.

I was diagnosed with anorexia at 18, just after I finished my A-levels. On the very last day of school forever, which is meant to be a fun day, and this was before exams, my form tutor and best friend said, 'You have lost so much weight'. The next day, my boyfriend suggested going to the doctor, which I did, and I said, 'I think I am a bit funny about food; at least everyone thinks I am a bit funny about food'. The doctor weighed me and said, 'Well, you are underweight and need to eat more'. She said to return in a week, and I did for the next two weeks. This was during the exams; by the third week, I had lost 8kg. By this third week, the doctor said, 'I am referring you to the eating disorder clinic'.

I thought the clinic would be like a drop-in thing. I didn't realise it would be the eating disorders unit. I thought I would rock up, get weighed, and leave. After all, I was doing it because Mum thought I had lost a bit of weight. When I went along, they said, 'You have anorexia nervosa'. I was so, so angry. I had no idea I had an eating disorder. I did not know anything about them.

We went to Sainsbury's that night, and Mum bought an orchid. She said, 'By the time the flower on this orchid dies, you will be better'. Which obviously wasn't the case. It was more like 20 orchids later. After this diagnosis, instead of not eating at all, I started eating slowly.

I was the eldest in our MFT group—most kids were 14 or 15. I felt quite maternal towards the other girls, although I did feel others were thinking, *'You don't want to end up like her'*, but that was okay.

Each lunchtime during the MFT week was traumatic. I was not expecting such massive food challenges. A therapist sat beside me and tried to get me to eat a whole quarter of a sandwich, and I eventually did so, which was a massive breakthrough. We would have two sessions before lunch, and we all brought our own cut lunch. On the day we were told to sit with other parents, I initially refused but then sat with a dad. I enjoyed conversation with him, and as for eating with him, I trusted him, and that was a big step forward.

So, I got to university as planned, did my first year, and then had a big dip. It crept up, although I knew I wasn't eating properly, that I was depressed and needed help. I didn't realise how bad it was until I saw a psychiatrist. I had stopped taking my meds, and that probably contributed.

I had gone from seeing someone at the Maudsley almost every week to not seeing anyone when I moved out of London to attend university. That was Error One, a massive mistake. I stopped taking my meds, Error Two. My moods became worse; my eating became worse. I thought that everything would be okay when the new university year began. But it was not okay. I could not function, basically, and Mum came to visit to try and look after me. I was admitted to a private hospital.

The first time I became ill, the anorexia was masking the depression, but the second time, the depression was the main thing. Eating was hard, and loads of weird eating habits came back, but not as bad as the first time.

At MFT, I felt I could get well enough to attend university, but this second time, I felt like, *'Full stop, I don't want even a little bit of illness left'*. There were parts of the illness that I was holding onto. I didn't go to university for a year, and when I resumed, I changed courses. The past few years have been like banging my head against a brick wall. I did my A-levels, had a year off being ill, did my first year at university, had another year off, was ill, did my first year at university again at age 21, and became determined to make it. For support, I had a therapist, and I liked her.

During my relapse, Mum and I did some work together, and this was really helpful and really difficult. Our relationship is good now. For ages, I hated going home, but things are much better now with Mum and Dad. I have learnt to accept that Mum and I will have differences. We won't always be on the same page about everything. And that's okay; she won't die if I do things she disagrees with. It won't kill me, either. We can have a good relationship, but we both have to accept we won't agree on every subject, and this is a challenge.

I grew up feeling that if I didn't act in a certain way, Mum would not be happy, and it would be my fault. I was afraid of disappointing my parents. Now I realise that even if that's true, my parents are responsible for their own happiness.

MFT was the first step in allowing me to become my own person. Like, I didn't have a strong sense of self. My sense of self is taking a long time to grow up. When I was an inpatient, I spent three days at home for Christmas and found it difficult; at Easter, I went home for three weeks; in summer, for three months, and my relationship with my parents felt better each time. Now, I love going home. We go shopping; we go to the cinema. It's great.

I don't see Mum as a friend. No. She's still my mum, but we are a little more separate. Before, we were too much in the same circle.

Having good friends around me helps to give me something to strive for: connecting with people. I must motivate myself to keep doing this.

Today, if I feel the eating disorder thoughts getting strong, I call Mum or go and see a friend. I am determined not to relapse again. When in the hospital, I thought, *'I will get pretty much better but not fully better, just in case',* and then I thought, *'Just in case of what?'*

I took a pen and paper and tried to think of reasons and ways in which an eating disorder would be beneficial, and there wasn't one reason, which was scary. I would have been hanging on to a little bit of the eating disorder just in case of *'nothing'*.

I became determined to let go of all the eating disorder. This remains difficult, but I know myself well now. I'm excited about my studies and have millions of life plans. I want to have five kids, starting at about age 30. That's only eight years away, and I want to go into clinical psychology or something.

So, with MFT, I had that one big life-changing moment— deciding to eat fast. However, generally, I think I did not go deep enough in strengthening my self-esteem, in accepting I was different from my mum, and that I was good enough. I thought I would upset Mum if I did not live the way she wanted me to. This was horrible and was kind of based on true things, like when Mum found I was sleeping with my boyfriend and smoking joints, which for a lot of my friends' parents would be quite normal. I felt she cried every time she looked at me. Mum was emotional and did not deal with these situations well, and neither did I. But now we communicate more easily. I have deep respect for her; going through the therapy with me must have been harrowing. To admit you have made mistakes, especially in raising a child, is difficult, and my mum was able to say this.

Chapter 10

A mother and son can do this, too

JAMES

James's parents divorced when he was young. By age 12, James knew he was gay, and then he developed anorexia. James began developing an image of what he thought he should look like as a gay man—straight, dyed black hair, tight dark clothing, and eye make-up. He believed gay guys were 'really slim, pale and attractive' and thought this was the only way to be gay. Not eating was his only coping strategy to appease his anxiety. His dad was not interested in multi-family therapy (MFT), so James and his mother went alone. I met James when he was 19. He was passionate about nature. He was volunteering with Greenpeace and studying environmental sciences. His mum had a high-risk professional career and worked full-time to support herself and James. This is their story:

The mother

James was 14 or 15, and we were apple-picking when I noticed his bare arms —he had lost a lot of weight. As the days rolled on, he became withdrawn and uncommunicative. He retreated and lost interest in eating. He grew his hair long to cover his face. He was hiding. He began missing school; he couldn't get up in the morning; he stopped seeing his friends—unusual because he was quite a social animal. And he stopped playing his viola.

One morning, we had a crisis. I couldn't rouse him. He seemed almost unconscious, and when he did wake up, he came

DOI: 10.4324/9781003641070-13

out swinging, not that he was trying to hit me. I thought, *'He is just so angry and outside of himself'*. Then I thought, *'I think he is going to hit me'*, but I knew I could hold on to him, no problem. But he was not wearing a shirt, and I saw his emaciated torso—I could see every rib.

At first, I thought the reason was street drugs, but James was adamant he was not taking drugs. Our family doctor had known James all his life. She had helped me through my pregnancy with him and he agreed to see her. The minute she saw him, weighed him, and drew blood, she was concerned that this was anorexia and provided an immediate referral. I had been suspecting anorexia by now, although my only experience with this illness had been when singer Karen Carpenter died from it in 1983. I thought, *'This is not just a physical illness; this has to include a huge mental component'*.

At the time, James was experiencing difficulties with his father. His father had a new wife, a new life, and had pretty much said to James, *'Whenever you are with me'*, which was one week on, one week off, *'you are pretty much on your own; you are old enough now to take care of yourself, to cook for yourself'*. I think James felt an emotional abandonment. He was an only child from our marriage. I had an older daughter from my first marriage who had little to do with James, and James's dad had a new stepson.

To have the general practitioner's (GP's) confirmation that James likely had anorexia was a relief in one way because there were many possibilities.

We were referred to the children's hospital's Eating Disorders Unit and connected with the MFT programme. It was presented to us as a time-intensive commitment. Because I worked full-time, I asked myself, *'Can I actually manage?'* It was a huge commitment. Basically, the day-to-day treatment was loaded back to the parent for food, nutrition, and observations, and weekly visits—a 90-minute car ride each way—to the clinic to meet with the team. (But) There was medical support, and

I accepted the offer to join the MFT programme because, by then, I suspected James might die.

Thankfully, we started this treatment within two weeks, and my boss agreed to flexible work hours, although I couldn't work from home. This commitment took everything I had. My life consisted of caring for James and his nutrition needs, nothing else. I was singing in a choir, rehearsing on Thursday nights and Sunday mornings, and I had to give that up. When we got home from the hospital, I would prepare food and feel exhausted. It was the hardest thing I've ever done.

When we started MFT, James was 15. I thought this MFT group would be a good way for him to experience his peers, and I was looking forward to meeting other parents.

James's schoolteachers and principal were supportive, but my family was not. My mother was from a culture where there was little food when I was a little girl, and there were many of us for her to feed. She believed James would eat when he was hungry, and she did not understand the loss of hunger cues.

James's dad came with his wife for one or two MFT meetings before pulling out. So, for the time of James's treatment, because he needed three hot meals a day, plus two snacks, he had to stay with me.

At MFT, what I found helpful was reconnecting with past achievements and successes, such as where we would build timelines. Every child in James's group had become emotionally detached, so reconnecting with good memories was helpful. The kids had lost sight of how life had been for them before the illness developed, and when they remembered happier times, they could say, *'Oh, I would like to be there again'*.

I developed a white hatred for James's illness. It was a monster that invaded our house and family. I had to learn to ignore its rudeness, the cold rejection; that wasn't my child—that was the illness. Besides listening to the other parents and the treatment team, I did a lot of reading and researching and learnt everything I could about the illness.

The biggest lesson I learned from being in MFT was to open up. I grew up in a culture where you kept everything quiet—if there is conflict in the family, for instance, you don't talk about it—so talking about James's illness freely in this beautiful, supportive group where everyone had common denominators was hugely beneficial. I also took my cue from James, who said, 'I'm sick; I have a mental health issue'. He was open about it because he has grown up in a different culture. Adopting this attitude has helped a lot in my wider circle, too.

One time at the Eating Disorders Unit, I became fearful. I was tired and thinking I was failing to help James despite doing everything I could. He had lost weight that week. So I was emotional, and James turned to me, very angry, and said, 'Don't be like that in front of me', and this was good because I realised how much he was relying on me to be strong, confident, calm, to help him battle this illness.

Secondly, I reached a point where I realised I could really use somebody to talk to. James was supported—he had this great team at MFT. I was working for him and could use someone to share with, too. At work, I applied for employee assistance, and a counsellor who had experience in adolescent–parent conflicts provided a phone consultation and gave some coping strategies.

I have a strong, supportive church family, and I came out and shared and said, 'James is sick'. I said he had an eating disorder, and everyone enveloped me and provided love, support, and understanding. They were empathic and sympathetic and gave unconditional acceptance. James was very sick; it didn't matter what the sickness was, the church community supported us and became my spiritual feast every Sunday.

There were times during MFT when I felt alone, and the other families, especially the parents, would raise my awareness that nobody is alone, and knowing this helped a lot. So, most of the time, being a single parent was okay because I was with this group, and no one questioned why I was without a partner.

When James was ill, he lied, and one of the MFT messages was, *'Do not take it personally; your child will lie to you'.* I had been telling James that his lying was devastating, upsetting me and 'Making me take a big step back from you'. At that point, the illness was winning. When I heard other parents saying their child was lying too, I realised this was the illness—this was yet another way the illness was trying to isolate the child from its source of greatest support. So I decided, *'Okay, you are not going to win. I won't let this lying affect me'.*

I'd cook and prepare his meals at 5:00 a.m. before going to work, and at the end of the day, we would do a briefing, and I would say, 'So did you eat your breakfast?' 'Your snacks?' Then I would find food thrown out, like the entire meal I had worked hard to prepare—something tasty, perhaps a chicken breast with broccoli, with cheese on top, his favourite things. Quite labour intensive, stovetop. To find the whole thing swept into the trash felt like rejection, made worse when he said, 'I ate the whole thing'. I found snacks intact in the bottom of his backpack. This was shattering until I could see, by attending MFT, that to react would be to feed James's illness.

Because it was just James and I, I treasured our nightly suppers, our meal of the day—this time together was important. But James got to the point where he would not eat with me. He would eat upstairs in his room, and I would eat alone at the table. I found this very lonely and thought, *'This is just us; this is our relationship disintegrating'.* It turned out the other families were saying the same thing. Their ill children wouldn't let them see them eat. Knowing this helped a lot, too.

I let James eat in his room. You have to pick your battles. There were times when I was adamant and forceful, and there were things like eating in his room that I would let go of. He eats with me now, but it took a long time.

At the MFT group, I asked the other families how they coped with this. One family insisted that their child join the entire family so they could witness the consumption. I had to get James to promise me, and when he makes a promise, it is difficult for him to break it. So that was our strategy. He did not want me to witness him eating, but he would show me his empty plate. He may have lied to me—which I learned not to take personally because that was his illness—but he trusted me.

After MFT, James's hunger cues returned, and it was great to hear him say, 'I'm hungry'.

Other parents were experiencing similar challenges. We could see our children were very different, so clearly, behaviours such as hiding food and being untruthful about it belonged to their illness. With understanding came strength and confidence. Through all this, I learnt about resilience. For support, I had the MFT team and families, my church and faith, James's school administrators, and physical exercise—I also ran long distances with a girlfriend, and this helped a lot.

I kept James away from his grandmother for the duration of his illness. We could not waste energy trying to be defensive of inappropriate suggestions and strategies. I felt angry at James's dad for not being involved in MFT, but that anger was unhelpful. The MFT team leaders pointed this out: 'You are wasting valuable energy; you need to focus on what you need to do to get through this'.

I gained self-awareness. I learned to filter, shove things away, and draw other things in, doing whatever I needed to get through this. James and I were definite partners in his recovery. Once James grasped recovery, he worked hard to make it happen.

Near the end of the MFT week, they asked us to draw posters about our achievements and where we wanted to go from here. It was very specific, and James wanted an 80 per cent average in his studies at the end of the year so he could attend university. That helped crystallise what the kids had accomplished, what they were grappling with, and what they still needed help with. The future was bright for them, and they were all looking forward to it. When James was stuck deep in his illness, there was nothing except a deep black hole. Now, he could see a positive life beyond. The timeline was helpful for me, too, because sometimes I got so caught up in the here and now that I forgot how much had been accomplished.

Six months after we started MFT, we celebrated James's weight restoration. His hair had stopped falling out and was glossy again. I took him shopping at a special mall, and he bought armloads of clothes to fit his new physique—armloads that now fit him. We had a way to go, but we had come a long way.

There was only one scary moment when James was approaching 18—he lost weight, and I panicked and took him back to the MFT team. We worked out a programme to help him regain the weight. Soon after, he got the exam results he needed to get into the college course he wanted.

Single parents can do MFT. A family is a family, no matter what the configuration. James and I were a family, and we were in a group with a family of five and a family of three. We were all families.

My job kept me busy. I had flexibility but worked 60 hours over seven days. Initially, I thought my childhood had equipped me well to work confidently in a high-risk career. Still, it also prepared me for helping James recover from anorexia, which was a far greater and more important challenge.

The son (James)

I was an anxious kid. I wasn't happy about anything, was extremely picky with food, and developed my eating disorder in early adolescence.

I became an outpatient at the eating disorder unit, and every week, they checked my vitals, took a urine sample, weighed me, and gave some counselling—I had a social worker for my family, a psychiatrist for myself, an educationalist for my parents and me, a nutritionist, and doctor. As I got better, the sessions were spaced out every two weeks. I despised these people who were making an enormous effort to meddle in one of the few things that was just my own. Like, they were trying to get me away from my one coping mechanism, food, which was helping to ease my anxiety.

After one-on-one therapy for a year or two, Mum and I began MFT group therapy.

Emotionally, MFT was unpleasant for me. Teenagers with eating disorders are really mean and hard to be with. I was one of them, but being surrounded by these people made me feel emotionally exhausted and drained.

I could see myself in all of them. For example, I could see myself in the way they would lash out and shout at their parents, as I had done. They were incredibly stubborn and weren't open to seeing that things could be different. Their parents seemed like very nice people who cared for their kids but were at a loss for what to do.

It is different when you see someone else's parents—because you have so much baggage with your own parents, it is hard to see them the same way.

MFT helped me gain confidence. That is the number one thing that helped me get out of my eating disorder—developing self-esteem and confidence. I stopped caring about other people's opinions and what they said about how I looked. I had cared intensely about this, but now I let this go and felt happier.

I have been openly gay since age 12 or 13. I knew before I developed anorexia nervosa that I was gay. I told Mum one-on-one before Grade 7 started, which wasn't a big deal. I didn't tell Dad until Grade 9. I felt anxious about the way I felt, especially regarding my self-image. Pop culture and the internet were my only real exposure, my only source of information, on what it meant to be gay. In middle school, I was bullied badly, mostly by males, because I was openly gay, and that period remains triggering. Anorexia was developing at this time. I began restricting food intake because I was becoming more aware of my body size.

Besides becoming more self-aware, I was developing an image of what I should look like as a gay man—straight, dyed black hair, tight dark clothing, and eye make-up. I only knew that gay guys were really slim, pale, and attractive, and thought this was the only way to be gay. Regarding the therapy, both parents were accepting of my sexuality, but the abuse at school was definitely gone over, and I was learning how to cope with that.

Putting weight on was scary. If I did not eat according to the MFT meal plan, I would be made an inpatient, so I followed the plan, but my anxiety skyrocketed. In Grade 10, I missed school a lot because the eating task was all I could focus on. I also started to smoke weed. My parents didn't know about the weed, which I bought on my allowance, for a long time. I was very good at hiding things.

The MFT gave Mum and me some closure because we were there together, and I could see that other parents were anxious. Mum had been a bad worrier, and now, I could see other mothers reacting with worry in the same way as her, and I was able to give her a little compassion. I had always been a sponge for Mum's worries. She loves to help people, and it was good for her to reassure these other parents and give them support. This MFT was good for her.

When Mum refers to my eating disorder, I still have trouble talking to her about it. I can speak to other people, but I have difficulty talking about it with her because she has seen it all and seen the worst. I usually just shut down. I feel I deserve trust because of the work I have done, and when she brings it up, it is like she is saying that I am still ill and anything could set me off, and I could go down that path again. I feel she is not respecting or trusting me.

After leaving home, I lived in a college residence, several hours from both parents, and visited each regularly when not busy with study or volunteer work with Greenpeace. Greenpeace was fulfilling and therapeutic for me. Becoming technically skilled at climbing, my speciality, added to my confidence—it was sometimes scary. Still, I could do courageous things, like climbing 25m on an installation. Because of my experiences, I could do this. I was successful when I developed anorexia and successful when I decided to get better. So, if I wanted to do a dangerous climb, I could do this, too, and afterwards feel a surge of confidence.

I am still working on acquiring coping strategies and replacing the bad, self-harming ones, such as weed. To cope in a positive way, sometimes I talk to people, but this isn't easy because instead of opening up, I tend to close and withdraw.

I find running effective. Sometimes, if I can't run, I might make music, which is also therapeutic. I play several instruments, like the ukulele, and let problems go, which helps me get rid of anxieties. It's hard, after having an eating disorder, to find a balance between a healthy lifestyle and a healthy lifestyle that is also unhealthy because of how stressed you are about it.

I learnt through therapy that perfectionism drives a lot of my anxiety. So, I have learnt to let this go—because perfectionism was causing me to work into a frenzy. I have learnt to fail rather than cling to perfection. I have learnt to realise when an anxiety attack is coming and how to let go; this is a big thing, to learn how to let go.

Anxiety would happen a lot—like at school. I would be afraid of starting a large assignment—I would be so afraid of not doing well that I would wait until the night before. I felt that if I allowed myself a long time to work on the assignment and it wasn't a good product, then this meant I was stupid and incapable, so I would do it all at once—like in five hours—and if I got a good mark, then that meant I was awesome. But this way of coping also meant I was always under pressure.

There are certain things I have learnt to replace negative coping mechanisms and to feel better, like making a pot of tea. Mostly, it is the ritual of making tea using tea leaves. I have several favourite types, such as Earl Grey—and I love bergamot. When I was self-harming, it was not just the pain that helped.

What made the ritual soothing for me was treating my wounds afterwards—I liked the pattern of going through the motions. So, tea-making is a more positive and comforting ritual than self-harming.

Being gay added to the pressure regarding body size. Pop culture is improving in terms of representing more kinds of gay people. The reality is that people come in all shapes and sizes, and every shape and size is valid, but when I was young, I only saw one stereotype in the media: slim and beautiful.

When I developed anorexia, half the problem was that I really, really hated myself. Harming myself felt good. I would think: *'I hate myself and want to suffer slowly',* and on top of that was *'I don't like my body and this is how I can get there'.* I have had to learn to love my body the way it is. I can only count on one person in the world to love me: me. If I don't love myself, I will have a really tough time.

Chapter 11

When MFT is the last in a long list of therapies

MILLIE

Millie developed anorexia nervosa just before her twelfth birthday. For the next four years, she was hardly at home—she was in and out of hospital, with treatment, therapies, everything. Her parents had the philosophy that when treatment was offered, they would try it. Millie was 15 when she began multi-family therapy (MFT); this was the last in a long list of therapies. Millie says, 'By then, I could not take any more. I had had many hospital admissions, but this was the hardest. I thought, "New girls are coming in; they don't know what is happening, but I have been doing this for four years. I don't want to do this re-feeding thing again". I never knew what direction I was going in; I never knew how anyone could imagine what they would be doing in three months, let alone three years. I couldn't. I didn't know if I was going to be dead, or back in hospital, or at high school. I was so preoccupied in the moment with my illness thoughts.

By the time I got to MFT, I resented my family so much. It was such a stretch for me to get there. I was angry with them for agreeing to be part of that treatment and fought tooth and nail not to go'.

The mother

When we first felt worried about Millie, our family doctor said, 'I think Millie has depression'. He sent us to a paediatrician who said, 'Millie has an eating disorder'. He wanted to admit Millie to the hospital immediately. Unfortunately, the hospital

DOI: 10.4324/9781003641070-14

was full, so he emphasised that we must closely monitor her. Her condition worsened that very night, so we took her to the emergency ward, and she was admitted and remained an inpatient for five months.

From there on, there were many ups and downs. After being an inpatient, Millie became an outpatient, but her illness was stubborn, and the hospital staff recommended that she get help at a private facility in another country. We had tried to get her into the eating disorders programme within several hours of home, but there was a year-long waiting list, and Millie was sent to a treatment centre in another country, 5000km from home. She was 12 and was admitted for six months. Leaving her there broke my heart, but that facility played a part in saving her life.

When Millie came home, we thought she would go off to school, but within weeks, an opening came up in the children's hospital several hours from home; it was a day treatment programme, and Millie started there in September. Every time a clinician or professional said, 'This is available for Millie', we jumped on it. We never said 'No' to anything because we had been told to take whatever professional help we could get; otherwise, Millie would not get better. We knew this was true because we had tried to help her but couldn't. We couldn't do this alone.

So now I had to do a lot of driving, some days three hours, to get Millie to the Eating Disorders Unit, five days a week. She attended the clinic for about a year and was made an inpatient at times when her weight began to slip. Millie hated going to the Eating Disorders Unit. She wanted to be home and to be going to school like a normal kid, but although her weight had been restored, she still had eating disorder issues.

Fortunately, my workplace was flexible and had an office near the hospital, so I could continue working while Millie was an inpatient. Several nights a week, we would stay with a family member in the city to reduce the amount of driving.

Every Thursday night, my husband George visited, and we would attend a family group therapy session at the Eating Disorders Unit. During this time, Millie seemed to come out of her shell, but bounced back and forth the whole time she was in day treatment. She didn't want to be there but couldn't leave until progress was made.

Millie had no formal schooling for three years. The hospital staff tried to offer classes, but she was too focused on her disorder. They said, 'Don't worry about her schoolwork; it is more important to heal her'. So, the gap in Millie's education wasn't a big concern for us.

Throughout the four years of therapy, Millie was not happy. She wanted out. Eventually, we were offered a place in MFT.

By this time, though, Millie was done with therapy. She was done with hospitals. This was a turning point. Just the idea of being admitted again, going through the re-feeding again, gave her the strength to say, 'I can do this'. She seemed at the point where she was willing to attempt and accept the challenge of recovery. At MFT, I felt we were more supportive of others rather than benefiting ourselves. For us, MFT seemed like a pep talk; it capped things off. It gave us a boost.

We attended the MFT for a week. We drove every other day, getting up at 5:00 a.m. to arrive on time. After that initial week, we returned for a follow-up visit every month.

The food sculpture was a fun event that encouraged people to share their experiences. I also enjoyed the lunch hour, which many others hated, because I found it relaxing. We sat at round tables and chatted, helping the children with eating disorders be part of a normal, relaxed environment. During Millie's illness, meals at home had been pretty hairy. Mealtimes fell apart, which was horrible, especially when we had company.

At MFT, when another couple's child was at our table, we didn't feel the emotional burden of this being our child and were more relaxed. I found this a good teaching environment.

From participating in MFT, I was able to appreciate how far Millie had come compared with other children there—some were just at the beginning of the illness. Everyone was at different stages of the disorder. We were a little more advanced on the recovery path. I noticed that Millie, who was pretty stubborn most of the time because she did not want to be there, started contributing more. We thought that was great because she had experiences to share at that point, and I felt proud of her because by sharing her experiences, she was helping others.

MFT reinforced that other people are there for you and that you, in return, can be helpful to them. My family makes fun of me because I love participating in therapy groups and encouraging and helping others. But I get strength out of participating, and it gives me confidence. I tell families they cannot help a child get over an eating disorder on their own; they need to reach out for support for the child, learn about the illness, and gain coping skills for themselves.

I found the social side of MFT more positive than attending one-on-one sessions with the therapist. Meeting with the therapist every week started to get stale, but the social environment of MFT helped Millie open up more. It provided the last little push she needed to say she wanted her life back.

Millie has required no inpatient admissions since MFT. Eighteen months after the therapy, she left home to go to university. I felt concerned, but she chose to live in a residence where she could cook her own meals. She had control there, and this was important to her. I visited her once a week. In the second year, she got her own apartment and continued to be capable and independent.

The father

My wife has left out all the bad parts. Mealtimes were hell. We secretly called Millie's illness 'Cybil'. We would say, ' "Cybil" is coming home today; everybody, get ready'.

Things were especially tough during Millie's first two years with anorexia when she was 12 and 13. Millie's hair was falling out from stress, and her sister, Jacinta, 15, was ready to leave home, saying, 'I don't want to live here anymore'.

I was secretly ready to give Millie up and keep what family I had left. I was watching my family falling apart. We were all arguing. It was horrible. Trying to get Millie to eat sparked all the arguments. Mealtimes were terrible. I felt helpless. When Millie's first illness first developed, I went to work—I'm a shift worker—and asked for a few days off, saying, 'I've got to fix this. I'm going to fix it, and I will be back in two weeks'. My supervisor said, 'You will be gone for a while'.

Well, I can tell you that little girl sure did show me. I'm sure I made every mistake there is. If there is a book on eating disorder care mistakes, we have ticked them all.

Early on, when sitting with Millie while she ate in the hospital, she convinced me that the food looked awful, so I tipped some out. I thought, *'How can they expect her to eat this?'* Later, I learned that the food was not the problem. No matter what was on the plate, Millie would not have wanted to eat it. I had no understanding of an eating disorder before Millie developed anorexia. I was an old-fashioned guy with the attitude that the child would eat when hungry.

One weekend, the hospital sent Millie home for the weekend and said, 'If she doesn't eat, take her back to the hospital'. Millie was in a Cybil mood and was not eating, so I got ready to take her back to the hospital. She said, 'No, I am not going'. I said, *'Well, I will make you go'*. And she said, 'No, you are not going to make me go'. I said, 'Well, we will see about that'. I physically grabbed hold to put her in the car and sat in the back seat with her while my wife drove for 40 minutes to the hospital. Millie tried to jump out when we were almost there, and I had to grab her again, and I was thinking, *'Oh my, what if the cops see me? What will I say?'* No seat belts on. Very stressful.

One time we took Millie back, and the hospital put her on suicide watch. This was before she was sent to a residential centre in another country, thousands of miles from home. I couldn't afford the treatment, but our government kicked in. We could not tell Millie about this plan until the day [we would leave home] because she would refuse food and drink as soon as she knew, and she had to be medically safe to be allowed on the plane. We got her on the plane, but by the time we landed, hired a car, and drove to the centre, Millie had had no food or water for 24 hours and passed out several times. She passed out in my arms when we pulled up at the centre, and I had to carry her in.

We visited her the next day, and she was a little better, though mad at us for leaving her there. We went home and were to come back a month later. That month felt like someone had thrown stuff off our shoulders. We didn't have to watch and care for her. She was in a good spot, being cared for. We had time for our other daughter, Jacinta; we toured around and did things. We went to restaurants!

This residential facility, I think, saved Millie's life. But it didn't cure her. She needed to go there or somewhere. I mean, the hospital near home wasn't helping. Millie gained enough weight at the residential centre to get safe, the bare minimum, and then came home. She was still suffering from her eating disorder and soon lost weight again and was readmitted to the local hospital. Finally, that hospital said, 'There's nothing we can do until the kid opens up'. That's when we went to the children's hospital.

Millie was 15 when we attended the MFT. I was totally not thrilled because the hospital is several hours' drive from home, and we would have to drive in traffic during rush hour both ways. But at the preview meeting, the MFT team said, 'Yes, Millie should come'. And my wife always says, 'Don't refuse any help that anyone is going to give you'. So, we figured the logistics out.

The game I remember, which didn't work out so great for us, was the pyramid, like where you are now and where you will be at the end. Millie was supposed to tell us when she would no longer have her eating disorder, and she did not have an answer. My wife kept saying we must finish this pyramid, and I said, 'We are finished. Millie's not ready to finish it yet'. I had to stand before the other families and say, 'We have had great difficulty with this project. This is as far as we have got because Millie is not ready for recovery yet'. And this was accepted. It was hard to say but true. We had thought we were further along the recovery road; we thought we were near the end.

We were thinking positively at the time because Millie was maintaining her weight. She was out of the hospital and knew she would be back in the hospital if she lost any weight; she was smart enough by now to at least maintain her weight. Even though Millie's stance with the pyramid showed we weren't finished on the recovery path, we could see we were further along than most families.

I don't think MFT would have worked if we had taken part earlier. I don't think Millie's recovery was due to one thing, but everything together. First, there was the local hospital—where we learnt how not to do things because they let her get away with everything, including exercise when she was an inpatient; next, there was the residential centre in another country, which helped Millie survive and come home with a little more of herself and a little less Cybil. After that, at the children's hospital with the day treatment within several hours' drive from home, Millie was slowly gaining, and finally, the MFT helped a lot. After MFT, she continued to recover, but it still took time. So, I don't know if there could have been a shortcut.

On one of those Thursday nights at MFT, when families ate dinner together, we were eating a pre-packed meal, and I had a chocolate bar. I was joking around and told Millie, who was 13 or 14, 'I bet you won't eat this'. She said, 'No'. I offered her $100 to eat that chocolate bar. She grabbed the chocolate bar. The other kids were chanting, 'Come on, Millie, eat it; it is worth $100'. That was a lot of money for a young kid, but she could not eat that chocolate bar. And I knew we were in trouble.

Many health professionals, along the way, said they knew how to 'fix Millie'. But they knew nothing. That is scary. If a parent is feeling worried today, I would say, 'Seek professional advice right away and hold on, don't give up'. I said to Millie, two or three years in, 'We've been doing this for this long, and we will do it another two or three years if we must'. We never gave up, but I wanted to, trust me.

Before Millie developed anorexia, she was full of fun and outgoing. She had a funny, sarcastic streak. She would usually do anything I asked of her. She always did well at school. I don't know how she managed to get her Grade 12 education on time with her peer group after missing three years of schooling because of her illness.

The sibling (Jacinta)

I was 13, starting in high school, when Millie got ill. Millie and I were always close in relationship as well as age, with just two years between us. So, the fact that she suddenly wasn't there for four years because she was away from home being treated for her eating disorder, was pretty different. It affected me that way in that she was not there.

When Millie was home, she was so preoccupied with her illness that we had no fun. I felt like I lost my sister for those four years, which basically comprised our adolescence. I was by myself a lot because Mum and Dad were at the hospital or taking Millie to appointments, but I never felt neglected. My friends and extended family were there for me when I felt upset. I had school, too. My best friend was right next door, and a cousin talked on the phone with me every night for months. I never felt alone.

When Millie was home, I was never really involved with the meals; I left all the authoritative stuff to Mum and Dad. However, there was fighting every night, and I could hear it from my room. Mum or Dad would come and talk with me after the fights, debriefing and venting to me about what was going on.

The best advice I got was not to pretend that nothing was wrong but to treat Millie the same way I always had. I tried to ignore the illness and to focus on her as my sister. I think it was because Millie and I had been close until this point, and then she wasn't there. So when she came home, I was happy to see her. It was easy for me to treat her like I always had.

Millie could only talk about what was happening in the hospital because that was her world, so I gave her the lowdown on what was happening in my life. Talking to her was difficult because her illness had such a hold, and I think she often faked that she was listening to me. Also, her moods could change quickly, and as much as I tried to treat her like I always had, I was having to tiptoe around the illness.

Millie and I shared a best friend, and when we were together, the best friend and I would take Millie out somewhere, like to the local mall. 'Let's go out and do something', we would say. Millie would dress herself in the most terrible clothes. They didn't fit her properly, were not clean, and were grungy-looking. She would put her ball cap on. She did not want to be seen, but our perspective was, 'If you look better, you might feel better. The reason people are staring at you might be because you look like a nine-year-old boy'. So, we took her to the mall, but first, we would try to fix her up a little, and she would get pretty upset about that. Simply being out in public was enough to upset her.

Millie didn't seem to have a problem if we ate, like pizza, in front of her, but of course, she wouldn't eat anything herself. Sometimes, we watched a movie, and she would make snacks for us, but not for herself. Trying to help her socialise didn't really work. Sometimes, there were pockets of time where

I could almost forget that she was sick. And these pockets gradually increased.

When we went to MFT, I was 17, and Millie had been ill for about four years. Most of the other siblings' perspective was that going to MFT was a day off from school. Maybe they didn't want to be there, were too shy, or did not know how to articulate their feelings, but there wasn't a lot of communication, and when there was, it did not usually involve our sick siblings.

My family was probably further along in the recovery efforts than everybody else. I was familiar with the therapists, who often asked me to share my experiences. I felt my role there was to inform or try to help answer other people's questions. I'm not sure how much I got out of it for myself.

The activity I remember most was the skit where we played out what it was like to have anorexia, and I was always chosen to be the child with anorexia. I probably should have known how to play that role, but I had not been able to understand the illness even by then. Like why it happens or what it is. So, I felt awkward playing that part and did not know what to say or do. I tried to behave like Millie—mostly to sit there and pretend nobody else was around. With all the families looking on, I did feel awkward.

I still don't know much about what causes anorexia, though I know quite a lot about how to cope with it. I know you don't give up. Mum and Dad would sit at the table with Millie for hours while she ate a meal. It was almost like she had reverted to being a little kid and was being told to sit there until she had finished what was on her plate. The fighting was the worst aspect of the illness because Millie would scream and cry and pace around indoors. Once, she brandished a frying pan and came out of the kitchen, trying to run from the house.

The patient (Millie)

At age 10, I felt guilt after eating some foods, and at age 11, the illness took off. I didn't know why I had to go for a run after

I had eaten. I just had to do it. When you develop this illness, you don't know what is going on. When you are first admitted to the hospital, you think, *'Okay, I can do this'*. And as soon as someone puts food in front of you, you think, *'No, I can't'*.

As much as I needed to be in hospital because I was on my deathbed, it spiralled me into a dark place. I got into a state of *'I never want to get better'*. I did not want to recover because recovery means, *'You eat dinner'*, and I was not ready to do that, right? Looking at the food made me feel horrified.

The health professionals and my family did everything they could, utilised every opportunity, and tried everything to get me to eat, and I resented them and hated them for it. I wanted nothing more than to do my own thing and for everyone to let me be the way I wanted to be. I was always in the darkest state; it was devastating, and I hated everything.

With anorexia, there is no happiness in your life. Things that used to make you happy, you don't allow yourself to do that anymore, right? Throughout the whole hospital phase, and when they sent me away to the residential centre, I felt a lot of anger.

By the time I got to my last hospital stay, three years after this illness started, I could not take any more. I had started back at school and had relapsed. Even though I had had many hospital admissions before, this one was the hardest.

I said to myself, *'I have done this all before. I have seen this all before. New girls are coming in; they don't know what is happening, but I have been doing this for four years'*. I am thinking, *'I am done with this. I don't want to do this re-feeding thing again'*. I had an agreement with myself that I would never get better. But I wanted to stay out of the hospital. So my deal with myself became, *'I am not going to recover, ever, but I am not going to come back here to the hospital'*. As much as that sounds like a negative turning point, it was nevertheless a big stepping stone. I was, like, *'I won't recover, but will do whatever I have to do to stay out of hospital'*.

I never knew what direction I was going in; I never knew how anyone could imagine what they would be doing in three months, let alone three years. I couldn't. I didn't know if I was going to be dead, or back in hospital, or at high school. I was so preoccupied in the moment with my illness thoughts.

By the time I got to MFT, I resented my family so much. It was such a stretch for me to get there. I was angry with them for agreeing to be part of that treatment and fought tooth and nail not to go.

We had been in therapy for four years. I said to my parents, 'I'm finally out of the hospital; I weigh enough so that I don't have to be in there. I'm trying to move on with my life, so why on Earth do I need to go to MFT, back among people who are just starting on their journey? Why are you putting me back in this environment? It is the biggest trigger'.

I was like, 'Let me just go and move on'. I was 15. On the first day of MFT, I felt awful. I knew that whatever this therapy was, I had already done it. If anything, I expected to leave this latest treatment feeling more upset because I would see kids who were thinner than me, and although now in a normal weight range, I still struggled in my mind.

After four years out of everyday teenage life, I had a lot of adjusting to do, and now they expected me to return to the environment I had worked so hard to get away from. I did not want to do it. I tried to explain, 'I can't be here; this is so triggering for me'.

This is where I disagree with my parents. They say you should take every opportunity. Even now, if someone said I should join a therapy group where new kids are just starting, they would probably agree it would be good for me. So, this is where we disagree. I resented them for making me go to MFT.

When I got there, yes, I felt awful, like I was basically watching myself three years earlier. It was a kind of Catch-22. I would sit there, looking at these other girls, thinking, 'I want to be that thin again'. Come mealtime, the girls would sit there, determined not to eat, and I would sit there, eating my meal, and think, 'I don't want to be like them'.

So, going to MFT turned out to be a positive thing for me. It was challenging, so challenging, to sit there because, of course, that eating disorder voice was so loud in my head. The voice was especially loud when I was among people with the same illness. As much as I disagreed with it and hated it, there were negatives and positives about MFT for me.

The MFT was good for my parents. Mum especially needed it—she had struggled; she was the one who got the brunt of the illness; she was the one who mostly took me to hospital appointments, tried to get me to eat; she was the one going through the most stress. MFT provided her with emotional support to help her move on. I suppose now, looking back at all I put them through, the least I could do was go to MFT with my family. MFT was good for Dad and Mum, as the families shared and opened up about their feelings.

MFT was good for me to be around the other girls with anorexia, as much as it was triggering because I was now trying to get accustomed to everyday life. If I was going to be triggered when I saw a girl with anorexia, then I still had work to do. So, MFT allowed me to see if I could cope and forced me to deal with that.

Many triggers in the hospital environment had automatically set me back. Like, when I had been an inpatient for five months, by which time I had gained 30 pounds, and a girl was admitted looking like I did five months before, I would look at her and think, *'My goodness, why can't I be thin?'* It would trigger me right back, and the next week, I would go home and start losing weight all over again.

So being in MFT, seeing all these girls, much thinner and much younger than me, I would go home that night and think, *'Oh my goodness, I am so fat, I need to lose weight'*, but then

I would think, *'No, I am not going back there'*. These pros and cons were very challenging, but I got through MFT with no significant relapse.

For me, the challenge of recovery came back to two options: *'I can be thin and miserable'* or *'I can be fat and deal with it and move on'*. I would look at myself and think, *'I am not happy with how I look right now, but hey, my life is so much better now: I am going to school, I am going on vacation, I am going out with friends'*. I might not like the way I look, but I would rather deal with that than be in the hospital feeling too afraid to eat. So, this was a big step, learning how to separate the two worlds and the thoughts of illness from mine.

Being at MFT, seeing the girls and their families, seeing these people, and seeing where they were, helped bring this all home to me.

The activity I remember most was one lunchtime when I had to sit with another family. I looked around the room and saw the other girls struggling to eat. While with the family I was with, I had eaten my lunch and everything, and we just chatted. It was, like, ever so normal. And this was so easy for me. I was happy and enjoying the conversation, and the other girls were crying. I walked away from that session, thinking, *'I have moved on'*. MFT helped me realise how far I had come.

Six years have gone by; I am 21. Even today, the eating disorder voice can hurt, so to go to MFT when everything was still fresh, like when I was fresh out of the hospital, was a big challenge.

I have thought I would always have to deal with the illness thoughts. There are still bad days when the thoughts are strong, but the difference is that I know how to deal with them now. If I am worried, I call my friends rather than my family because they would worry. I don't believe I will relapse, but they would probably think so. My friends know what to say.

I also like to go for a run, and this helps a lot. It sounds weird that to cope with an eating disorder, I go for a run, but this helps me feel rejuvenated. Anything to keep myself distracted is good. I still have 'awful' days when I feel disgusting and so down; my friends say, *'You are a little negative today'*, and I say, *'Yeah'*. They look out for me; the good thing is that I have new and old friends. With my new friends, I would never dream of telling them that I had anorexia because they might pick up the cue that I am feeling down and automatically connect it with anorexia. As it is, they think, *'Oh, Millie is down today, let's cheer her up'*, and it goes no deeper than that. On the other hand, my old friends are there for me if I want to go deeper and talk about it.

I suffer from depression more than anxiety and do not have therapy for it. I always bounce back. I know the eating disorder likes to isolate you, so I want to be around people, especially when feeling down, and friends are all I need. Being with friends is much better than spiralling down. I studied overseas for six months and coped well.

I think the best lesson is that you can give a person all the support available, but that person has to reach their own turning point. Until that person decides they want to get better, you can do all you want, but recovery won't happen beyond a temporary effect.

Constantly being in a supportive environment that you need to be in to recover can make all the difference.

My parents were right to insist we go along to MFT. Many times, I looked like I had got there, that is, in achieving recovery, but slipped, so it was understandable that they wanted to make double sure and take up this one more therapy opportunity. This was frustrating for me because I knew I was doing well, but the experience turned out to be like insurance for me and strengthened me more.

Today, I live a relatively normal life, using coping skills and supports, which include friendships, running, and reflecting on when I was sick. Like, if I think I would like to be 40 pounds lighter, I ask myself, *'What was my life like when I was 40 pounds lighter? Not very nice'*. I decide to keep the 40 pounds.

Chapter 12

'Only I can get myself out of this illness'

CASSANDRA

When someone tells Cassandra to do something, she wants to do it less, so when told, 'You have to eat', she refuses all the more. This was the theme during her recovery. However, when Cassandra began eating, she started thinking differently: 'I really wanted to do kickboxing, so Mum said, "You can do it when you get better", That spurred me on because it was what I wanted to do. The kickboxing was something I could do for myself'. The recovery path was not easy. Cassandra's mother, Harriet a single mother for much of her daughter's life and needing to work full-time, felt shame and blame when Cassandra was diagnosed with anorexia. Five years after multi-family therapy (MFT), at 21, Cassandra remains strongly independent; she has completed a university degree and is living away from home. This is her story, and also that of her mother, Harriet.

The patient (Cassandra)

First, at MFT, we had to draw a picture of what anorexia was like, and everyone had creative ideas. There were drawings of people being held back from their food by loads of iron or something like that, and I drew a big burger with a big red cross through it and a little stick of broccoli with a tick. It was pretty blunt.

MFT was better than single therapy, that's for sure, because they did things in a fun way. However, I didn't like the bit

DOI: 10.4324/9781003641070-15

where they put us in a room—like an interview room—to talk about things, and the adults stood behind the glass in another room, murmuring among themselves. It was kind of voyeuristic, nosey, and creepy, even though we had a therapist in the room with us and another was with the parents.

I got something out of MFT in that I liked the other kids— I hadn't met children with the same illness as me before. We talked about the annoying things that parents or others say and laughed a lot. For example, when your family tells you you look better, saying, 'Cassandra, you look well!' 'Cassandra, you've got curves now!', this was the worst thing anyone could say. I did not want curves.

It was good for the parents to hear this. Mum definitely found MFT helpful because she had worried that she had pushed it on to me. Dad came along for several sessions, but his attitude remained the same. He thought my illness was a phase—when he was young, he did not eat for a while and got over it, and he believed that I would do the same. He did not come to MFT often enough to get any benefit. My stepdad came for a few sessions, too. He would get frustrated and leave it to my mum to enforce.

Mum became more vigilant at home because when listening to other people and talking about how annoying their kids were, she got backhanded tips to try. The parents would say to each other, 'Oh, I hadn't thought of that one!' We children also got tips—even the doctors inevitably slipped up. Like, after Christmas, we were in MFT talking about how Christmas was, and Mum said, 'Well, Cassandra didn't want to eat the outside of the potato, but then she did eat it with some gravy', and one of the therapists said, 'Oh, she ate the gravy!' I thought, *'Crap, am I not meant to eat the gravy? I won't eat that anymore'*, So, the doctors put their foot in it sometimes.

By the end of the MFT year, I was pretty much near the end of recovery, definitely with weight. I think my attitude was helpful to the other kids. I was the first to gain weight, and in a group situation, if one person does well, this inspires the others.

The hospital was at least a 40-minute journey on the train. I missed a lot of school going to appointments, but I needed something to do on the train, so I studied and got really good results. I started taking antidepressants near the end of MFT. This helped, and I was taking the medication when I did Year 11 exams. I was not seeing any more therapists when I started my final year of secondary school.

I was not getting the same sort of anorexia thoughts in Year 12 but was still unhappy about my eating. I was bingeing occasionally and restricting, yo-yo-ing; I was not out of the clutches. In my first year at university, I joined a lot of clubs, and my eating started to get out of control, so I pulled back some. I knew where it would lead, so I stopped doing so much exercise. Then I felt upset, as I had more free time. I didn't tell anybody and continued to cope in this way through university.

For instance, I would get angry and upset with myself if I could not complete a full exercise routine. That's when I knew I had to be careful. On Mondays and Fridays, I would have an exercise session at 1:00 p.m., another at 3:00 p.m. and athletics at 5:00 p.m. I would try to return to my room to eat something between the sessions but began to think, *'I don't feel like eating'*. Eventually, I recognised the signs and realised, *'This is going badly'*.

Mum always gets suspicious if she sees I am losing weight. She is always the first to point that out. She trusts me more now, especially since I have started eating cheese and stuff like that. (But) Since leaving the MFT she has had like a built-in warning bell. Even when I'm at a healthy weight, she insists I have a snack at this time and a snack at that time. 'Have you had your snack?' 'Yes'. 'Where is the cup then?' 'I've already put it in the dishwasher'.

Mum is less watchful now, for sure, but I can always tell when someone is assessing my levels of fat, just by the way they look at me. Mum still does this sometimes, though she would never admit it. And I think, '*Well, I won't wear shorts when I'm near her*'.

My illness was around for a while before it was noticed— perhaps 18 months before—because I cut down on food a little at a time and increased my exercise a little at a time. At first, I went through a healthy living stage, with a lot of fruit and vegetables; next, I cut out milk in the morning and other foods, not so much to lose weight but to be more healthy. Then I got into a spiral. After recovery, as soon as I started to exercise a lot, like in my first year at university, I began to spiral again. Like, as soon as I got to a certain stage, I could never do enough exercise, and I think that urge will remain.

I don't eat butter, so I still have some food phobias. But I like avocados. I like brown bread toasted with avocado, chilli relish, and bacon. I have had many bone scans. I take a multivitamin, drink milk, and eat yoghurt. I think my calcium intake is okay; it is just that my bones don't click.

I got to the stage of thinking, '*Only I can get myself out of this illness*', probably from stubbornness. Even at MFT, I did not connect closely with anyone. I could have found a connection if I had wanted to because there were plenty of friendly people in that group. I guess the point is I didn't like therapy at all. I went along to humour them. I didn't rely on friends for support, either.

I learnt at a young age that if there is one person I can count on, it is me.

My inspiration is not my mum because she differs from me in many respects, but I do admire her, still. Mum always has been a close-friend person. She is a connecting person. She has a big group of friends and likes to have them around her. We differ a lot in that respect. I'm not a loner because I have close friends, but I don't relate to them in the same way as Mum. It was nice that Mum found a special new friend at MFT, and it was nice for me that she did, too.

I have a half-sister, eight years younger than me, who lives with Mum. I have a stepbrother several months younger than me—I don't see him much; he is my stepdad's son from a different woman. On Dad's side, I have a half-brother and half-sister who live with Dad and split time with him and their mum. Everyone is split around. I get along well with all my half-siblings, and I am the eldest, but having many family members on both sides seems odd.

I usually hang around with older people. Age is not a factor for my friends. If Mum is having a cocktail party, I fit in well with that.

For me, the illness is in the past, full stop. I don't feel the need to understand it or discuss it again. I know how to stop myself if I feel myself going down that road again. I have told my flatmate that if she thinks I am doing too much exercise, she should tell me so. I don't see a nutritionist or dietician or count things. I want to get away from all that. If I start thinking like that, I will want to do more of it, that is, keeping track of in-flow and out-flow, and that would be a bad sign.

I like to get out every day, even if not to connect directly with people, to walk around the block at night, that sort of thing. Making sure I have gone out because another warning sign is when I feel unfulfilled several days in a row. A good day contains exercise and a feeling of fulfilment. I feel really good if I do a lot of exercise and do not eat much afterwards—but I like chocolate fudge cake, and my happiest day is when I exercise and earn the chocolate fudge cake. Because I work now, I have less time for exercise, which is annoying. Endorphins help me feel I have achieved something. This feeling peaks just before I finish exercising. After I stop, I spiral and feel I should have done more.

I am so stubborn and determined that telling me to do something will make me want to do the opposite. This was the theme during my recovery. With eating, I started thinking about things in a different way. I really wanted to do kickboxing, so Mum said, 'You can do it when you get better'. That spurred me on because it was what I wanted to do. I couldn't do things because people wanted me to do them, but if I wanted to do something, this made a difference. The kickboxing didn't seem like a reward or achievement. It was something I could do for myself.

The mother

Being a single mother for much of her daughter's life and needing to work full-time, Harriet easily felt shame and blame when Cassandra was diagnosed with anorexia. Little did Harriet know that in helping her daughter recover through MFT, she would also help herself and gain a life-long friend. This is Harriet's story:

Having heard MFT was an essential part of recovery, I wanted to start as soon as possible, but there were no spaces available, and the eating disorder nurse believed Cassandra 'wasn't ready' to engage with it. I felt frustrated that treatment could be with-held until she 'was ready', as I feared that time might never come. Despite Cassandra's apparent unreadiness, I pushed and insisted as I thought this treatment should be tried. Cassandra continued to lose weight, her anxiety rose, and hospitalisation was considered.

I shared anxieties with my partner and Cassandra's father (separated), and emailed and wrote to other close family members. Conveying information about Cassandra developing anorexia that way was easier than being subjected to a cross-examination or the anxieties of others being added to those I was already trying to manage. Some family members responded in a supportive way; others didn't. I found myself regretting sharing such personal news as it left me feeling ashamed and uncom-fortable about the sense of exposure for Cassandra and us as a family. I confided in only a few close friends. In hindsight, I would choose carefully with whom to share this news.

Cassandra's dance teacher, on the other hand, expressed concern, and we had a productive chat. She had suffered from an eating disorder, too, and I felt relieved to know that Cassandra was having contact with someone who understood and had recovered.

At the initial session of the MFT, a child who was recovering from anorexia and her family shared their stories, and this was immensely helpful. The child represented hope that recovery was possible. The MFT also helped to align the differing approaches and attitudes to the illness between myself and my partner, who felt angry about it and responded accordingly as he saw it as attention-seeking rather than as a serious illness.

The most powerful exercise at the MFT was illustrating a mealtime with the anorexia 'voice'. This was an invaluable and painful insight into the immense struggle a person with anorexia has when faced with eating food—something so easy for someone with a normal appetite.

By far, the most helpful thing was the bond that developed between myself and another mother. Following the first four-day workshop, we kept in touch regularly. Initially, we communicated by text, and then, when texts became 12 messages long, we moved to email. At times, we were sharing experiences daily. We shared crises, successes, ideas, and disasters. We offered each other perspective without judgement, support, and encouragement. We could safely challenge each other because we were in the same boat. We shared our pain and laughter. This friendship played an immensely precious role in supporting me in our process towards recovery; it was a consistent source of joy and humour throughout the MFT process and beyond.

Cassandra never 'accepted' therapy as such but did attend the MFT sessions. When she objected, I said that everything I had read had said MFT was an essential part of recovery and that when she could show me she could have a healthy relationship with food, I would believe she did not need therapy. Cassandra was reluctant to open up verbally, but the therapist was incredibly skilled and developed insights and emotional shifts through creative work. I would dispute the *'right time'* theory and suggest a *'right therapy'* approach to replace it.

Cassandra was opposed to her school knowing about her illness, and I respected her wish against opposition from my partner, the specialist nurse, and others. However, if anyone expressed concern about her or asked me if she was unwell, I said I would not lie. This proved a helpful ace card, as it became motivating leverage for getting Cassandra to stick to her meal plan. If I had doubted she was sticking to her meal plan, I would have involved the school and insisted that someone sat with her to eat lunch. The consequence of not informing the school was a barrage of letters regarding poor attendance and punctuality—almost all absences were a consequence of hospital appointments or MFT days—but amazingly, no one from the school contacted me to ask why.

Several times, despite the immense effort to support, follow advice, and remain patient for signs of improvement, there was no progress. I would feel sad, exhausted, ineffectual, and demoralised. I wondered about surrendering to the experts and if Cassandra would be better in a residential unit. Often, after these cathartic moments were discharged, my resolve was slowly restored. I didn't want to give in; this was my daughter's life I was fighting for, and this belief was like restorative fuel when I felt weary. Giving in wasn't an option.

Most palpably, I felt like giving up when the eating disorder staff considered hospitalisation—the specialist team's concern about Cassandra's continued deterioration added to my sense of impotence and inadequacy. I felt beaten and ready to hand her over to hospital care despite the immense sense of failure and betrayal of her I was experiencing. Cassandra was never hospitalised, thankfully, and I found that threatening it was enough to motivate her to sustain her weight.

There were many points when I thought, *'We are winning'*. The first time was when Cassandra gained weight, though it wasn't sustained. I was to discover that gaining weight was associated with Cassandra feeling much worse, and it was not something I could openly rejoice in.

There was a time when Cassandra had a crisis where her mood became increasingly low, and she felt panicky and suicidal. I arranged an immediate appointment with the psychiatrist. We discussed the option of antidepressants, and Cassandra did agree to try the medication. One of the MFT young people had started medication and was feeling better, so this example helped to promote the idea with her. Once the medication began to take effect, there was a sense that anorexia had released the tightness of its grip. Cassandra's thinking became less rigid, and she was more relaxed about the meal plan and more amenable to negotiations to develop it further. She made a steady recovery once her depression was addressed.

After five years, we have no ongoing issues, but in the early days post-recovery, there were still signs of eating disorder behaviours. For example, there was unforgiving perfectionism and rigidity in eating certain foods (though weight was normal). At one point, I found evidence of what seemed to be bingeing, in complete contrast to the earlier restricted eating habits.

Cassandra's weight exceeded her ideal before returning to a stable normal, as it has been for a year or two now. Thankfully, we were warned about how the weight would redistribute once the oestrogen levels returned to normal. Otherwise, it could have become a source of worry. One thing Cassandra would always avoid was butter and cheese. She will always dislike butter but now eats everything, including cheese, cakes, puddings, and chocolate.

Through the process of helping my daughter through this illness, I felt sensitive and distressed by the mother-blame culture. There are undercurrents of it in society, and our general practitioner (GP) gave it a professional 'stamp' at the outset. 'Controlling mother' was a theme, but it was also suggested the illness may have been caused by the fact that I am a working mother. At the time, there was a lot in the press about preschool care and its value to children of stay-at-home mothers. As a lone parent at the time of Cassandra's birth, I had no option but to return to work. I would have loved the luxury and choice of extended maternity leave, a career break, or part-time work. I suppose this regret fed into my sense of blame.

People often seemed more focused on coming up with theories about why anorexia had happened rather than thinking of what support they could offer. A few friendships and relationships with family members were 'reframed' during this time. I became more distant from those who made unhelpful comments and from those whom I feared judgement, and closer to people who I felt wanted to understand our experience and trusted we were acting in Cassandra's best interest. Through this process, I learnt that, regardless of what some people thought, I am a good mother, and the quality of the relationship with my daughter, particularly concerning trust, has been instrumental in her recovery.

My most important lesson has been understanding the need to be more assertive, especially in close relationships. I thought, *'What example am I setting to my daughter about how to get my needs met?'* Before this, I was too busy juggling everyone else's needs and keeping everyone happy, sacrificing my own needs, and ending up pleasing no one. I learnt to risk rocking the boat, throwing in a grenade, and risking the fallout; I learnt to challenge things, create a storm, and hold on to ride it out, knowing the essential things would remain intact. Taking risks was a vital part of managing anorexia. Parental guilt and fear of getting it wrong can crush the impetus for risk-taking—this is why support for the family is essential and instrumental in recovery. A big fear for parents is that their actions might make things worse.

Any family crisis can expose existing difficulties and precipitate change. Some of my family issues relate to competing needs and demands. As well, personality and past experiences caused differing interpretations of anorexia-driven behaviour and opposing perspectives on how to respond. This was perhaps caused to some extent by, and certainly more complicated due to, our blended family. Anorexia acts like a plough that turfs up the things buried under the surface, forcing you to confront them. Everyone has these issues to some degree, and troubles within a family can expose the cracks that may be superficially hidden and avoided to prevent rocking the boat. Sometimes, though, a bit of boat rocking can lead to improvements.

Although the young person needs some privacy in consultation, the family also needs support. While I recognise that the specialist team has expert knowledge of the illness, the family may have expert knowledge of their child or young person. Collaboration between these two is essential, and sometimes, advice can be modified or risks taken in a managed way in light of this collaboration.

Guilt is the most destructive and unhelpful experience for parents, as it can undermine and inhibit the important contribution a parent can make to supporting recovery. Doctors need to tell parents, 'It's not your fault'. If not said explicitly, parents will often believe the doctor is thinking, *'It is your fault'*, even if the doctor appears neutral. This was my experience.

- See Chapter 7, to read about Harriet's special friendship with Lydia's mother, Lisa.

Chapter 13

'There is no cookie cutter for this illness'

AMY

> Peter had no hesitation in putting his child before his career. He
> relocated his family to a country that could help his daughter Amy
> recover from anorexia. At multi-family therapy (MFT), he learnt
> to replace fear with hope, keep calm, and stand beside his wife.
> Together, the parents discovered the key to recovery was not about
> culture or control but science and love. 'During the MFT week, we
> were told a story about research on monkeys isolated in a cage—it
> showed that friendship and family are critical to living a normal
> life', Peter said. 'Isolation leads to many problems—and we could
> see this was true with anorexia. The group setting with other fam-
> ilies was good for us and Amy. The trigger for her wanting to
> recover occurred when she realised this treatment could help her—
> the friendship, the connections, the bond with the other children,
> all this was important. She began looking beyond her illness—she
> wanted to go to school. She knew the nutrition better than anyone,
> and when the doctor said the effect of starvation on bone density
> could impact her future life, make her hair brittle, and so on, she
> understood and was motivated to eat'.

The father

We were living in Asia when Amy developed anorexia. She was
11, and most eating disorder programmes there don't accept
children as young as this. We searched the internet and made
two trips to an eating disorder unit in the USA. The first time,

DOI: 10.4324/9781003641070-16

we participated in part of the five-day intensive programme. Amy restored weight and was engaging less in compulsive exercise. We returned to Asia for about eight months. We stayed in touch with the eating disorder therapist by teleconferencing, but while this was helpful for us as parents, Amy had difficulty feeling connected. She needed face-to-face. We tried with Amy a few times, but she lost interest.

The first time we took Amy to the US, we were getting to the fundamentals. The second time, we were able to focus on recovery. The treatment team knew what they were doing; they were pragmatic. It was a shock and reality check to learn that Amy could die from this illness. One thing that Amy could relate to was the medical explanation regarding bone density— her scientific mind could understand the need for motivation.

The parents' meeting once a week eased our fear and embarrassment—we found others shared the same issues. Another thing that helped was that Caroline and I learnt to be united. I am too soft-hearted, and Caroline is more upfront, so we were able to discuss and present an unbiased voice on the meal plan and so on. This united voice helped counter the anxiety experienced by Amy.

I am soft-hearted because my work requires me to be away from home often, and I feel guilty that I don't spend enough time with my children. So, when home, I pamper and give them what they want, and sometimes the children play on this as they know how I feel, and this is very difficult for me. One lesson I learned at MFT is that giving a child some hardship is okay. If parents don't provide boundaries when the children are growing up, they are denying their children the full growing-up experience.

Every patient is different—there is no cookie cutter for this illness. We know Amy is strong-willed, and forcing her to do something never works. She needs to see hope, and then she can achieve miracles. She could see recovery taking place in the other children and felt inspired that she could accomplish this, too. The programme was teaching coping skills and self-awareness not only for recovery from anorexia but for life. I learnt, too, to replace my fear with hope by watching other parents in our parent group. I also saw that when parents don't see hope, they get caught in a downward spiral with no win in sight, so I learnt to keep calm because hope is half the battle. To hear stories of recovery, share in the parent group, and see the children making progress, we experienced hope.

One breakthrough with our daughter was with medication. I was terrified of the impact on Amy—I mean, no parent wants their kid to have psychological medicines. But we were able to understand this would help ease her anxiety, and soon, we could see that the benefits were much more significant than any side effects.

We understand Amy is on a lifetime journey and may not require medication forever. Amy is doing well on her medication; she is swimming again, has more flexibility and independence in her day, and her weight is on her recovery curve.

Amy's health was my prime reason for moving my family to the US. I wanted to put my family first to provide the support system necessary to care for Amy. To help her, I had to put her before my career. Her condition can relapse, so even if we stayed in the US until Amy recovered, and returned to Asia for her to attend college, the illness could come back, so we are basing our family life in the US.

The contract was something that Amy liked and gave us parents something to use—for example, it set boundaries for us, like not nagging during mealtime, not talking about food or weight all the time, and not being anxious. The bottom line is to get our child to feel part of the treatment collaboration and for the family to work together. It is a delicate balance; some psychology is involved—for example, we want Amy to be involved but not for her to have control, so we try to guide her carefully. Not allowing Amy to go to school was not a good consequence of maintaining the contract. Her issue is largely anxiety, and to miss school would have caused more anxiety if implemented as a penalty. She loves school, and it helps to get her mind away from both anxiety and her eating disorder, so school is good. The consequence needed to be something the child wanted to do, but for us to say 'no school' to Amy would have created more anxiety. When we moved to the US, Amy wanted to go to Disneyland, and we did not cut it off totally; we did other activities, so it was a penalty but not a total turn-off. Anorexia is not a black-and-white illness. You have to be thinking all the time.

During the MFT week, we were told a story about research on monkeys isolated in a cage—it showed that friendship and family are critical to living a normal life. Isolation leads to all sorts of problems—and we could see this was true with anorexia. The group setting with other families was good for us and for Amy, who was very resistant to change. The trigger for her wanting to recover occurred when she realised this treatment could help her—the friendship, the connections, the bond with the other children, all this was important. She began looking beyond her illness—she wanted to go to school. She knew the nutrition better than anyone, and so when the doctor said the effect of starvation on bone density could impact her future life, make her hair brittle, and so on, she could understand and was motivated to eat.

As a dad, I learned the importance of educating myself about the disease, talking to professionals, and being the backbone of my family. I must strive never to show weakness but rather show I am strong and convince my family the sky won't fall, because this illness can be scary. Dads also need emotional support to do their job. My wife and I shared with church friends— having friends who can offer support is important.

Coping with this illness has been challenging for my wife, who had to quit her job and be a full-time carer at home. Our church has helped her. We tended to blame ourselves, asking, 'What have we done wrong?' However, we have learnt that we can only control what we can control. At MFT, we received a tremendous education regarding mental health. We learned our child does not have control of her illness, and if she needs medication to live a normal life, we have to trust science. The illness causes the child to have strange behaviours, which can isolate the child, but they do not control this, and loved ones need to understand this so they can offer support.

The mother

We felt frustrated because we could not see what the problem was when Amy developed anorexia—we could not see her brain, right? She continued to lose weight. We tried hard as a family to help her gain weight—we tried to calm her down so that she would listen to and obey us. For us to sit beside her, telling her, *'We will sit here as long as it takes'*, would never work. If we told Amy this, she would purposefully not eat; she would get up and walk away. I tried to motivate her and tried distractions, like playing cards, but this never worked.

We needed more help as Amy developed a need to exercise compulsively after she had eaten. Even if rain was falling, she had to go outside. When her legs began to develop a fracture, I told my husband, 'We have to take her somewhere'. We were living in Asia, but a counsellor in the ex-pat community suggested that we approach a treatment centre in the US. We went there twice. We had several days of intensive family therapy, but not with other families, as we could not match our schedule with the programme. The therapist helped us to understand this anorexia—we were trying to understand so we could deal with Amy's behaviour. We wanted to know if this illness was due to anxiety, perhaps biological anxiety, or family relationships.

Eighteen months later, we were again in the US, this time for a month, for a week of MFT with other families. The first time, we were not in a group situation and did not gain enough skills and knowledge. We needed to learn how to manage when we left the clinic and took Amy home, and by now, we had decided to relocate permanently to the US to safeguard Amy's health.

I don't believe culture had much impact on the development of Amy's illness. I believe the cause is internal and biological in the brain. We have learned new ways of treating our children and encouraging education. Our culture believes children are born as they are, and we have the role of guiding them with the abilities and talents they are born with. With happiness, health, laughter, and emotional savvy, they can reach high. Our traditional culture was to push, push, push for an education, and this could be challenging. This societal attitude is changing for the current generation of children.

With MFT, I found the contract for Amy most helpful, where we said, 'You have to eat this much to get this reward'. This reward was very helpful because, at this time, she could not think normally.

Secondly, as a family, for the first time, we met other parents who had a child with anorexia. My husband and I had wondered if we were to blame. We have very close families, no divorce or anything, but we did not know what to do. We could not discipline Amy, for she was a perfect child basically. At MFT, we learnt other families were going through the same thing. This illness was not easy for them either, and we learnt from other parents and the group leaders that medication is sometimes necessary—until then, we had thought if Amy was strong enough, then she could cope without medication. Not so. I could now see that Amy's need for medication was no different to other members of our family needing medicines for diabetes or heart problems.

Thirdly, I am the first to notice a problem in our family. With parenting, I am the prime carer—my husband says I worry too much, but the MFT helped him to understand the anorexia and brought his understanding to a level similar to mine. We are more consistent, we agree more on our approach, and we are on the same front; he stands beside me rather than me standing alone. This enables me to feel much stronger—this is a more powerful way to face this illness.

I quit my very good job to take care of Amy. A family needs to be united, and I want to be here for Amy until she completes high school. I don't mean helping her physically or academically—all I want to do is make sure she is eating correctly and share my experience and knowledge about this illness.

Most importantly, I have learned that if we don't help our child as a family, no one can help our child. I truly believe that family support is 95 per cent of the solution to this illness. Sometimes, Amy looks at me and says, 'I hate you, Mum', and I know this is the illness talking. Amy, when she is relaxed, is so sweet. When she is feeling stressed or under too much pressure, I can hear anorexia kick in.

I have experienced tremendous stress in life, but my body can naturally dilute and handle the stress by eating good food, talking with friends, and watching TV. My challenge is to help Amy find out what coping skills are right for her. Her mind is too busy to focus on this—she seems to think about many things, though I don't know what.

Sometimes, people say the family controls too much, but some families control more, and their child is not sick with anorexia. So, control is not the main reason for this illness. For me, the leading cause is biological. I am careful to treat Amy in the same way I treat my son, and am careful not to be too controlling and pick the battles to fight. Like my sister says, 'Amy is a good child, and you don't need to worry about her—like with drugs or alcohol. She has no bad behaviours'. Her only problem is this eating disorder.

After Amy was prescribed medication, her compulsion to run eased—she had been very rigid and obsessive about running. Her favourite reward on our contract was exercising for, say, 20 minutes. We have not used contracts for eight months because she basically has been eating normally. Her latest thing is she wants to run and do cross-country; however, we won't allow this for another year for fear it may trigger her eating disorder. Another reward for Amy has been volunteering in charity work, and she enjoys helping older people with Alzheimer's disease.

Amy likes school, the teachers like her, and she has made good friends but has lingering anxiety. I think that for Amy to be occupied is very important, and I try to keep her active on weekends so that there is no time for her mind to be anxious. I take her shopping, she does her volunteer work, helps with the housework, and we have a little dog to care for. Besides wanting Amy, now 16, to recover fully from her illness, we want her to prepare for college in three years. We hope that she can do this with help from professionals and with support from her family. We want her to learn to care for herself, grow up, and become independent like a normal teenager. Otherwise, she will never grow up.

Chapter 14

When 'doing' with others makes a difference

EMILY

Emily, the youngest of three daughters, developed anorexia at age 14 and, together with her parents, participated in multi-family therapy (MFT) ten months before our interview. Since the five days of MFT, Emily, who also has type 1 diabetes, has required no further treatment for anorexia. Although her parents were well informed on evidence-based approaches, the MFT brought it all together. They had read a lot about the therapy and knew the model of care. But they did not know how to implement it. Being there and participating in real time for one week made all the difference.

The mother

Midway through our MFT week, the doctor and his colleague were talking about what happened physiologically with anorexia nervosa. I started crying. I think everyone thought I was crying about something to do with bone density or osteoporosis, but what triggered my tears was the realisation, the reality of the difficulties ahead—that to help Emily get better, we would sometimes have to do things we did not want to do.

We would have to do things we feared might hurt our relationship with our child, like enforcing the consequences if she did not eat the food on her plate. Standing up to the illness at every meal was already scary for Emily and painful for us. I already knew the importance of nutrition. The thing was, the MFT team

DOI: 10.4324/9781003641070-17

filled in the missing pieces educationally. Suddenly, I under-stood and got a good sense of what we had to do—the doctor's talk brought this to life, and everything became more real.

One activity that had a big impact was when the girls cre-ated a sculpture of what a plate of food resembled to them—it was big and grotesque, and they recorded on a tape the voices they heard in their mind when faced with a plate of food. The dialogue was very accusing and derogatory. Then, they did a role play with the parents. The mum was given the role of the daughter, sitting at the table, at mealtime, and the daughter was given the role of the mum, presenting this plate of food, and playing the tape behind the mum's head. To have that experi-ence of what it was like for our daughter at mealtime was com-pelling. Until that point, I was unaware of how strong those illness thoughts were that Emily was hearing. Now I understood what she was up against.

One set of parents had been through a lot in helping their daughter, over and over again, and were still going through it, but to me, they were a tower of strength. Like us, they needed the tweaking to have it all come together. This family's perse-verance inspired me.

I felt concerned for other families, especially the newcom-ers, and wanted to tell them that although this therapy would be difficult, it would be worth it. We had been fighting the ill-ness for about 18 months before we began MFT, and because everything that we had tried was not helpful, we felt we knew MFT would be the answer. Without that experience of previous struggle, I can imagine that it might be easy to give up when things got tough. I wanted to help the other families understand the importance of sticking with it.

Having background knowledge of this model and experi-encing it in this supportive environment was very helpful for us. An example was understanding the simple but extremely effective concept of starting with a daily intake of a certain number of calories, and your goal is to increase weight by a certain amount each week; if this does not happen, you add 400 calories daily, until you reach that weight gain goal.

Another helpful factor was the contract that we developed over the course of the week. The contract, to be adhered to when we went home, spelt out that life would pretty much stop unless weight increased by a set amount each week. The contract was between Emily and us, and the three of us signed it. We discussed some things together, but I would not be surprised if Emily did not like parts of it as her dad and I did most of the wording. Each family created their own contract. The MFT therapist helped us and offered guidance, for instance, on supervising Emily's meals at school.

The first week after we went home was difficult, especially the first night. Once we got into a routine of, 'You know, this is it; this is what we are doing now', it was easier. Emily did not have a choice, nor did we. Things started to get better then.

We had no monthly catch-ups with the MFT team due to the distance—we lived a five-hour flight away. The five days was it. I did call the therapist once or twice and she was wonderful. We were referred to a local family-based therapist based about two-and-a-half hours away. We drove there for an intake, but Emily did not get a good feeling, and I also felt concerned, so we decided that as long as Emily was adhering to the contract, we would not go again. That therapist seemed more task oriented and clinical rather than empathetic and understanding of Emily's feelings. Being empathic would have been helpful.

The most important thing for us at MFT was that the programme's therapist cared deeply, and this came across. Her empathy and care made all the difference. She 'got it'—she was matter-of-fact and caring at the same time. Emily liked her, too.

When Emily developed type 1 diabetes at age 11, we knew where to go, and she was quickly and correctly diagnosed and given treatment. But when she developed anorexia, we saw several doctors during those early few months, and none made a correct diagnosis. It was her celiac doctor, a gastroenterologist, who noticed the eating disorder symptoms and took action. Four previous doctors had not picked up on the symptoms. I had kept waiting for a doctor to tell me what to do, and valuable time was lost for early intervention.

The other treatment place that Emily went to, about a year before MFT, had been ineffective. It was a residential centre, and Emily was there without any family members. I attended for the last few days, saw first-hand how the program worked, and decided, *'Right, we are out of here'.*

What scared me most in these moments was that having worked in the mental health field for many years, I knew good, compassionate programmes were out there, along with the not-so-good ones. But how would I know which was which until we experienced them? I felt locked in a no-win situation.

As a therapist, I knew something about eating disorders, though I had little experience in treating them. I began searching for and reading anything I could on the topic. This included books on family-based therapy, other treatment approaches, and personal stories of the illness and recovery. However, I did not truly understand or know how to implement what was needed. I would read something and then think, *'Okay, I know what we have to do now'*, only to find that nothing we did was making a difference. During this period of rapid weight loss, Emily saw several doctors, none of whom seemed to grasp the severity and true nature of the problem. Not knowing where to turn for quality treatment, and because no doctor was suggesting we do anything more, we kept on as we were. If the doctors were not more concerned, perhaps she was not medically in danger, and there was nothing more *to* do at this point.

I first learned of MFT from the school nurse, who knew another family who had been through the programme. When things did not get better for nearly a year and began to get worse, MFT was the treatment we sought at that crisis point. MFT brought to life all that we had read about and propelled us forward in a way that simply reading the book could not do.

Before Emily developed anorexia, we were just like your typical family: loving, caring, and fun. Not perfect, but we all knew we loved and supported each other, no matter what. The illness shook things up a lot, and since treatment, we are still rebuilding relationships. It's a process, and I feel very hopeful about the future.

The father

I tend to be positive upfront and tend to maybe deny things are going on until after it is obvious they are happening, and for me, this has made Emily's illness harder to deal with.

I look back, thinking, *'Could I have helped Emily sooner if I had realised what was happening?'* Not knowing how to help was the biggest frustration. We made a big mistake in sending Emily to a residential centre early in her illness. In researching and looking on the internet for treatment places, several local people said some girls from the local university had been to this place. So we thought it was a good place, and the frustration looking back is, you don't know if your child is not happy because she is not dealing with the eating disorder or because of what she is telling us. That remains my biggest regret: we knew about family-based treatment and MFT, but the irony is we probably weren't ready. If we had tried it earlier, we might have given up. We were kind of laid-back, and my experience with the other parents at MFT was that they were similar to us.

I had preconceived notions of parents who had children who developed anorexia. I thought the illness was more associated with trauma, strict parents, and perfectionism. I have a long history of that on my side of the family. So I was aware of that, but I did not feel we were that kind of parent. We did not tell our daughters, *'You have to have that grade in school'*. Our expectation was, *'You have to do the best you can, and that's all we expect of you'*. To see the illness developing in our family was shocking, and also shocking for me as a father, not being able to protect Emily from it.

At MFT, the food sculpture helped me realise how difficult it is for a child with anorexia to eat. I thought at one point they were going to ask us to eat what was on the plate. That scared me, and the swapping of the roles helped me to realise how ineffective we had been—the kids took on the role of the parents and said the same things we would have said, and seeing that helped me to better understand how separate the disease is from the person. To understand that the illness was suppressing Emily helped us do what we had to do to find her.

I did feel mean to have to implement the contract. I'm the softie, I guess. I would be saying, 'Maybe we need to listen to Emily more; maybe we should let her have this or do that', and MFT helped me to realise that if I kept talking like this, she would not get better. I realised that being firm was not being mean to Emily; it was being mean to the disease. Being firm would help her come back. Knowing this helped me a ton. It helped me be strong.

My wife, Sandy, had read a lot of books about eating disorder treatments, and we had done a lot of talking before we did the MFT. We knew early on that we would be ineffective if both of us constantly ganged up on Emily. So Sandy took the lead on enforcement, and I was between that enforcement and providing a sort of refuge for Emily. At times, I would reinforce; other times, I would try to help her have that refuge where it was less stressful.

One MFT therapist told us about 23- and 24-year-olds in a treatment programme who felt angry at their parents for not having done more to help them. This resonated with me. I'm confident Emily did not doubt our love for her, so to know that our love was separate from what had contributed to the disease was difficult to accept. If we had not tried every other approach we could have tried, I doubt I would have been strong enough to do what we needed to do with MFT. Taking the softer approach has worked for us in every other situation in raising our three girls—we have three amazing girls. Each is unique and talented in her own way, and I am proud of the young women they have become.

To see how Emily is making good choices now is remarkable. She is a remarkable girl. I had autoimmune issues in my family, and Emily has diabetes and celiac disease to deal with besides the anorexia. To find out at MFT that anorexia has a biological basis, I was like, 'Wow, why didn't anyone else mention this in the past 18 months?'

I was really pleased when the doctor at MFT explained that the traits of the illness—perfectionism, conscientiousness, and so on—could be very effective when directed in the right way. But when consumed by the illness, these traits can be tough. The doctor also spoke about the bone density issues, and I felt really, really happy that we had come to MFT right then.

Another thing I learned at MFT that I wished we had known earlier was the concept of dense foods. Some foods contain more calories than others, and so the experience of eating those was not as challenging as eating more or less dense foods. I had not heard of that concept until we went to MFT. This meant we could get Emily to eat significantly more calories with a smaller food intake. This knowledge was comforting because we could work with that to make meal times easier for her.

The hardest thing was not being tough but watching Emily having to eat. You know, early in my professional career, I found public speaking devastatingly scary, and I remember realising, *'If I don't do this, I can't go on'*. I fought through it every time, and I'd throw up before every speech. In the back of my mind, I was proud of myself for having fought through the fear. I saw Emily having a similar experience in the fear she faced with each meal. Knowing how debilitating that anxiety was and realising that same anxiety was true of people having to eat when they have anorexia, opened my eyes in terms of the empathy I had for what Emily was going through. She didn't have a choice. And we didn't have a choice but to implement this plan to help her.

My wife and I have had a lucky marriage when it comes to negotiating decisions. We are polar opposites but instinctively know the right way to go. For the most part, I'm saying this, and she is saying that, and we meet in the middle. With Emily, I tended to say, 'Maybe we need to back off'. My wife would say, 'No, I think the MFT contract says we have to make sure we enforce this rule', so every time there was a question about whether we should let something go, an example being how much exercise Emily could do in a day, we would talk and talk until we agreed, and then say to Emily, 'This is what we have decided'. We knew we had to have a unified front.

The most challenging time for us all was when we came home from MFT, and Emily felt up against the wall. We almost lost her that first night. I tend to be optimistic and think, *'This is gonna work, this is gonna work',* so discovering that Emily was feeling like she had no options was dreadful.

We knew the MFT approach was right and had to do it. I think logically, and this situation was like dealing with two people, one of whom was horrible and not even a person. We had to deal with that horrific part to get Emily back, and my constant comfort throughout was in knowing this illness was a thing we had to get rid of.

What made the difference for us with MFT was the team's empathy. Empathy is essential. We had to learn how to be tough and empathic at the same time, and that was not easy to teach. A combination of empathy and toughness is needed to help a child recover from anorexia.

The technique of MFT is important, but that's not all. The delivery is important, too. This made all the difference for our family. We always had empathy by nature, but we did not have the skills. We had read about it but didn't know how to implement it until we did our week of MFT. The skills gave us, the parents, something to hold on to—the knowledge that this is how we have to face this, and we did not waver. I love having my daughter back!

Middle sibling (Brittany)

I was 22 and stayed in college a long way from home when Mum, Dad, and Emily took part in MFT. When they came home, I talked with Mum a lot about my role with Emily because I was one of the few people who knew about her illness, the monster that it was, but I was not a primary caretaker involved in the contract.

I saw my role as providing a sort of refuge for Emily because our home for her, I am sure, was really hard. That was where she was told, 'You have to eat', and that was scary. I would have her over to visit to provide relief away from that high-stress environment. I lived in a big house with nine other girls in college, and this, I think, was fun for her—there were always lots of people there, and we played cards, spent time on campus, or had sleepovers.

My struggle was always, if Emily was there for a meal, *'How much do I push for her to eat it?'* How much do I hold back and say, *'Well, she ate most of it and is going home later'*. I did not want her to feel like, *'I don't want to visit Brittany again because it is not a safe place any more'*. It's not that my parents created a bad environment, but that's where most of the tough conversations about food happened.

I noticed a difference in Emily before and after she went to MFT. For me, one of the biggest struggles was that I felt like she had lost who she was, and I didn't know who she was anymore. The time she had anorexia was a defining time for girls in general, figuring out who they are, and so she lost this time, about 18 months. It was like she was nothing during this period.

Like, in middle school, before everything really started, I could name things that Emily liked and describe her personality, but after the anorexia developed, about the beginning of her first year in high school, I did not know what made her laugh any more or what she was passionate about—I couldn't see any more of that there. My family tried many things to help her improve during that time, but nothing seemed to work.

One of the most difficult things was watching her—she seemed bound, trapped, captured. Like watching her walk from the kitchen to the living room, walking the long way through the house to get there, or knowing that she would wake up early in the morning to run on the treadmill downstairs. Knowing she was running on the treadmill after she had already been to a challenging gymnastics practice earlier that day. That kind of thing was hard.

Trying to figure out how not to give in to the eating disorder but also to show Emily kindness was a challenge. For example, when she was still really sick and fragile, she would want to go on walks all the time. I would want to spend time with her, but I felt if I went on the walk with her, the eating disorder was winning, and I would be contributing to the problem and making her sicker. I thought not going on the walks was a way that I could protect her. When our sister Jessica came home, she would go on the walks, so I felt bad for not going but couldn't bring myself to do it.

One time, my family was at Disney World, and we were looking at a map to see where we wanted to go in the park. Emily was trying to convince us that we should go to the rides in a certain order that would cause us to walk back and forth over the park all day. And I was like, 'No, that doesn't make sense'. I insisted we walk around the park in a circle because that made more sense. I felt it wasn't Emily who wanted to go the long way; it was her eating disorder. Normally, it wouldn't have been a big deal to me, but I felt if I were to give in, I would be giving in to the eating disorder.

So there were times when I could be pretty stubborn about it because I was like, thinking, *'This eating disorder isn't going to control me too',* and I thought I was helping to keep it from controlling Emily, too. Now, as she gets better, I don't feel I have to keep myself from doing anything athletic with her...like, the other day, we played tennis together, and that was fun.

Ten months after MFT, Emily's personality has come back; she is laughing more, and I see life in her eyes. I think it was really, really hard for her to implement the contract and hard for my parents, too, but I reflect that MFT was worth it because Emily is better.

Maybe I would not have said that immediately after the MFT week. I would have said, 'No, try something else', because I knew how hard the contract was and felt it could hurt her more.

Helping people with anorexia to recover, they have to eat, and eating is the scariest thing, and at times, my parents were like, 'You have to eat this'. I wasn't there much, but when I was, I could see the fear and pain it was causing Emily. I felt like saying, 'Can't we try something else?' But the bottom line was, 'She has to eat to get better'.

Today, when we were leaving home to come here for this interview with you, Mum and Dad were bringing us lunch, and Emily said, 'Yeah and for me, too', and I thought times like this would never happen again.

MFT is difficult but worth it, in the end.

The nine girls with whom I share a house and my faith were my greatest support system. My family was always supportive, but I also had another family in my best friends. My faith was the most important thing for me in getting through this difficult time. Jesus was about healing people; most of my hope came from the Bible.

Eldest sibling (Jessica)

I was 23 and living away from home when my family participated in MFT. When I first noticed there was something wrong with Emily, I wondered if she had an eating disorder and decided, 'No, she does not meet the criteria'. My perception of anorexia was that the illness evolved from a severe body image issue, but I never heard Emily say she was concerned she was overweight or fat. Yet clearly, she was losing weight and not eating.

In November, I came home from college for Thanksgiving, and we drove interstate to spend it with my cousins. That weekend I noticed that Emily didn't interact with anyone the way she used to, not even with cousins who were her age and whom she normally loved being with. I don't remember what she did or didn't eat—that had nothing to do with why I was worried about her. She looked thin but not strikingly so, but what stood out was that the carefree sister I knew was gone, and now she seemed preoccupied and unhappy and just kind of not there in general. We drove home after a five-hour trip, feeling exhausted, but as soon as we arrived, Emily jumped on the treadmill. That scared me.

In December, I came home again for Christmas. At this point, she was really unhealthy and thin. I had had conversations with my mum and sister Brittany about it, and I was getting worried. But it still didn't seem like an eating disorder—at least not my perception of an eating disorder. Emily never talked about her body or being too thin; her illness onset was quiet and subtle.

Another thing that stands out is what happened after that same trip home. I woke up to a really loud sound while it was still dark outside. I was super groggy and thought maybe the fire alarm had gone off, and I was trying to get back to sleep (I guess I'd be screwed if there really was a fire). But it kept going...I got up to see what the sound was, thinking maybe Dad had left a clock on the desk in his office. But when I opened the door to my room, Emily's door was open and the sound was coming from there. I went in, and she was gone, but her alarm clock was ringing. Once I turned that off, I heard another weird sound, which I followed downstairs. I got down to the second level of the house, and the basement door was open. The sound was getting louder. As I started walking downstairs, I realised it was the treadmill, and I found Emily working out; it was 4:00 or 5:00 a.m. That's when I was sure something was wrong. I didn't know what to do. So I sat there with her, trying to seem natural. I asked if I could bring her water. She said, 'No thanks!' She said she couldn't sleep, so she thought she'd run. That was one of the scariest moments in the beginning.

I was worried, too, when Emily and our parents went to California for the MFT, as almost a year had passed since her previous treatment at a residential centre, and that had not helped at all. I felt helpless. I was at college more than 1,000 miles away, but worse than the distance was that I seemed emotionally far from Emily because the illness was making it hard for her to have a relationship in general. Maintaining our relationship was hard because we could not communicate—the only way I could try was via email.

When my family came home from California, that was hard too, but in talking to them on the phone and Skype, things gradually seemed to be getting better.

Emily's whole personality had suffered during her illness. She had always been lively, confident, and spunky, and we would make each other laugh. Because I was away from home most of the time during her illness, the change was noticeable. When I came home after MFT, she could smile, not faking it, and this was really special. Until then, she had had to fake happiness because she was barely laughing or smiling.

Before Emily's illness, we had been a happy, normal family, and I found the secretiveness of anorexia to be distressing. It made me want to be more open and honest in my life, too. There weren't many things I could offer to help Emily, but one thing I could offer was sharing and showing those sides of myself that were hard for me, like that I was not perfect, and she did not need to be, either.

When I left home for college, Emily was 11, and I was 18. It was like, when I left, she was a little kid. When I returned home just before this illness started, I realised how much she had grown up, how much we had in common, and how much we had to offer each other. So when she was sick and we could not communicate, it was tough. The experience made me realise what I wanted in relationships with my family and that I would have to work for that more. Now that Emily is getting better and more able to share, I don't want to miss this opportunity to get to know her.

The patient (Emily)

I was 14 and starting my first year at high school when my anorexia developed. I was aware I had lost weight, but was not aware that it might keep getting worse. I was in competition cheerleading in September, October, and the beginning of November, and I did gymnastics as well until I got too sick. I managed to finish the gymnastics season. And then that was it.

Early the following year, I was sent to a treatment centre for almost a month. My memories of that place are not good; I felt very alone the entire time.

Going to MFT with my parents, I felt a lot less alone, and I felt connected with the other girls. We cared about each other, and I did not feel triggered by them, even though we were able to share experiences. We shared our phone numbers and Snapchat on our iPhones; we set up a Facebook group to keep in touch after the MFT week. We would post good things about our day. We would post funny things, too, so our messages were only sometimes about struggle. I felt close to these girls even though we had only five days together. I was 16, and we were all close in age.

I enjoyed doing that food sculpture activity. Until then, I didn't know what I saw when confronted with a meal. We piled food on a plate. We had a bagel, pudding, sugar, and a gross combination of foods; it looked disgusting. Gummy worms and stuff like that. I hoped my parents would understand what we were trying to show them. Like, that plate of food was one-millionth of what the food felt like to me. We each said one thing we heard in our head, and those words were recorded together and played back to our parents. I guess that is the closest thing to reality you can do in an exercise like that, but it is very different because the parents knew there was a recording right there beside them, but in real time, you think that it is you saying that. So it was different in that way, but it gave the parents an idea of the voice and how it sounds. That voice is really like an abusive relationship. It's like constant verbal abuse. I didn't see it like that until taking part in this activity. It helped my parents and me a lot.

The other girls found this insight helpful, too. At mealtimes, we began to think, 'Okay, *I have heard that before'*, and *'Maybe that voice telling me not to eat is not the real me'*, and we began to back up these thoughts with stronger thoughts like *'That's not me', 'Not true'*. So when we had our next snack, we would look at each other and think, *'I hear that too'*. This helped us feel more connected and, at least, slightly disconnected from the illness voice. But it was still very scary.

We girls had a lot of opportunities to share, like exactly what we felt from the start of a meal to the end; everyone was very open. We helped each other in this way, and when I got home and got stuck at a meal, I would remember, *'That person said she felt the same way'*, and just to have this perspective that someone else was going through this too was helpful.

About that contract—we spent most of the week crafting it. I still feel ambivalent about it—it is a good idea in that you have to do some things, 'Like this is what you have to do', and 'This is why', but I have a hard time understanding that the contract helped. Sure, some rewards were helpful. Like, you need some reason to help you stand up to these voices in your mind. One of my rewards was a car, which, well, you would think would help, but no, it did not at the time. I was 16 and wanted my licence to be able to drive and gain some independence. But the car didn't make me want to eat more food. I remember thinking, *'You can invite me to write down anything I want in that contract, like, say, a million dollars, but I still won't want to eat my meal'*. My parents could offer nothing that would have made me want to eat that meal.

I did eat, and I did get the car, and so long as I maintain a healthy weight, I can drive it. At first, the thought of getting a car if I ate was no help at all. Now that I am at a healthy weight and can drive the car, I appreciate it. But when you get to this point, recovery is about other things, too, so it is just a plus now that I happen to have a car.

Everyone has their own way of recovering, and the contract helps some people more than others. It didn't help me because, at first, I felt utterly hopeless. I knew my parents would not budge; they would uphold the contract. We had each signed it, and that was that. I felt that if I went home and followed the contract, life would suck because I had to do all the things the eating disorder didn't want me to, but if I didn't, then I would not be able to do things that meant a lot to me, like walk to the neighbour's house, or my friend's house. I felt that either way, I did not have a life; I did not have a good life at all.

Like, I felt I was being got at from all sides, and while I understand that sometimes you have to go to those measures where everything is taken away, at the same time, if denied all freedoms for too long, you can reach the point where you don't see the point in recovery. That's where I was on my first night home and injected an overdose of insulin. You have to try and find a balance in the contract with what is too much, and what isn't helpful. Something was needed to remind me, Emily, of who and what I was and that I was respected. I felt I had no rights at all.

On the flight home and during the first week at home, I did not like the contract. But after that first night at home when I did not want to live and spent a night in hospital, yes, it was hard, but I had this new motivation to get better, and I had never felt this way before. In some ways, this was the easiest time. I wanted to get better. It was physically challenging—I had to eat a lot of food. I did not want to eat, but I made myself do it. My parents thought this was the hardest thing to do, but now I knew I wanted to get better. Wanting to get better was by far the best part for me. I was nowhere near better, but now I was feeling motivated.

Going home from the MFT week, I had not felt that way at all. The moment came in the hospital emergency room after taking the insulin overdose. I woke up and thought, *'I want to be better'*. It was the day of the Super Bowl. This was the second year in a row that I was watching the Super Bowl from a hospital bed, and I thought, *'I don't want to be in the hospital next time the Super Bowl is on'*.

I felt, at MFT, that the therapists encouraged us to make friendships, and they tried to make it fun, even if we did not feel like fun. I am glad I met the other girls there as we are really close. We use Facebook a lot for eating disorder things, like good things that we have done in coping with it, and we text or Snapchat about other everyday things. An example on Facebook is when one of us says, 'I am having a thought, and will it be triggering if I say this?' We always like to start by saying this, just in case, but none of us has been triggered by anything we have shared. And then we proceed to share what we are experiencing, and for some reason, for me, it is hard to do it to yourself, but when you are seeing someone struggle with an eating disorder, it is like, 'Oh, come on, you can have such a good life'. So, we try to help each other in this way, and this helps us, too. It is like, I can see that this is the best way for this other person, so can I see it for myself, too.

When I was told we were going to MFT, I was at the point where something had to give—my eating disorder did not want to go, but I was mentally exhausted and didn't care. I had felt nothing for so long; I was almost not a person. I felt no emotion and didn't have a personality anymore. I couldn't care about things. I didn't have an opinion on anything.

The MFT experience has brought my family closer. It was hard on the parts to do with the eating disorder but not on our relationship. I felt like my parents were understanding and didn't feel they were mad at me. I don't think they will ever understand what anorexia is really like, but they had empathy and knew it was hard for me.

We don't refer to the contract now—I still have to maintain a healthy weight and get weighed every week and a half. Under the contract, I had to reach a certain weight. If I lost weight, I would lose privileges. The contract is still in place in this way.

Ten months after MFT, I rarely have anorexia thoughts, and if I do, well, it is almost like a voice in my mind, and I recognise it and say to myself, *'Okay, I heard that, but I don't do that anymore'*, and, *'That's not who I am, anymore'*. Now, I don't have to pretend to laugh or have fun. Life is fun. I am in my third year of high school and enjoying sport again—doing track and cheer squad. I like San Diego and want to go to college there. I want to be a nurse and maybe eventually a doctor.

Chapter 15

The sparkle behind a belly button piercing

AMELIA

Amelia developed anorexia at age 13 and took part in multi-family therapy (MFT) at age 16. By looking at the other girls, she began to understand what she was inflicting on herself. As the MFT week progressed, Amelia began to realise how 'great a person I can be without anorexia' and that she needed to eat. Her mum started to understand the seriousness of the illness and how hard her daughter was working to recover. Inspired, the mother became willing to work hard to get out of her comfort zone. Mother and daughter still don't agree over many things but are learning to meet in the middle sometimes. This is something neither had been willing to do before.

The daughter

Everyone else in my family was perfect, and there was me, unable to eat the bit of pasta in front of me. When everyone else in the family is perfect, and you are dealing with an eating disorder, you feel like the problem child. You don't understand at the time that your parents don't see you like that. I have become a lot stronger as a person due to MFT. I don't get hung up on small problems any more. If I don't fit into my jeans in the morning, screw it, I'll buy another pair. If I hear a girl say, 'I have gained two pounds, and my hair has gotten more oil', I push myself past this small talk.

I was nervous and confused on the first day of the MFT, but then I found that I got on really well with the other girls. We

DOI: 10.4324/9781003641070-18

still stay in touch on Facebook and chat on the phone. I was 16, the eldest in the group, and I felt a responsibility to mother the others; I have a mothering instinct and wanted to help look after them. I tried my best to make us close-knit, and the girls were like, honoured that I was doing this, and this helped me too because if I didn't eat, I was going to be *'all talk and no walk'*.

The thing was, I could see the other girls were sick, and then, what happened was they helped me know that I was ill, too. I got the mirror effect with them—by looking at them for the first time, I could see and understand what I was inflicting on myself. On the first day, when snack time came, all the girls started complaining and saying, 'I don't want to eat that', 'You can't make me eat that'. On the second day, I was watching this girl, and she was crying, and I could see how fearful she was of the food. Suddenly, I saw the effect of her eating disorder and how it had taken over her life, and I realised how we had the same thought processes, so it must have taken over my life, too. So, I had to show the girls that behind all my talk, I could eat my meals, too. It really sucked. It was horrible, but really pushed me to do well. I had to eat. On the third day, we girls all decided to eat lunch, and we were all happy and laughing, talking about boys and high school in general, and we didn't notice, really, that we had eaten all of our lunch. I was like, *'Wow, this is a step in the right direction'*.

Another day, at one of the sessions, we took all this disgusting food and, like, we poured pudding over cold pork, and lemon, and sugar cottage cheese, and other food to show our parents how food appeared to us. We each recorded one thought of our eating disorder on an iPhone and presented the meal to our parents, one by one. Behind them, we played our taped recording to put them in the role of how we felt at mealtime and what the food looked like to us. This helped many parents understand how hard it was for us. Our reluctance to eat was not about us just trying to get attention, but about that we were feeling physically nauseous.

I have always been goal oriented and responsible in working towards the goals that I set for myself. I have wanted to go to college and get a degree. At MFT, now that I could understand the effect of anorexia on my mind and body, I wanted to do what I had to do to get my life back and be normal. I could see I had to work on controlling my eating disorder. I was a top student and already had missed a lot of school. I had been taking a lot of advanced placement subjects, like taking a college class in high school. I had missed school because I was nauseous; I missed school because I had a bad headache; and I missed school because of doctor appointments. *Enough!*

On the first day, the MFT leader was talking about all the things you can't do when you have this illness. Suddenly, I could see why I had to eat. I had just got a car and my licence, but if I did not recover, I would not be able to drive myself to school. Things like that, going to the beach, doing what I wanted to do when I wanted. Our leader made me think about what I was missing out on. My pretty timeline, which hangs in my bedroom, starts with me turning 17 and includes the birthdays of my parents and me going to college and graduating.

Independence has never been an issue. My parents and I set guidelines, and they have always encouraged me to do what I wanted. I was not their little puppet. I controlled what I wanted to do. I made my own decisions. If I were horrible to myself, I would have to accept the consequences that would come with it. This is how my life was, and this is how it has been during my recovery process.

I hated my contract. I thought it was the most rigid thing. I hated it. It was authoritative, like a dictatorship, very *'I am holier than you because I am your parent, so suck it, and you can do this'*. That's how I felt at the start of this recovery, but later on, I realised that my parents were doing what was best for me by setting strict guidelines because if they did not stand up to the illness right then, it would have been much harder for me. So the contract sucks, and you hate your parents for it.

Only later do you realise your parents are setting these rigid boundaries to benefit you. You just can't realise at the time that your parents are fighting the eating disorder for you because you don't have the awareness yet.

My contract reward was to have my belly button pierced, and it sparkles. A belly button piercing was important to me because it was something my parents would never let me have. My very old-fashioned dad definitely would never approve of it—getting my ears pierced was bad enough. I can drive around in my car with my bathing suit on, and my belly button sparkles and attracts attention. Every time I look at the sparkle on my belly button, I am reminded of how hard I had pushed myself to get it. It gives me strength.

I chose the piercing rather than a tattoo because I can take it out one day if I want to. When I walk around in my bathing suit, I know I own my belly button piercing. I know what I did to get it. Other people don't know how hard it was for me. They don't understand how hard it was inside my head. They just thought anorexia was my personality; they just thought I was telling myself not to eat. They didn't understand there was another voice yelling, *'You can't'*.

MFT helped the parents understand more, too. I felt more hopeful that my parents would understand what it was like for me and would avoid saying unhelpful and offensive things, especially my dad. I don't like the way Dad talks about my anorexia. He was born in a state where feelings were not talked about, and he is a businessman and conservative-minded with a viewpoint about solving problems. So, he thinks, *'if you are sick, find a way to cure it, and then you will be okay'*. He has had to learn that life isn't always like that.

Dad would often set my eating disorder triggers off. Like he basically said, 'You are killing yourself, and you are excited about the thought of it. Otherwise, you would eat'. He said, 'It is because you have let your body get so out of control that you no longer know what you are doing to yourself'. I felt deeply offended that he would think I was purposefully trying to do this to myself. I could see why he thought I was deliberately doing it, but he did not understand the effects of anorexia on me.

Dad compared my illness with having cancer. He said my refusal to eat was like a cancer patient refusing to have chemotherapy; therefore, recovery would not happen, and I was going to die. He talked in a condescending and negative tone about my illness.

That said, I have inherited many good traits from my dad—I am good at handling money and handling myself in front of other people. When Dad and I talk to each other, we act as if nothing is wrong because we both want to avoid the problems relating to my eating disorder. I am an extremely emotional person, and he is extremely unemotional. So, I put on this act.

However, the MFT week definitely improved communication between my mum and me. I get more privileges than I used to have, like more freedom in having friends, including boys, over to visit, and getting my school lunch by myself, and I have a later curfew until 11:00 p.m. I can stay over at my friends' homes more easily. I don't drink, smoke, or take drugs, and I go to elementary school and talk about the importance of being drug free, like how drugs can negatively influence your life.

With the other parents, I could see that some did care about their children but were not expressing their care in the way that their children needed. This helped me realise that my parents did care about me, even though not always in a way that I needed or that was helpful to me.

I was 13 when my anorexia started and 16 when I did MFT. Now I am 17, and the illness is still powerful in my mind; I still suffer from images of my disease experienced before recovery. But recovery has taught me how to deal with it. I figure this is something I will have to deal with my entire life. I will not wake up one morning and it is completely gone.

If I had not gone through MFT, I don't think I would have realised how great a person I can be without anorexia. One of the best things about this illness is that you get a lot of time to reflect on yourself.

MFT is like 50 hours of intensive—I don't want to say training, but, well, a 50-hour-long pep talk. You have five days with people who are in the same situation as you. Maybe not everyone has the same social, economic, or cultural background, but everyone has come to this same point in their life due to anorexia. It is like a horse race: you are all placed at the start line together, and the five days are getting you past the first mark on the way to recovery. You have all come from the same place and are all doing the same thing, and the whistle blows. The rest of the race is like you going through recovery.

MFT is like 'here are the ropes'. You are encouraged to do things to help heal yourself; you are helped to find the best parts of yourself; and you do a lot of reflection. You learn how to talk to yourself and cope with your fears. The therapists help you with the first lap of the race, and then they kind of push you to do the rest, like they nudge and guide you for the first lap, and when you come around to the start line again, they let you go.

I don't know what I would have done without MFT—its role in recovery from anorexia is kind of like your crutches straight after knee surgery. I made friends there, and I like sharing with others who are going through the same situation. We are crutches for each other. The other girls and I have our own little private Facebook group and keep in close touch, especially when having a tough day, because we understand what each is going through. It is helpful to know that no matter how hard my day is, I have five friends to talk to, ready to understand. We give each other inspirational messages. I am a senior now, and I want to focus on psychology and work in the field of eating disorders.

Besides anorexia, anxiety has been crippling. I would get panic attacks anywhere—at concerts, a fair—and would get too afraid to go out with new people, like I would become so afraid, I would have a panic attack. It got to where I would go to school for an hour and have to leave due to a panic attack. I am having ongoing therapy to learn skills to cope with this anxiety and am on medication for it. I tried to do without the medication, but I accept I need it for now.

When going out to dinner with my parents, I try not to think about the menu until I get to the restaurant because the more I think about it, the more anxious I get, like *'Will I have this, or this, or this?'* The waiters don't know what I am going through, so I pretend everything is okay and place my order. I suffer more when alone, but in company, I don't like to let people know. I eat with friends a lot more than I used to. Like no one really understands what I have been through. I look at myself and think, *'I weighed 30 pounds less than I am now, and I am still skinny'*, and tell myself, *'I have to eat this food because I am determined never to go back there'*. I have so many more things ahead of me than I have had in the past.

The mother

We started MFT within two or three weeks of the doctor diagnosing anorexia. I had searched on the internet and found there were a lot of places in our state that treat eating disorders, and this was confusing. We tried a nutritionist first, but this did not get us anywhere. So I began searching for someone who actually specialised in eating disorders. I was drawn to the MFT programme because it is research based. Most therapy places were offering a weekly visit, a treatment session here, a discussion there. In those sorts of programmes, it is hard to find someone to really associate with, and I knew that we might not get along with the first, second, or even third one we tried. I was not willing to take that risk.

Fortunately, we found MFT, and I really liked how the programme was set up. It was offering information to us, the parents, and at the same time, our daughter would be getting help. We were very happy to find such a programme.

My husband, myself, Amelia, and her brother attended for the first day. My husband has an extremely busy job, and I was stunned that he came along on the first day. He could not be there the remainder of the week, but to be there even one day meant a lot to me. Coming along to that first day was both scary and not scary. We knew we needed information. We needed to listen to people who had studied this illness. I felt comfortable right from the start. It also helped that the MFT team took a positive approach with Amelia.

At first, we knew there was a weight issue and that this was causing other issues with Amelia, but we had no idea about the seriousness of the illness, how to go about dealing with it, or how to force the issue. Just to learn how to cope, from people who had studied and treated this illness, was huge for us. We could tell Amelia all day long, and the doctors could tell her all day long, 'You must eat', but she could not respond.

You never know how you will feel going into a group situation. On the first day of MFT, everyone was sitting around, looking apprehensive. But this changed pretty quickly. The girls were all comfortable, and we met other parents who had been dealing with the illness for longer than us and had similar issues to solve. Some had travelled a long way to attend the MFT.

The way the MFT programme was run was helpful and positive. The leader kept things moving, which helped to overcome any deeply emotional moments. The girls felt comfortable with this, too, and interacted with each other and the team. I felt involved, and Amelia felt involved. I think we retained more because of this. People were not talking *'at'* us.

Plus, we were applying what we were learning as we went along. Like, everyone knew that a certain amount of food had to be eaten for lunch and for the snack, and it had to be *at this time.* We learnt that the food is first, regardless of anything else we do. Dealing with this can be hard: watching a child who does not want to eat. I was glad not to be the only person saying, 'You are not eating enough'. Just having a number given by the therapy team was helpful, like saying, 'You have to eat so many, whatever the number was, calories every day'. A firm guideline on how much food needed to be eaten was very helpful. This helped me, as well as Amelia. I don't think she would have been able to do what was necessary for recovery if we had not been in a group situation, and I don't think I would have been able to do it either.

Before we started MFT, Amelia would eat only oatmeal and apples. She now realised she had to start eating pancakes and butter and as much food as we could get, the more, the better. We had gotten into worrying about the small print on labels, the fat content, and so on. Now, all that was out the window. We were off in the opposite direction. Now, we were buying whole milk on the way home; forget about the non-fat.

The attitude to eating and nutrition was also the opposite of what I had been doing for my personal health, so this experience was also heralding a big change for me.

We did a timeline, and this still hangs in Amelia's room. The timeline was a very visual and positive experience. Looking at everybody's timeline and seeing their goals helped us all see that for our goals to be realised, we had to move forward from this point on. The contract would be the centrepiece. All the girls had something they wanted as a reward, and Amelia wanted to do the one thing that her father would never let her do.

The contract impact was huge because we had different goals, expectations, and thoughts on how to get there. My husband had thought there would be a quick solution and that this illness could all be dealt with quite soon. We negotiated over every point in that contract. There were little button heads over the whole thing.

Part of the contract stipulated that Amelia must eat a certain amount of food each day. She was not supposed to be involved in meal preparation, and she was supposed to sit at the table and eat what was put in front of her. That was a big point of contention for Amelia because she wanted to fix her own food.

She wanted to be involved. Until we took part in MFT, this was something else that I thought was good—that Amelia wanted to cook with me. Now, cooking was out. And exercise, also listed in the contract, was out. There was no room for negotiation until she gained some weight. I think the contract helped Amelia to see that we were taking a stand: she could not get out of things any more. We were standing up to the illness on her behalf.

MFT helped Amelia see the importance of going out with us to eat and do other social things. We built this into the contract. Once this contract was all sorted, Amelia was fine with it—she realised she had to do it. Her mind was able to see that this was what needed to happen, whether her eating disorder liked it or not.

Until MFT, I had not really thought about why Amelia would not eat. I had not realised how nauseating it was for her to even think about or look at food. I thought she was not eating simply because she did not want to. Learning about how she thought was helpful to me. I realised the seriousness of the issues and how hard my daughter was working to try and beat this illness, and I found that I, too, was willing to get out of my comfort zone.

The biggest issue going into MFT was that we didn't understand what this illness was like for Amelia; we did not understand how she was feeling inside. At MFT, every aspect of the illness became easier to understand. This was huge for both of us. Until this point, we had been trying to treat each symptom as a medical condition, for instance, headaches. Now, we could see that they were all related, and this was big. Now we understood that as Amelia regained some weight, many of those symptoms would be minimised.

I personally got a lot out of meeting the other parents. We got a lot of support from them, and 'You know, if this does not work, try this'. 'If your daughter does not want to eat that, maybe try this'. The parents discussed things like this when the kids weren't in the room, like, 'What do you do when you find your kid walking around the house in the middle of the night to get more exercise?' and 'What do you do when you find your kid doing star jumps in their bedroom?'

Until then, I thought it was great that Amelia was working out. We hadn't realised that exercise was an issue as well. We found that other children were doing the same thing. We learnt a lot from other parents, especially about the behaviours they had experienced with their children. We learnt that certain words could be triggering.

More than anything, I learnt that a lot of people don't know much about anorexia. They think that once you gain a few pounds back, then you are fine. Until MFT, I didn't understand this, either. Now, I felt good because we didn't know what to do, and we were learning what to do.

On the Monday going in, I didn't know what to expect; I didn't know if this week of MFT would help my daughter. I felt a lot of uncertainty. *'Was it going to be the right program or a waste of time?'* Amelia, obviously, did not want to be there. So, getting through the first day was a big thing. Getting a schedule and a routine was helpful; every day, there was more progress. Soon, Amelia was thinking about what she wanted to eat.

The MFT has helped me to be more understanding with Amelia. Before, when I did not understand, I would get impatient with her. We still don't agree on many things but are learning to meet in the middle sometimes. This is something neither of us was willing to do before. I wanted it my way because I was the mum, and she wanted it her way because she was the teenager.

Teenage years are difficult anyway, and this was another thing that masked the anorexia symptoms for us. We didn't know if her behaviour was just a normal teenage thing going on, or if she just had a bit of an attitude.

Anxiety was an issue for Amelia before she developed anorexia, and has remained an issue. During her illness, when the symptoms were pronounced, she would not want to go to a restaurant. She felt safe and comfortable in her room and her home. She didn't feel like being social with friends. The MFT has helped Amelia see that re-engaging in social life is important for her recovery.

MFT has helped us understand the illness and has armed us with the right information to make the right choices. We still have the contract, but Amelia has reached all its goals. She is continuing weekly therapy sessions to help manage her anxiety, and I am happy with this. She is receiving support in a private environment where she feels safe.

Chapter 16

'I am not my mother; I'm me'

CHAROLETTE

Charolette had been to family-based therapy (FBT) and was a hospital inpatient before going to multi-family therapy (MFT) at 14. At home, Charolette's mother was a 'type-A personality', and her dad was a peacemaker. Charolette was afraid her parents would divorce. Until starting MFT, Charolette and her parents really didn't communicate with each other. Perhaps the most helpful thing they got out of MFT was learning how to talk with each other more, how to listen, and to tell each other how they feel. Charolette has learnt that she can't change others and can only change herself. Two years later, this is Charolette's story:

The patient

With FBT, we would go for an hour's session and talk to this therapist, then leave for home and try to do what she had told us to do. But the therapist never made time to get to know us. She was never really *'there'*. At MFT, the therapists were with us all day, and they got to know me, which made it easier. And having my whole family there for those multiple days was helpful as they could see how we got through each point of the day. MFT was real life, whereas with FBT, we went into a consulting room for one hour and then left. I didn't care what happened in that room during that hour, like, because the therapist was looking at her clock and getting ready for the next client coming in.

DOI: 10.4324/9781003641070-19

I would think, *'We are paying you, and you are not even listening to me'.*

I liked the therapists at MFT. Before we went to MFT, my parents and I really didn't communicate with each other. I think this is the biggest, most helpful thing we got out of MFT—we learnt how to talk with each other more, how to listen, and how to tell each other how we feel.

We did a lot of stuff where the parents were able to get an insight into what we went through, and this helped me talk to my parents more. Especially because we were in a safe environment and because I liked the leaders, it was easy to talk to them. There were three families; one girl was older, and one was younger than me.

When I feel like restricting or feeling triggered by something, I have learnt to write down how I am feeling, take a break, and not act on that thought right away. This skill has helped me gradually learn to focus on other things that are important to me. I write down what these things are. I have also learnt to apply this skill to areas of life other than food.

With stressful situations, like during finals at school and when a big test is coming up and I feel anxious, I now stop studying for a bit and take a break. This allows me to refocus, and then I can go back to studying without impacting other areas of my life. If I did not stop and refocus, the anxiety would build so much that I would not be able to concentrate, and this would affect me and the way I interacted with other people.

Before I learnt these coping skills, I would kind of back away from everyone and shut myself in my room and not want to talk to anyone. I wanted to escape from real life and have my own peace. Now I can express that I am feeling stressed and kind of work through it. By being really aware of myself, I am more able to respond to my body's needs.

I can say to Mum now, like, 'I am feeling very stressed right now and want to go back to my eating disorder. Can you just help me?' Maybe she does not know what to do all the time, but she can be aware for me. MFT helped my parents understand what I need in the way of support.

My family has come a long way since this illness started. My parents used to fight all the time. I was super worried for a long time that they might split up and get divorced. It was horrible, and I worried a lot about it. Now, I have found that when I am doing better, everyone else is doing better, too. I know everyone has a role in the family, and I can't change others around me. I can change only myself.

Dad and I have always been close. I relied a lot on him to help me because it was hard for me to talk to my mum. I didn't get on so well with her as she has an A-type personality; she was highly strung and stressful. Dad was like the peacemaker, and things would get pretty angry between Mum and me, so he was the one there to keep everyone calm and safe. It was comforting when he was there. Before my illness, I would hide from all the stress rather than deal with it, but now I have learnt to express my feelings more.

Mum and I had a lot of tension, and I didn't need to say anything, but the MFT leader could just tell things were difficult between us. In a group session with the girls, she focused on me and helped me understand how to express my feelings a little more. That she noticed I was struggling without me saying anything to her meant a lot to me. She suggested that I focus on little things at first, for example, the colour of an outfit that I like, and build on the expression of that feeling because, you see, I had always done what Mum wanted me to do, because otherwise, she would get mad at me. So, I was to start making more decisions for myself. I am not my mum. I am me. MFT helped me see this.

During MFT, each girl made a stress box, which contained things like a scented candle, special lotion, and a stress ball, and I put a bunch of quotes in mine, like inspirational verses, such as, *'Sometimes the hardest thing and the right thing are the same'*. I covered my box in a collage of pictures from magazines. At home, either my parents would remind me, or I would remind myself to go to the stress box. Like, if I were worrying about dinner, I would go to the box, play with the stuff inside it, and then go to dinner. Or my parents would suggest that I take the box, go upstairs, chill out, and then come back down. I would use the box during such times to connect with myself.

The MFT team prepared me to adjust to life at home. They told my parents that transitioning home would be difficult and that the contract would be helpful. They knew we would struggle and helped us prepare for that.

The contract helped me feel supported, with a helpful protection plan to stay in line. It put the responsibility of eating onto my parents rather than me, and this made it easier to eat, like it was not my fault I was eating; it was my parents who were to blame. If I didn't eat breakfast, I was not allowed to go to school, and I did not like missing school. It was the same if I did not eat dinner the night before—if I did not eat, I could not go to school the next day. Pretty much, if I missed a meal, I could not go to school. I had already missed a lot of school, probably two months, due to being in hospital with my illness, so I had a lot of catching up to do. This was before and after MFT. But this year I have missed no school.

Before, when I did not feel respected or acknowledged by my mum, I would separate from her and go into my own little world, the eating disorder world, and it wouldn't matter what she wanted. Now, I must be super aware, like if I feel I am going back into the eating disorder thinking, I plan ahead.

Like, I knew that transitioning to home would be stressful, and going on a family vacation is always stressful too, so now I do an hour-by-hour plan in advance, like for the first couple of days. I will list what I like to do each day: go to tennis, come home, eat lunch. I put my plan on my cell phone or print it out, decorate it, and stick it on my computer. If we are going out to dinner at a restaurant, I will go online beforehand, check out the menu, and make my choice so I am not anxious about it.

I learnt these skills at MFT. For example, I know I am healing, and these challenges won't be unbearable if I take small steps. These are all positive things, whereas I can see now that the eating disorder was one big negative experience. Now, when I feel the urge to hide away in my room, I call a friend to go for a walk, take our little dog for a walk, or text some friends on my cell phone.

While I was sick with anorexia, I did not have a social life, but now I enjoy going out with my new friends. It's nice to fit in with everyone and feel normal. I still see a therapist regularly, learning to manage the eating disorder and anxiety, and I will be glad when I don't need to go anymore.

One reason I missed a lot of school was because of panic attacks. Now, I am careful not to let things get too much for me. I tell myself I will do the best that I can; I may not be able to do 100 per cent, but that doesn't matter—because realistically, it is not possible every time. I complete my work well before the due date. I like to be punctual. Like, I would panic if I did not start an assignment until the night before. I would say, 'I cannot go to school until I finish my homework'. I know that learning to manage stressful times at school is an important skill because there will always be stressful times in life. Other people who have not gone through anorexia don't always have this skill, so it is one good thing to come out of all this.

I appreciate where I am now. I was not happy with my eating disorder. It was horrible, and I hated it. Our family was falling apart. It was really bad. Now our family is back, and we are all really happy. To go out with friends and for my parents to have normal dinner conversations instead of focusing on me and making sure I am eating is special. When locked in the eating disorder, everything seemed to revolve around me. Now we can talk about other things.

We moved house in the past six months, and I am in a new high school, in my second year, and I feel very happy. A lot of kids at my old school knew about my illness, so it was good to get a fresh start where nobody knew about my anorexia. Now, I can be who I want to be. I am getting my driver's licence in a month, and right now, it is the girls' tennis season after school, and I'm pretty involved in that. I also want to start volunteering in an eating disorder organisation and help others. I have realised how good living is and want others to know this, too. For my career, I want to be a gynaecologist and deliver babies.

I am working on becoming more independent and having confidence in my decisions. I don't want to be judged by my mum for my decisions, so the more I feel she is not judging me, the more I think it is okay if we disagree, and the easier it is for me.

Chapter 17

Understanding the illness helps mother take charge

DIANA

Diana, 17, is high achieving, perfectionistic, hardworking, asks a lot of herself, and has a high anxiety level and some obsessive-compulsive disorder (OCD). She is the third of four children: boy, girl, girl, boy. Her dad works full-time, and her mother works full-time at home. When Diana was diagnosed with anorexia at age 15, her mum felt a failure for being unable to persuade her daughter to eat. This is their story.

The patient (Diana)

When the doctors found I had anorexia, they recommended treatment for a long time, but I got angry because I didn't want to miss school, the perfectionist that I am. So they found a one-week treatment—multi-family therapy (MFT)—and Mum signed up for it.

I did not want to go to MFT but knew I had been sneaky in hiding food. Mum got upset when I would not eat, and she would cry, 'I am a horrible mother if I can't feed my girl'. I was angry because going to MFT would mean missing school, and I was trying to let Mum see this, but I'd been seeing the hurt in her eyes at mealtime, and I knew I was going because I could not disobey her to that extent. This family treatment was to help the family help me recover, and although I arrived angry, I soon secretly began to love it.

DOI: 10.4324/9781003641070-20

At MFT, we learned how to train our thoughts in preparation for going home after the treatment. Learning why I need to eat has helped me gain insight and motivation to recover. My hair started to grow again.

From the first day, I knew that I would recover. I saw how bad anorexia is, and I wanted to be healthy, not low on energy. Mum and the treatment people said I was just saying that, but I thought, *'I will show them that I have changed and that I can do so quickly'*. I enjoyed all the food, and I stopped counting calories and worrying how much I ate, which was a big relief. My stomach was always full, and I threw up a few times. I hated how they were suspicious of everything I did, as though I was a small child. But being with the other girls helped a bunch.

The contract felt like a punishment, but was helpful in that my mind was saying, *I don't want to eat*, and yet the contract was saying, *I have to eat*, and I liked to do the right thing. I understood that if I did not eat, I could not go to school. So, I ate. A year after MFT, I feel so much better and more alive.

The mother

When we got a diagnosis of anorexia, it would have been better if we had been referred straight to the eating disorder centre. However, our family doctor wasn't sure what Diana needed the most help with first: her anxiety, OCD, or eating disorder. When we arrived at the eating disorder centre some three weeks later, we chose the MFT option. The following week was Thanksgiving break, so we had to wait a week for treatment to start. The MFT leader helped pass that time by calling nearly every day, explaining things, talking about what to expect, answering questions, and talking to Diana. Diana was eating really well, obviously trying to prove that we all had it wrong. I started doubting again and shared my concerns with the leader. She explained how this behaviour was very typical and not to be fooled by it.

We were expected to meet with a psychologist at the treatment centre on Monday at 8:00 a.m. I had to promise to take Diana there, and if she really wouldn't come, call an ambulance. With that threat, I got her to come reasonably willingly. So then the treatment started.

The other two girls in our group had been hospitalised and refed before starting MFT. For Diana and us, this treatment was our first help of any kind, and her re-feeding was to start that same week.

The MFT week gave me the confidence to look after Diana. One of my first questions was: 'I don't know how to help her. What do I do? I don't know where to start. Just saying, "eat more, eat more" only makes it worse'. I felt guilty about Diana needing help because I believed I must be inadequate if I could not help her as a mother. At MFT, we learned practical day-to-day, meal-to-meal things. The team helped us to start re-feeding Diana that week.

We learnt it was helpful for Diana to think of the eating disorder as a bad person taking over her brain. She had to work hard, and we had to work with her to get 'the eating disorder' out of her brain. We learnt we were all in this together, that this was *not us against Diana*. There was more to anorexia than merely looking skinny. Even for the girls that were done with re-feeding, their thinking was still obsessive. We were taught how our brain functions, or doesn't when it is starving and the consequences. The seriousness of this made us more determined to be firm on Diana through the tears and yelling. We learned that once her body was starved, her brain could not reason any more, and so we had to think for her until she was refed, and this meant making food choices for her.

At MFT, what I found most helpful was the education on why and how kids develop an eating disorder, what happens next, how serious it gets, and the confidence I acquired to persevere in helping Diana. The explanation by the MFT leader about how the brain acts and reacts really helped us understand and took the blame off both the kid and the parent, which was a huge relief.

The MFT leader also explained the dangers of weight loss and what body parts start to fail, like heart rate, bone mass, brain cells, and kidneys. I gained confidence in knowing what would be helpful to Diana and what was not. I got practical day-to-day advice and guidance, such as what not to say during dinner. For instance, I learnt to avoid label reading. I also really enjoyed the sessions when the girls and siblings were taken to one room with one therapist to discuss things together, while the other therapist talked and listened to us as parents. We could ask each other, and the therapist, questions about things we could not really talk about with the girls there.

I learned it is wrong to call skinny girls 'anorexic'. I learned that not every skinny girl has anorexia, and not every girl with anorexia is too skinny. The girls that were in treatment with Diana looked really nice and healthy but still had enormous issues eating. I also learned the importance of every child following their own personal growth curve. For Diana, we were relieved to learn she did not have to gain weight until she was fat, but just until she was back to where her usual growth should be.

One reason we chose the MFT programme was because the part-time/day treatment would take many weeks. Even though she could do school there, Diana would have missed her own classes too much. Also, I would have had to do a lot of driving, an hour each way, every day, for many weeks. Also, I would have had to leave Diana there and pick her up, and I wanted to be part of the treatment so I would know what to do at home. I wanted to know what the treatment leaders said to her, how they got her to eat, and to see that she would be treated kindly and so on. Also, I was concerned she would meet other kids with eating disorders, try to be the best one, and learn tricks from them.

We were one of a small group of families at MFT, and it was a much more controlled situation. We were able to see how other family members were suffering and talk with these other families about strategies that were working for them. The first few days were the most difficult. Diana was in denial and angry and fought us; her behaviour made me feel like a bad parent. Also, Diana was really angry about the contract. It made her feel like a small child. To her, it felt like punishment, even though the leader explained repeatedly it was just a guide to help us know where we were headed.

In those first few days, I almost gave up with MFT. Every morning, the girls' vitals were taken, and they were weighed. Diana had to be refed starting that week and had many tummy aches. We would get home pretty late, and I still had to cook for the whole family, as Diana had to eat proper meals. We were all tired. Diana was sore, upset, and angry, and would throw up after dinner because she had been eating too much. Her weight went down and down, and along with it, her heart rate. I was scared the amounts she had to eat were too much for her and that she would have to be hospitalised. On a Wednesday evening, she threw up again, and I was leaning against the outside of the bathroom door, crying and saying to my husband, 'This is not working'.

Surprisingly, the following morning, Diana's weight was up a little despite the throwing up. The MFT team explained that if Diana could keep the food in for even half an hour, most of the food would be absorbed already. It showed. Meanwhile, the other girls who had been refed before coming to the programme encouraged Diana, were sympathetic to her, and suggested that a hot water bottle on her tummy would ease the pain and provide comfort. It did.

Also, drinking hot tea helped. The girls were not allowed to drink empty-calorie drinks a lot, but were allowed to cradle a mug of hot tea during the day. The girls compared which tea they liked, and this became another comfort. Even we mothers were drinking hot tea in the second half of the week. Diana had admitted by now that she had an eating disorder and started to bond with the other girls. They made things for each other in their evening hours and exchanged email addresses.

The contract gave me backbone, helped my husband and me be on the same page, and made me feel more confident in helping Diana. Even though Diana just wants me to help her, I am not always around and have three other children to care for as well. After MFT, my husband pitched in more often, and we both had the same guidelines. For this, the contract was really helpful. Diana says we did not use it, but it was there for us to draw on.

This week of treatment really worked for Diana. It kind of gave her a 'shock' treatment back into normal life, but I could see how one week might not be enough for some kids. In the family therapy, they did address the anxiety issue and tried to give the girls stress coping strategies, but Diana needed more of that. This was where the psychologist came in, and Diana was scheduled to have weekly sessions after MFT.

Our contract included that Diana would see the psychologist, even though Diana kept saying she was healed after the week's treatment and wanted to be left alone. She agreed to work on the anorexia but nothing else. Once Diana's weight was restored, after three months or so, the psychologist wanted to work on anxiety issues and social skills, but Diana refused to cooperate. Diana would benefit from such help as some issues made life hard for her. Like, Diana would say things and then say she did not mean them 'that way' if she noticed friends being upset with her.

Physically, she is doing okay—she eats well and makes all food choices herself. Last week she compared a sports physical test for school, with a year ago when she wore a heavy jacket and jeans, the pockets filled with stones to increase her weight on the scales. She laughs about that now. I think the eating disorder is gone, but I am on guard. Diana remains per-fectionistic, obsesses about things—her grades, but less about her appearance—and is learning to cope with a high anxiety level. For kids like Diana, follow-up therapy after MFT is very helpful.

Chapter 18

The getting of communication skills leads to breakthrough

SAMANTHA

When the emotion is taken out, a resolution can be achieved more quickly. This was one of many skills Samantha's parents learnt to employ in resolving issues with their only child, who was treatment-resistant. Multi-family therapy (MFT) enabled the parents to understand and listen more, while their daughter saw how she could get a resolution without throwing things. Through the group sharing, they learnt that a resolution could be achieved more quickly when the emotion was taken out. What was important in MFT was communication, learning to listen and talk in a way that was not victimising, accusing, or blaming, and was more open.

The mother

We had travelled internationally over the summer, and Samantha was fifteen and a half, in her second year at boarding school, when her eating disorder was noticed. We took her to see the therapist at the nearest children's hospital, where she was admitted straightaway. This was a shock for Samantha and us. It was mid-November, and we were told she would likely need to be an inpatient until Christmas. Samantha was extremely unwilling to stay at the hospital.

There were many rules. Everything was taken from Samantha, including her cell phone, which she depended on for social connection. Immediately, the staff started policing and

DOI: 10.4324/9781003641070-21

insisting that she eat, but she refused. Samantha always disliked rules, sanctions, and orders. She would do all she could to avoid them. This was a nightmare.

We took part in recommended family therapy, but this was unsatisfactory. The therapy was between us as a family and a social worker. The dynamics between my husband and me and our daughter were stressful, and Samantha felt she was singled out as the problem and everything was about her. She did not want to be cooperative. She saw the therapy as another attempt by us to get her to be different and claimed we were judging her. She would constantly say, 'Please get back my phone', 'Let me out of the hospital for half an hour', and 'Please let me take a walk'. We were in constant conflict.

We saw the therapist infrequently—she was busy running the whole unit—and due to high staff turnover, we often didn't know who to talk to and had no bearings.

We were told to expect Samantha's recovery to take a minimum of two years and possibly much longer. We were told that it was great we had picked up on the illness early, but even so, recovery would require a lot of time and work. At the same time, things were getting dramatically worse as Samantha was not eating.

We took her out of hospital before Christmas as we lived several hours away, both taking time out of our jobs. Samantha had insisted, 'I will get better if you take me out. Take me out'.

She deteriorated further. She was admitted to several other hospitals but walked out or was asked to leave. We could not find the right help, and no matter what we did, Samantha was refusing to cooperate. We had no options left and were forced to take our daughter to the psychiatric hospital, where she was admitted to a locked ward. Again, as in several hospitals she was admitted to, there was no eating disorder unit. That hospital also discharged Samantha with no treatment plan or advice on where to go. By now, Samantha had experienced about six months of mistreatment.

We took Samantha home and called the therapist at the children's hospital. We pleaded with her to take us, and she agreed, even though we were not in the hospital's client region. We had no illusions, as the treatment hadn't worked before, but this time, she stayed in the hospital for five months and recovered up to 80 per cent of her body weight.

Samantha was forced to take additional supplements and had been told 80 per cent body weight was the point at which medically she would be allowed out of hospital. She put us under constant pressure, 'Let me put weight on my own', and 'Let me go to school', but we knew if we took her out early, we would have more trouble. She was wearing us all down, including her therapist. By now, I had moved to the same city as the children's hospital so I could visit Samantha, and my husband was commuting back and forth.

When she left the hospital, Samantha was enrolled in a day programme, and she had agreed beforehand to do the right thing. But on the first or second day, she refused to eat a cookie, and the staff said, 'We will call your mother and ask her to take you home. You can come back when you are ready to eat the cookie. Otherwise, you are out'. So, she was out.

We were getting nowhere. Samantha had dropped to about 70 per cent of her target weight and was becoming extremely violent. She smashed the stovetop and coffee table in our rented house. We had to call the police as we needed help to get her back to the hospital. By now, we had had more than a year of unbelievable stress with virtually no family therapy.

We started MFT soon after. By now, she was back to 80 per cent weight, and her therapist was strongly promoting MFT. We had a lot of confidence in her as our main therapist. Within four months, Samantha was ready to leave the hospital. She had to go back briefly for three or four days the following month, but after that, she had turned the corner. 'I don't want to go back to the hospital', she said and began to eat enough to stay out.

At MFT, we met other families. In the previous family therapy, the triangular unit of us with one therapist would never work because of the power struggle. For me, having therapy with other families was invaluable, to be with other mothers and talk with other mothers in front of Samantha but not targeted at her. She could hear without being made to feel guilty. This was important for Samantha and me. Also, it was important for us to listen to the stories of others and their terrible times. This was the best way to get this message across—in the company of others, without making individual people feel bad.

The way the MFT programme is designed—with activities splitting us up, combining us with others, and role-playing— helped me vividly see the way the eating disorder had pulled our family apart and how it had pulled our child out of the family. This was especially helpful in our context because the eating disorder, together with the anxiety, got channelled in a very self-destructive way for Samantha.

Of course, we had our own particular issues, including difficulties with attachment and the influence of a nanny in Samantha's early childhood. We started to make some break- throughs in those issues, and Samantha began to see that we were trying to understand and help her.

We were not a candidate for family-based treatment because Samantha was too resistant. What was important in MFT was the communication, learning to listen and talk in a way that was not victimising, accusing, or blaming, and was more open.

For instance, we parents sat together, and girls rotated around and spoke about a social problem they wanted to resolve. For example, they asked, 'I want to stay out until 2:00 a.m. Why won't you let me?' The parents had to work with someone else's daughter to resolve the issue, explain the response, and remain calm. I learnt that when the emotion is taken out, in this case, because I was helping someone who was not my child, a reso- lution could be achieved more quickly. So now I could employ this skill in resolving issues with Samantha. As parents, we understood more and were more able to listen, while Samantha saw how she could get a resolution without throwing things.

I especially liked the timeline exercise—which looked at what was going on with the eating disorder and family over an upcoming time—I found it helpful to plan something because, for a long time, I had not been looking forward to anything due to the illness. The past eight years had been filled with Samantha's anger and rage. Hopes had been dashed as parents. We had not had a relationship that we wished for.

This MFT was not easy for my husband. Having to expose himself in the MFT setting was challenging for him. He had to relive the trauma, and his way of coping was to repress it and work very hard. He was an executive working long hours. Samantha saw the effort he was making at our therapy sessions. He was committed, and he was willing to do this for her. Samantha might as well be a carbon copy of her dad; he was trying to help by sharing his emotions, and she has matured a lot emotionally. She still has some verbal abuse problems, but is getting her anger under control. For years, there had been no possibility of having an exchange with Samantha without grief.

MFT was the first time in years that we could hear each other. Samantha is now 21. She still has an eating disorder and issues with food, weight, body image, and self-abuse with laxatives. She still sees a therapist but not in a family situation now. She attends university in the States. School is something she can do. Our mother–daughter relationship has improved greatly, and we can exchange and share feelings.

MFT contributed to a breakthrough in our family relationship—it was the catalyst. The commitment we made to attend MFT—which Samantha could see—was painful, but importantly, Samantha began to see and understand that we loved her.

Chapter 19

Creating a caring environment at home to support recovery

EMMA

Bella and Mick were about to 'chuck' daughter Emma, 12, into a 'not-very-nice' residential facility that was 'for all sorts of kids with problems, not just eating disorders', when offered multi-family therapy (MFT). Suddenly, the parents realised they had to create a home environment where Emma could recover. The answer was not in sending her away but in caring for her at home. This was empowering. Totally. The MFT week was the turning point. It was not the cure but the method for the parents to help their daughter reach another level; it was a breakthrough. Earlier approaches were unhelpful. They fed her illness. The parents were not given skills training and did not know what to do. With MFT, all the families were going through something similar, and while every kid and every family dynamic was different, ultimately, they were dealing with the same illness. Seeing their situation and themselves in other families was helpful.

The mother

Emma was ten when she lost a lot of weight at summer camp. On returning home, within several weeks, she was not eating at all. I took her to her paediatrician, who said, 'You must take her to the children's hospital'. We took her to the emergency department, and she was admitted as an inpatient for several months. The psychiatrist became concerned, as Emma was not

DOI: 10.4324/9781003641070-22

responding to recovery efforts. She started to turn against us to the point where we didn't want to visit her.

We were encouraged to persevere and be involved, but nothing was happening. Eventually, the hospital staff said, 'We can't keep her any longer, but we can't just discharge her and let her go home because she won't eat for you, so we have to find another option'. We had been having Emma at home for overnight stays and day visits, but she would not eat with us. She would have all her food measured out from the hospital and come home with her bag of food. We would sit at the table, and Emma would refuse to eat her food, throw it out, or run away.

We called a residential facility that was for troubled kids with behavioural issues, kids that were acting out and were more delinquent-type. I didn't think our child was like that, and this facility was not equipped or experienced to treat a child with an eating disorder. Emma was not well mentally and did not fit the profile, but we didn't have a choice. This was where we were going to send her. We were getting ready to move her the next day when we got a call from the MFT therapist at the eating disorder unit of the children's hospital team to come for a meeting about MFT.

The therapist, aware Emma was being discharged and that she was treatment-resistant, offered to take over her care. This therapist became Emma's psychiatrist. She said, 'Even though Emma is young, we feel she should be part of our MFT that is starting, actually, tomorrow'. To us, as parents, this was a miracle. Desperate, we said, 'Yes', and the next day enrolled for MFT. This was six months after the diagnosis.

We were told the week's sessions would be from 9:00 a.m. to 5:00 p.m. with several other families, and we did not know how to get Emma to cooperate, even to get in the car to go there, because she was shut down at this time. She was reticent and non-verbal, which was a problem because we, plus the psychiatrists and social workers, didn't know what was going on inside her; we didn't know what she was feeling. Somehow, we got Emma to the first session. To be in a room filled with other families, with parents, siblings, and other girls just like her, was empowering and supportive for all of us.

MFT was the treatment that we needed for our daughter at this time. The breakthrough did not happen on Day One, but things were changing; things were shifting among and within each of us. Emma's sisters were angry with her. They did not understand what was going on with her; they didn't understand the disease; they didn't understand how it had taken such a grip on her—until they sat through MFT day after day and saw other kids older than our daughter, who could express what was going on, who could talk about their feelings, and who could share their negative self-images.

The activities helped us to understand how each person in the family was feeling and deepened our understanding, as a family, of the importance of being involved in recovery. We began to see that we needed to take an active role—and not withdraw, which we initially felt was best when Emma was in the hospital, being angry and dismissive of us. Now we knew that we should not be running away; now we knew we must confront this illness on our daughter's behalf. We knew we must love, support, and be firm with her when needed. We needed to learn all of this.

That week of MFT gave us tools to equip and help us manage what we were dealing with.

I particularly remember the role-playing activity. We were a family at a table and had to act out what would happen at mealtime. One child, an actual patient but not our daughter, chose me to be the mother. That, for me, was a real light-bulb moment. I was trying to get this patient to eat, and then we had siblings who were played by other people, and another person played my spouse. The way I was trying to get the child to eat was not working, so while role-playing, I had to change my approach, be a little gentler or whatever, and not put so much attention on the food but, 'Let's talk about some fun things', and that shifted something, even in that acting. The girl started to eat a little bit. I thought, *'Well, now I can take what I have learned in this role-playing lesson into my own family when we have meals at home'*.

In another activity, where I was more of a listener, the kids who had the eating disorder drew pictures on a poster of what the eating disorder represented to them and talked about it. Each kid would get up and put different things on the poster. Black blobs, monsters, and hands around someone's throat provided images and verbal descriptions to help us understand how these kids were feeling. This helped me see this illness was more than my kid; it was this monster that had a hold on my kid.

We saw we had to fight this illness and not let it take our daughter over completely because it was making her a different person. We saw how this illness was something separate from her.

An MFT leader suggested we tell Emma we were not transitioning her into that residential facility because we wanted her to come home with us. He wanted that message to be clearly conveyed, to let Emma know we loved her and would do whatever it took to save her. So, we were to take Emma home, and the MFT therapist discharged her, telling her, 'You are not going to the residential facility, and you are not staying at the children's hospital any longer'.

This significant breakthrough occurred somewhere in the middle of the week's treatment. Emma was kicking and screaming when we went to the hospital after that day's family therapy to pack her bags for home. But the FBT (family-based therapy) therapist said, 'You must leave. You can't stay here; we no longer have a bed for you. You must go home with your family'.

I said to Emma, 'We want you to come home'.

In the car on our way home, she was trying to get out, trying to jump out and run away. Her two sisters were in the back seat with her, trying to hold her down. My husband was driving, and I was in the front passenger seat, trying to keep her down and hold the car doors shut. It was horrible. When we got home,

Emma jumped out of the car and ran away. We had to chase after her and drag her into our home.

Throughout that night, we had to guard the front door. Not only lock the door. We had to sleep by it. We had to unhinge the bathroom door and remove it so she could not lock herself in. We had to be one step ahead and think of places where she could lock herself in and do damage to herself. We had to put anything with sharp points away because Emma had self-harmed in the hospital and would not even cry—she was so stoic, closed, and shut down. Six years later, I remember this time as if it were yesterday.

I don't know how we returned her to MFT the following day. When we showed up, the leader was like, 'Yay, you made it!' This was a horrible, horrible time. But we got our daughter back.

The big issue, our challenge, was that Emma would not eat with us. She did not eat much during meals at the MFT, either. She was very uncooperative. That week, all the other kids with anorexia were eating, eating with their families, laughing, and having fun.

We brought favourite food we knew Emma loved—like a bagel and cream cheese, which she had stopped eating. We brought this bagel, about half of one, and cream cheese. We brought sweet potato French fries. She loved grapes, so we brought grapes and chocolate milk. With that, she started to eat; she began to eat with us at the table.

Emma had been watching the other kids, and this big breakthrough for us happened on the third day. We weren't paying any attention to the eating. We were just trying to talk about life, about funny things like, 'Remember when this happened'. We were doing our best to have a loving, calm family meal. The other four or five families in the room, who seemed to be progressing, surrounded us with support.

I was very grateful for what the hospital did for Emma, but I also sought help for myself. I saw a health professional with eating disorder expertise once or twice a week because I needed to talk and needed more resources. I knew another parent whose daughter was a bit older and had been through all this, and I spoke with her. I was open to anything I could find to help get through this, like seeing spiritual mentors. I did so because this illness was consuming my whole life. It was taking a toll on my marriage and my other kids; it was consuming all of us, depleting us all: sucking out the life of each of us. Until MFT, we did not know what to do.

What happened next was that because Emma had returned to MFT after that first night at home, kicking and screaming, the MFT therapist used this as leverage and said to her, 'Look, if you don't feel ready to return home, we will write an agreement, we will draw a timeline, we will readmit you, and then that's it. You are going home. Your parents want you at home; that's where you are going to recover'.

We had maybe two more weeks with Emma in the children's hospital, and then this was it, her last chance. When she came home this time, she was much better. We had to make sure we were consistent, like making sure we sat down together as a family and ate our meals together.

By now, the school year was almost over, so we would invite friends over, but we could not let Emma go out socially unless she ate first at home. We had to wait until we felt that she would be okay. We told her we loved her; we strove to express our love, even when feeling angry and frustrated, and this also helped the breakthrough. Love is powerful.

Gradually, Emma's eating started to improve. We continued to eat together, and slowly, we could let her be on her own a little. Emma still had to check in with the hospital because she remained part of the outpatient clinic, and she really, really wanted to go on an overnight camp. We spoke to the camp director, and together, we agreed she could try it. The camp team was on board in supporting our daughter and arranged to weigh her every few days. But unfortunately, I was called after a week to fetch her.

We had a system in place. We had let Emma know that we trusted her to the best of her ability and would support her and try to make this work. It didn't work, so I flew out to the camp and picked her up. She was really upset, and I thought, *'Oh no, are we starting this again?'* I brought her to the children's hospital to check in with the MFT therapist and get weighed, and then we took her away for several days, and she started to get back into a good place. She continued to improve.

Today, six years later, Emma is in a much better place; she is more mature. She is not restricting, but I can't tell you the illness is completely over. I think food will remain an issue for her. She is always concerned about how she looks, and fluctuates with weight. She now tends to be more of an overeater than a restrictor, which frustrates her. The big thing now is that she can talk about it. When she asks for help, we send her to the therapist and nutritionist.

The MFT week was the turning point. It was not the cure but the method for all of us in the family to help our daughter reach another level; it was a breakthrough. The earlier approaches were unhelpful. They fed her illness. She had counselling for maybe one hour a week, and the doctors she saw wanted to medicate her. We were not given skills training and did not know what to do. We didn't know what other families were going through.

With MFT, all the families were going through something similar. While every kid and every family dynamic was different, ultimately, we were dealing with the same illness. So we could see our situation and ourselves in other families. This was helpful.

MFT saved Emma and our family and gave us tools not only to help her but also to give us relationship tools for each other. MFT helped us show each other more respect, unconditional love, and support. As a family unit, the illness strained us all, but the MFT strengthened us. Mick and I learnt how to be more united as parents. We saw the power in joining forces, supporting each other, and talking about things. We saw the importance of the family unit sitting down together and talking about fun things, having fun events for distractions in our lives, and being hopeful.

The father

The MFT helped me realise that my kid was not the worst. All the dads were equally frustrated in knowing how to deal with their daughters. Talking to other dads, we had all tried different methods. On the one hand, we were upset with our daughters; on the other, we wanted to sit and comfort them. Emma was a long way into the hospitalisation process before I realised her behaviours were due to her illness and not her. Everything began making sense when we went to MFT because I could now see the illness. I saw the same in other children. When just looking at your own daughter, you think, *'Why is she like this? What did we do that made her like this?'* You are feeling guilty. But when you see other families, you realise this is not your daughter; this is the disease itself.

Some fathers were still blaming their daughter, saying, 'Why is my daughter like this?' and they were angry. Some were more passive. MFT helped me realise that being upset with Emma would get us nowhere. Also, just being supportive, while okay, would get us nowhere. Ignoring everything would not help, either. Education was the most important thing I got at MFT.

When Emma came home after MFT, there was less tension. Also, there was less hostility because previously, we had felt we were on a battlefield. Mealtimes were always taking place in a hostile environment. I learnt that the less I talked about food, the better the environment. So, I began to talk about other subjects over dinner. I tried to engage Emma in talking about school. She definitely has a 'Me, me, me' personality, so I fed on that, asking what she was going to do and where she was going to go. This was the best diversion. In this way, I began talking to my daughter rather than her illness.

There were times when Emma was in the hospital, and we doubted if she really had an eating disorder or if her behaviour was masking something else. She was young and naïve, and we thought it was immaturity. My two other daughters were frustrated at their sister and frustrated that we were giving Emma so much attention. They were aged 14 and eight at the time and often had to fend for themselves. The MFT helped our other daughters because they could see the same thing happening in other families.

Until we went to MFT, I felt helpless. Once we went to MFT, I felt stronger, and I thought that maybe we could hope. MFT made a complete difference in our daughter's recovery. I saw her willingness to change. This was a big turning point for her—to decide that she wanted to get healthier. She could see it, and it got through to us, too.

Emma had been going down a very bad path. She had been in the hospital for four months. She was only 12 and was not going to live with us. After thousands of meetings with doctors and not knowing what to do, we had been about to 'chuck' her into a residential facility that was for all sorts of kids with problems, not just eating disorders, when we were offered the MFT option. When we told Emma, 'We want you to come home', this was the turning point. Not that we ever thought that caring for Emma was not our responsibility, but after all this time, all these interviews, therapies, doctors, and medications, suddenly it was on us—we had to make an environment at home in which Emma could recover. We suddenly realised that the answer was not in sending her away. Our responsibility was to care for her at home. We had to deal with it. This was empowering. Totally.

Six years have passed, and I have learnt to be more subtle, but I never forget about the time with the eating disorder. Even today, I don't ask my daughter, 'Well, what did you eat today?' Rather, I say, 'Do you want to go for lunch?' so I am more subtle, but as a parent, I am thinking, *'Is she getting nutrition?'* and *'Is she eating three meals a day?'*

I am always on the lookout.

• See Chapter 20, where Emma's sister shares her experience.

Chapter 20

'Oh, my sister does that, too'

EVA

Eva is the eldest of three girls, born two years apart, and was 14 when her middle sister Emma developed anorexia. Six years later, Eva is 20, and Emma is 18. Eva says, 'I have learnt to be more patient. Emma's illness introduced me to mental health issues. Until we went to multi-family therapy, I did not realise our brain can do things, and we cannot control it. After learning this, I did not get as angry. Understanding Emma had been difficult because she had never made herself vulnerable; she put up this guard and would never say, "I feel weak" or "I'm sorry". She never opened up. She put up a wall and put on a self-centred appearance'.

The eldest sibling (Eva)

Emma had been in the hospital for several months, and when our parents brought her home, she ran about, opening the doors, screaming, and crying. I soon learnt that when Emma got a kind of glazed look in her eyes, there was no getting through to her; she could not reason.

This behaviour deeply affected me. I could not think about anything else. I felt bad for our parents and my younger sister, and I felt resentment towards Emma. I thought she was selfish, like, *'How can you be doing this to us? We are so privileged; we have nothing to complain about. Why are you putting us through hell?'* I was frustrated, angry, and fed up. I tried a few

DOI: 10.4324/9781003641070-23

times to sit and talk to her, and she always seemed genuine and to understand what I was saying, but nothing happened.

Before this illness developed, Emma was fun. She was someone whom people liked to hang around, but with anorexia, she became angry. She put up a wall that no one could get through; she seemed to care only about herself and showed no remorse.

One time, she ran away from home, and we drove everywhere frantically trying to find her. When we did, she was yelling at our parents as though she had done nothing wrong and didn't want to get in the car. I thought, *'I can't believe this is my family right now'*. I thought we were a normal family until this issue.

At MFT, the doctor talked about anorexia, and I thought, *'I don't believe patients have a voice in their head telling them not to eat'*, and I thought, *'There is no way Emma could be like this'*. I was angry. I thought her behaviour was due to immaturity and being spoilt. To learn otherwise was unbelievable for me.

What helped at MFT was that once the other girls with anorexia started talking, I thought, *'Oh, Emma says this; she does that too'*, and I realised that this problem was something bigger than Emma being horrid. I realised, *'This is not something she can control. Other kids have the same thought processes, so, okay, this is the disease'*. It was good that other families were there because seeing their behaviours helped us to see what belonged to the illness.

Understanding Emma had been difficult because she had never made herself vulnerable; she put up this guard, and there was no raw breakdown from a different place within. She would never say, 'I feel weak', or 'I'm sorry'. She never opened up. She put up that wall and put on this self-centred appearance.

Our relationship has improved, but I have come to learn Emma has an obsessive personality. She goes to extremes on a lot of things, like eating, working out, shopping, and partying.

She does not seem to have an inner voice that says, *'I think you should stop now'*. Throughout her eating disorder, she was constantly angry with outbursts of major anger; now, she is happy with outbursts of anger. She likes things to be done her way. A plan forms in her mind, and if it changes due to outside circumstances, she can't cope. It can be a little thing, like not getting the keys to the car at the exact time she has decided she needs them.

That time with anorexia in our lives seems now, I hate to say this, like one incident in many more, like one phase in many issues with Emma over the years. Bingeing and drinking too much alcohol also have not helped.

I have learnt to be more patient. Emma's illness introduced me to mental health issues. Until we went to MFT, I did not realise that our brains can do things and that we cannot control them. After learning this, I did not get as angry with Emma.

That period of MFT was good for our family because we were always busy, and MFT forced us to be with each other all day and talk with each other about how we were feeling. This helped my youngest sister and my dad especially as he didn't talk much about emotions. Mum opened up, but Dad and I and my youngest sister didn't, and to hear each other out in the presence of other families and a therapist was constructive and non-judgemental. We were having conversations; it was not like an interview. We could listen, talk, and respond. Dad has become more understanding. He could be passive-aggressive, and a little thing could cause outbursts, but he can handle more things now. After MFT, life for us all slowly became better.

- See Chapter 19, where Emma's parents share their experiences.

Chapter 21

'Can I have some fries, Mummy?'

CATHERINE

Eleven-year-old twin Catherine developed anorexia in a country where treatment for eating disorders was unheard of. In a bid to save her life, the parents put the twins on a plane to their grandfather in North America. This is the story of a family's love, strength, and unity in the face of adversity, and the joy of a breakthrough. The mother explains: About 12 months after multi-family therapy (MFT), we went to McDonald's, which had been off the list for Catherine since she got ill. We were all sitting there, and I got them all the hamburger sandwiches. I didn't get fries or anything. Then, as soon as we were eating, Catherine, of all people, not one of her siblings, looked at me and said, 'Can I have some fries, Mummy?' My hand went straight into my purse to get whatever money I had, and I said to a waiter, 'Please get Catherine some fries'. I silently turned to my two other children and whispered, 'Did you hear what Catherine asked for?'

Right then, I would have let Catherine eat all the fries in the world. That was the moment when I knew Catherine would be okay. She ate every one of those fries. We have had to maintain our sense of humour through all this. We shared our fry story over the phone with my husband, and we laughed and laughed. If we could not laugh, we could not have coped.

The mother

My husband and I are citizens of an economically underdeveloped country. After 14 years in North America, we returned

DOI: 10.4324/9781003641070-24

home with our four children, aged seven to 16. Being born and raised in North America, moving countries was a big change for the children. They were clearly unhappy, and, for several months, they all had diarrhoea, malaria, and weight loss while their bodies adjusted to the new system. We enrolled them at school, but then I noticed one of my 11-year-old twins, Catherine, coming home with her lunch uneaten and her water bottle untouched. She would not even drink any water. Imagine, we were in a hot climate.

I said to my husband, 'Something is wrong'. Catherine was becoming more withdrawn, with no jokes or smiles. She stopped eating breakfast—she had gladly eaten eggs and cereal, but not now. She was losing weight rapidly. We knew she loved school; she was a very good student. We said, 'Catherine, if you don't eat something, you must stop going to school'. We took her out of school for one week, and that's when the battle really started.

The doctors had no idea what was wrong. They were asking, 'Catherine, why aren't you eating?' This skinny child just stared at them. Four months passed, and by now, we were desperate. We talked to everyone in the family and said, 'We are very concerned about Catherine'. We were afraid she would die. She was a walking skeleton. We called my dad, who had North American residency, and said, 'You know what? Maybe if we send Catherine and her twin sister over, just for a few weeks of the spring break, this will give her back hope and life'. My dad said, 'Send them over'. I could not travel with them because I had no visa or any sort of residency, and we had to act fast. There was no time to wait. We put the twins on a plane and kept our fingers crossed. That was the awfulest day of my life.

The twins arrived at my dad's place, and despite the descriptions we had given of Catherine's condition, he felt devastated when he saw her. He was amazed that she had survived the 17-hour flight. She did not want to eat or drink anything. So, the next day, he said, 'You know what? We have to take this child to a hospital'. He took her to the hospital, and she was immediately admitted to the emergency department.

The staff recognised anorexia. This was the first diagnosis. They admitted Catherine, inserted a nasal gastric tube (NGT), and, after one week, transferred her to the children's hospital. The doctor over the phone said that Catherine had acute anorexia. They had seen many patients, but Catherine's case was extreme. This was very, very hard for me not to be with my daughter. The doctors were saying, 'You must come. You have to be here. This is a very serious illness'. The situation was worse because Catherine had stopped talking, so I could not speak with her on the phone.

The nurses and the doctors would pass her the phone, saying, 'This is your mother; your mum is on the phone', but Catherine could not respond. I started feeling guilty, thinking, *I have upset my daughter, and now she is mad at me. Maybe she is upset we have sent her to her grandfather'*. For two months, Catherine would not say a single word on the phone. I would scream at the medical personnel and ask why she would not talk. They said the same thing, 'Catherine has not said a single word to us either'. She was numb; she was not talking, not brushing her teeth, did not want to eat or drink, and did not want to exist. She had given up.

The doctors wrote letters, and the consulate gave special permission for them to obtain a visa. I arrived in North America two months after the twins. I came with my two other children as they had a break from school. My husband had a new job and could not come. We went straight from the airport to the hospital. Diane was sitting by her twin's side, holding her hand. I entered the room and the sight I will never forget.

Catherine was on the bed, strapped so she could not move. If they did not strap her down, she would be violent and pull out her nasal tube. But what gave me comfort was that her face was rounder; she had gained some weight. She looked healthy, and this was amazing to see. She turned and saw me standing by the door, and after two months of not talking and no emotion, even then, she said nothing, but I saw tears rolling down her cheeks. I then knew something of Catherine was back. I had held and hugged her before she left home, but she could not respond or show any emotion.

Normally, if there is ever an emotional child, Catherine is that child. But now she was not saying anything, only staring at me, and I asked her, 'Do you feel anything?' And she said, 'I feel something, Mummy, but I can't show it'. Her tears were tears of joy for me, for they told me Catherine was in there.

At the time, Catherine refused even to stand up and walk to the bathroom, a few feet from the bed. She had to go in a wheel-chair. She was in complete shutdown. The doctors, every day, were trying to read into her mind how she had got to that point.

Five months later—she was in hospital for five months, all this time on the NGT—Catherine was discharged and became a weekly outpatient. She did okay for a little while but began to relapse and, in a month or two, had to be readmitted.

Catherine was readmitted to a hospital at another location, but this hospital was concerned more about the psychiatric care and not the eating disorder part of the illness. She was left alone for hours, and they would put food in front of her, and if she did not eat it, that was okay with them. I was thinking, *'My child is going to die; she has anorexia'*. Someone needed to be there to make sure she ate something. I went to the doctors at the children's hospital and said, 'Please help me. Catherine needs readmission'. She was readmitted to the hospital's eating disorder unit for another two months, and this time, when discharged, we were recommended to take part in the MFT group about to start. Catherine was, by now, 13, and I was ready for any help I could get for her. Already two years had passed since she got sick.

I walked into this room on the first day of MFT and saw husbands and wives and their children. I thought, *'Oh, wow'*. Even though I had been going to the hospital and had seen the kids as patients, to see the children in this room with their parents and to realise that they had the same problem as we did, this was surreal. I thought, *'Wow, so we are not alone in this'*. I wanted to know how others were dealing with this situation in their family.

We had to take a packed lunch each day. I had my four children to pack for, so we took a big cooler, something for everyone to eat. I looked forward to lunchtime because all the families would sit around this big table, side by side, opposite each other, and I could see how the other children were reacting to the food in front of them, compared with Catherine. Each child was in a different stage than Catherine—some had been ill for longer, some were new patients, and others were of various ages. We also had two young boys in our group.

It was amazing to see how each child struggled with their own meal—what they would eat and would not eat. Some children preferred sweet food and desserts. Other kids just wanted vegetables. Some refused to eat anything, so I thought again, *'Wow, we are not alone'*.

One time, we were asked where we would like to be and where we hoped to be in a month or so. We sat there and considered what we wanted our life to be like. We wanted Catherine's dad to come and share this experience. That was our one wish. It was hard for me trying to be strong for the children. Within, I was breaking down. I needed my husband's support; he dearly wanted to be with us. We were limited to phone calls and, occasionally, online.

Nothing was withheld, and all the parents understood that we needed each other and we would encourage each other. 'What do you do during mealtimes?' 'What do you do to encourage your child to eat?' We would exchange ideas. All this helped to bring back hope.

By now, Catherine's eating behaviours had started to change ever so slowly. She was beginning to eat certain foods. For example, one time I packed a tuna sandwich and cut up some egg and put it in the sandwich. She did not want the egg in the sandwich, so she asked me to remove the egg, but she did eat a few bites of the sandwich, and I was grateful for this. For her to see these other kids struggling and trying their best to eat some dessert, a piece of this and that, helped her.

All this time, we were living with my dad and stepmom, and my husband remained in West Africa. The MFT was new for all of us. We were trying to cope with things as they came. While Catherine was an inpatient at the children's hospital, I would sleep beside her, and my other children stayed in my dad's care. I cannot say that I just stepped into MFT and, 'Boom, things improved'. I would be lying.

While Catherine's eating behaviours were slow to change, she noticeably began to express herself more. We would sit in a circle at the therapy, and the leaders would ask each of us how we felt about this and that. We learnt it was much better to express our thoughts and feelings than to keep it all in, which was what Catherine was doing. Slowly she began to open up, like, instead of sitting alone and trying to deal with things by herself, she would tell me, 'I don't feel good today,' or, 'I don't feel happy today'. We learned to talk more about the illness even though it had been a taboo kind of thing.

We had to be careful not to say anything that might trigger Catherine. Even my young son, seven at the time, knew not to say specific things or words in front of her: for instance, the word 'fat'. We could all be in the living room watching TV, and often, the newsreaders and others would say that word. Someone's hand was always on the controls, ready to change the channels. It could even be just a 'fat' person passing by on the screen. I cannot believe I am saying this word to you right now. We were careful with what Catherine watched on TV and listened to; we kept her in a cocoon as much as we could to keep the illness triggers away.

For the children, I would generally cook one dish at mealtime, and everyone would eat it, but when Catherine was ill,

I had to make a special dish for her. Her siblings knew not to say to me about their dish, 'I don't like this, I don't like that'. They had to carefully choose their words at the table. If they didn't like what was on their plate, that was their problem. They could not say, 'I don't like it', or that would trigger their sister's illness.

During MFT, witnessing the children's behaviours regarding liking or not liking certain foods, I became more confident in giving Catherine new foods. Desserts had been a no-no for her, and I had focused on providing her basic nutrition. I had not bothered about desserts or cookies. But now I could see that variety was good, so I began introducing different foods, especially desserts. Within a month or two, she could eat the same food as the rest of the family.

After the MFT week, we went for a monthly check-up at the children's hospital, and Catherine had no more admissions as an inpatient. Now, she wanted to get better. That was the difference. She was a twin, and now she could see that if she did not step up, her sister would leave her behind. She could see she was missing a lot of stuff at school. Before, the illness would not let her see this. Now, real life was dawning on her.

Today, I am 100 per cent grateful, for I think I have my Catherine back. What we learnt at MFT is that you eat breakfast, snacks, lunch, and evening meals. This all has stayed with Catherine. She wakes up, she feels hungry, and she eats.

One time, when Catherine was in her worst shape, and we were all in the dining hall, trying to have a meal, my child was struggling to eat her food, and another older girl was busy eating. I was looking at the contrast and thinking, *'Things are so bad. I fear Catherine will never get to that stage'*. I feared she would never again be able to willingly eat her food. Now, every day, I watch her eat her meals. I am so thankful.

About 12 months after MFT, we went to McDonald's, which had been off the list for Catherine since she got ill. We were all sitting there, and I got all my children hamburger sandwiches.

I didn't get fries or anything. Then, as soon as we were eating, Catherine, of all people, not one of her siblings, looked at me and said, 'Can I have some fries, Mummy?' My hand went straight into my purse, and I got out however much money I had. I said to a waiter, 'Please get Catherine some fries'. I silently turned to my two other daughters and my son, and said, 'Quiet', and whispered, 'Did you just hear what Catherine asked for?'

Right then, I would have let Catherine eat all the fries in the world. That was the moment—the turning point when I knew Catherine would be okay. She ate every one of those fries. We have had to maintain our sense of humour through all this. We shared our fry story over the phone with my husband, and we laughed and laughed. If we could not laugh, we could not have coped.

My husband eventually could visit us—it took two years—shortly after we finished the MFT week. His presence was just what we needed for our family cohesion and helped Catherine greatly. Many positive things started to happen for her.

When my husband returned to his work, I stayed in North America with the children; we applied on humanitarian grounds. The doctors said, 'This illness is not something to take lightly'. I missed my husband dreadfully, but my dad, stepmom, sister, and brother were my support, and I made one or two friends. I found that talking about it was the best thing for me. Being conservative in nature, I try to keep things about myself to myself, but I found that talking about anorexia was the best way to cope.

Catherine continues to express her feelings. She has down days, but now she can tell us. We help her cope by watching a funny movie or reading a humorous book.

The father

I tried to be as supportive as I could. Hearing how stressful it was for my wife to be far away with a sick child all by herself made me feel helpless and sad. There was nothing I could do but pray that she was strong enough to do it all by herself. I was particularly happy to hear that Catherine was making small improvements.

For now, we are celebrating Catherine's huge progress in her state of mind. Although she is a sensitive child, she seems to manage her feelings very well nowadays.

This anorexia is very real and can happen to anyone, anywhere, regardless of race or socio-economic background. The children's hospital MFT programme has been great to us, and we are blessed to have had our daughter in their care.

The patient (Catherine)

MFT gave Mum and my siblings an opportunity to voice their opinions. As a family, we hadn't really talked about my illness, but being in the group situation forced us each to say something. This helped me understand better what Mum and my siblings were going through. Seeing many families there, with other kids like me, and their siblings, enabled me to see that anorexia did not only affect me, it also affected all of my family. Being in MFT is different from sitting alone and isolated in therapy with a doctor. In the group situation, I felt more able to speak about my feelings, and this was helpful for the whole family.

At MFT, just being among other people was helpful. We got to hear of other people's experiences, and I learned that I was not alone in what was happening. I made friends with a girl, and I saw that she was, like, gradually improving, getting to go to school, and I wanted to experience that same thing. Seeing her getting better helped me want to do the same.

The timeline helped me see how my illness had progressed, and I planned what I wanted to work towards. I wanted to stick with my goal of being able to eat by myself and try to get back to normal that way. Eating new foods was very scary because I was not used to this—I was not happy to do it, either. I had to force myself to do it, to get back to a regular eating pattern. When I got the courage to try a new food, I found the experience was not as bad as I had imagined. Watching the other kids, I decided that if they could eat dessert, maybe I could too.

When I was really sick, my sisters and brother would get frustrated, but eventually, they became more understanding and supportive, and I could talk to them more and explain that eating was really hard for me. Spending a lot of time with them has been helpful for me. They have helped to distract me from whatever illness thought I was having.

Looking back, I am thankful for what all the doctors and nurses did for me, even though I was not very thankful to them, like, in the moment.

I am in Grade 11 now and enjoy going to school. I still get stressed, like with tests and whatever. Eating is not a problem now, but sometimes I still feel anxious at school. I try to do other stuff that I enjoy, like watching movies, reading a book, especially about fantasy and science fiction, and playing board games with my sisters and brother. I want to go to university, and I want to travel. I am learning French and look forward to using it when I travel. I also look forward to spending more time with my family.

Twin sister

We had a long plane trip to stay with our grandfather, and as it was pretty rushed, we hardly had time to say a proper 'goodbye' to our family. Catherine didn't talk much on the plane, so I felt alone and sad, but I wanted to be with her.

I am feeling very happy now because Catherine is almost her old self and we are going to school together, in the same year, and able to spend more time together. We both like reading books.

Talking to other siblings at MFT helped, and it was comforting to know others were going through the same thing. We were told to be patient with Catherine and spend as much time with her as possible. We were told to act regular and keep things as normal as possible around her. Sometimes, it seemed like all the attention was on Catherine and my siblings, and I would feel left out. We found comfort in each other because we were going through the same thing.

I had to try to be more independent because I was used to always doing stuff with Catherine. Before she got sick, we liked to play outside together and share secrets. Growing up through grade school, we weren't always in the same class, but we would always be together at recess and lunchtime. When Catherine was really sick, I wondered if she would always be like that; I wondered if she would ever get back to a normal life. Now, it is hard to believe she was like that because we are doing things like we were before she got sick.

We were almost 12 when Catherine got sick, and I think I pushed some of the bad memories to the back of my head; they are only a blur. I tried not to let it affect me. I was sad but wanted to stay strong, especially for my younger brother.

I felt relief when Mum arrived after those first two months at my grandfather's home, and I was no longer the only one in our immediate family with Catherine. My grandpa would need to go to work, so I would stay at the hospital. It was a lot of responsibility. The doctors helped me understand that Catherine's behaviour, like not talking, was not really her doing it but her illness. This was hard to understand, but eventually, I noticed other patients and could see more clearly that not eating or talking were behaviours that belonged to anorexia.

While I had seen other patients at the eating disorder unit of the hospital, it was only when I saw them with their families at MFT that this made a lot of difference to how I felt in our family situation. I could see we weren't alone.

After MFT, Catherine could express her feelings more and let us know if she was unhappy. We were all encouraged to share more about our feelings.

Life is much better now—we are thinking about school instead of worrying about what Catherine might eat, and it is the same for her. The food thoughts no longer consume her. This is a big relief. Catherine is more positive, not all the time, but much, much better. Catherine was always more of a worrier than me. I can feel anxious, too, but I try to control it more. She gets more anxious, like, if stuff doesn't go as planned. I like to plan things, too, and if things don't work out, I feel disappointed but can cope with it, but it is harder for Catherine.

If I see Catherine looking down, I ask her what is wrong. She is not really talkative anyway, but if she goes really quiet, this is a sign she is down, and I might think, *'Oh, we talked about a test we did today, and she is not feeling good about her mark'*. I just sense this. Being a twin, I think I have a unique sense, as we are together most of the time, and I can easily tell if she is not feeling good. I first try to talk to her, and if she does not want to talk, I try to distract her, like doing something funny. I tell her a joke or joke around about the situation. Especially at school, when I am stressed out, I just try to laugh it off. I try to encourage Catherine to take stuff lightly and not be too serious about it. Usually, after a little while, she will start to feel more comfortable. She is more reserved, and I tend to be more open.

The MFT has strengthened me going through this with Catherine and has helped me be a stronger person in coping with problems that come along.

Older sister

The scariest aspect of my sister's eating disorder was at the start of her illness. Due to the lack of proper medical facilities and knowledge on how to treat anorexia in that country, our situation looked grim. Catherine was wasting away day after day, but we couldn't help her or convince her that food was not the enemy.

The first few months after she was admitted to the children's hospital were equally challenging. Although she was slowly being nourished back to health, I felt for a long time that the real Catherine I knew was long gone. Anorexia puts a toll not only on your body but also on your mind, and my sister was no longer the affable person she used to be. I had increasing difficulty in having a conversation with her because she hardly responded to things I said or asked her.

I began to dread the days when I did 'lunch duty' and had to sit with Catherine until she finished her meal. I feared Catherine thought I was betraying her by taking the doctors' advice, which further stressed our relationship.

At MFT, we learned the importance of always being encouraging and supportive of our sister, even when she refused to talk to us or cooperate with anything we told her to do. As long as she was aware that we loved her unconditionally, she had a greater motivation to return to her old self and quell the thoughts that were fuelling her eating disorder.

As the eldest child in the family, I didn't feel overlooked or left out during this experience. However, I thought that I needed to step up and make sure my brother (the youngest child) was getting enough attention when our mum had to make frequent trips to the hospital to be with Catherine. If anyone were more affected by this, it would be Catherine's twin, Diane. Used to doing nearly everything together, Diane had to become more independent in Catherine's absence.

Young brother

When Mum, my older sister, and I arrived at my grandpa's place, we went straight to the hospital and asked for Catherine's room. When we saw Catherine, Mum was sad and devastated.

I was surprised to see Catherine in this state, strapped to her bed. I was still happy to see her, though, as I had not seen her for two months. I was really happy to see my sister Diane sitting beside Catherine, my grandpa, and my grandma.

On the first day of MFT, all the parents were in one room, and I was surprised to see other kids. I had seen other kids with the same illness as Catherine, but to see them all together, with their families, was helpful because I liked to know that we were not the only family going through this.

In one session, all the family members sat in a circle. I think you had to say your name, and I liked this because everyone was encouraged to talk, like families. We talked about what we were doing in the moment.

Sometimes, the kids went to another room to do activities, and then we were called back to show our activities to our parents. I liked that a lot. One of the activities was to show a picture of anorexia. I drew a picture of a superhero riding the anorexia—I wanted a superhero to take the illness away from my sister. I like drawing. Around this time the MFT also provided a snack bar, and I liked this too, and we could choose what we wanted. I usually liked fruit best, especially fresh strawberries.

I did not understand Catherine's illness until we went to MFT, and they started explaining it more, and that's when I began to get worried. They said that sometimes the illness is life-threatening, and that was scary for me. We discussed this and what it meant when we went home that night.

When Catherine would say, 'I don't like this' and 'I don't like that', I would ask, 'Why don't you like it?' She couldn't answer. When she started to eat more stuff, I began to feel happy. When Catherine got sick, I was young and didn't have much time with her. But now she talks and plays with me. That's why I am grateful for the help we got. She would not be back if she did not receive MFT.

My understanding of anorexia is that it is something you can't see. Of course, it can happen to a boy or a girl, it does not matter; and it is really bad, and the person who gets affected by anorexia can't eat, and sometimes they don't talk much. When this illness happens, it is essential for the family to get help and to remember that they are not the only family going through this.

Chapter 22

Anorexia does not care who you are or where you are

SHIRA

Shira's family settled in North America when she was two. When Shira developed anorexia at age 14, her parents had no idea what was going on. When the family began multi-family therapy (MFT), Shira was eating, but mechanically so. She ate only to avoid readmission to the hospital; there was no enjoyment. When in her rebellious state, she would say to her mother, 'I eat but hate you for it'. The mother says, 'I would not know how to respond, and this is where MFT helped me to cope—the MFT therapist would raise this in our group situation and say, 'Let's discuss your problem, how you are handling this, and what we can learn from this situation'. At MFT, other kids were eating pizza, no problem. Shira saw this, and it gave her a push—maybe she could eat that food, too. In the group sessions, the child with anorexia didn't feel targeted, and for me, it helped to know how other parents were coping and what methods were working for them that I could use.

The mother

When Shira was 14, she progressively cut out her favourite foods and began exercising like crazy. That Shira did not eat, did not make sense to me. When she fainted, I rushed her to the hospital emergency department. The medical practitioner said, 'Shira has an eating disorder, a genuine illness in this country'. He said, 'People can die', and suddenly, my eyes were opened. I realised we could lose our child.

DOI: 10.4324/9781003641070-25

The doctor said, 'Go home, and I will get someone to call you from the eating disorder unit to help'. I waited weeks, but nobody called, and being an immigrant, I did not know how the system worked, so we kept waiting. Eventually, I asked my general practitioner (GP), and he said he would get someone to call, but again, nothing happened.

Meanwhile, Shira was clinging to her studies as a lifeline. All day, she would say, 'This is what I have to do'. The whole house was a nightmare. Shira was irrational, highly strung, mean, and rude, and her screaming fits scared me and my other kids silly. My son would hide under his bed. Our whole life revolved around trying to soothe her so that she would not become emotionally distraught and have screaming fits. She would cook a lot, make us eat, and eat nothing herself. She insisted I take her grocery shopping at all odd hours and pick up stuff, but she wouldn't eat it. She was reading the labels of every food item.

We had not heard of anorexia and had no idea what to do. Things got worse. Shira was picking at salad leaves and running for kilometres.

One Friday, she got up to go to school, and I went into the bathroom and could see every bone, every rib, on her body. This was frightening. This was not the daughter I knew. I said, 'You are not going to school unless you eat something'. She threatened me with a knife. At this point, I realised that this was not my daughter speaking. I said to my husband, 'Call 911'. Police and an ambulance came and took Shira to the emergency department. Her vitals were low. The examiner ordered fruit juice and crackers for Shira and said, 'If you eat this, you can go home for the weekend, and we will see you on Monday'.

Shira forced down the juice and crackers because she wanted to go home—she must have run 20km on five spinach leaves over that weekend. We took her to the day clinic on Monday morning, and the nurse took her vitals and went running. Shira's condition was critical.

She was put on drips until she could be admitted to the eating disorder unit in a children's hospital. She gained weight
over several months, and I got my daughter back. I took her
home, thinking all was fine, and didn't realise she was gradually
relapsing after six weeks. By then, it was too late, and she had to
be readmitted to the eating disorder unit. Shira was not happy.
This time, she got the MFT therapist as her psychiatrist. Shira
initially fought but began to appreciate this psychiatrist when
she arranged for the schoolwork to continue in the hospital.

This time, Shira was in the hospital for about a month and
was about to be discharged when the psychiatrist suggested our
family participate in MFT. I said, 'Yes', because I did not want
to be unprepared this time. Shira did not want to attend, but the
psychiatrist told her she would be readmitted to the clinic if
she did not come, so she came. I wanted support and guidance
from others because I hadn't a clue how to handle this illness.
Talking to other parents at MFT, I found we were not alone.
Other parents were feeling guilt and shame, too.

Our extended family lived on another continent, so we had
to manage without family support. This is why MFT helped; it
gave us a support system and showed us how to proceed. We
learnt this illness does not end when the child walks out of the
clinic; the illness takes a long time to heal. The MFT therapist
said she had seen people die of eating disorders and was determined not to let this happen again, and this gave me confidence
in her. I clung to the thought *'This is someone who cares and
will look after our daughter'*.

Shira was eating but mechanically so. She ate only to avoid
readmission to the hospital; there was no enjoyment. When
in her rebellious state, she would say, 'I eat but hate you for
it'. I would not know how to respond, and this is where MFT
helped me to cope—the MFT therapist would raise this in our
group situation and say, 'Let's discuss your problem, how you
are handling this, and what we can learn from this situation'.
At MFT, other kids were eating pizza without a problem. They

were enjoying it. Shira saw this, and it gave her a push—maybe she could eat that food, too. In the group sessions, my child didn't feel targeted, and for me, it helped to know how other parents were coping and what methods were working for them that I could use.

The kids had to put on paper what their eating disorder looked like to them, and Shira, the girl who did not want to come to MFT, drew someone lost in a maze, and this showed me, *'This girl is still confused, she is not done with the eating disorder'*.

The parents shared how they handled meals and so on. We would think, *'My way is not working, so maybe I will try another person's way'*. We all gained confidence and the strength to go on. The team was always positive, and the sessions were always positive. I always left for home feeling tired but saying, *'I am ready to face it again'*.

During the MFT year, I had to return to work, and my manager was supportive. One day, I arrived late due to another argument with Shira, and I was in tears—Shira had always been honest, warm, and generous but, since the illness, had developed a selfish side and showed little consideration for her family. My manager pulled me aside and, on hearing my story, offered Shira a part-time job. Shira was excited, for this job gave her something other than her illness to focus on. After several weeks, she came home one evening and said, 'You know, Mummy', and this is the girl who knew how many grams of fat, carbs, and protein were in every supermarket food package, 'I noticed fries on sale, can I go get them?'—and she brought them home and ATE them. Later, I cried for an hour. I was so happy.

This was a breakthrough, but the battle was uphill all the way. Shira loved mathematics and wanted to go to a major university and live on campus, so she needed to work on recovery as well as her studies. She worked hard on both.

After MFT, Shira required no more hospital admissions. She had been very sick for one year. At the time of this interview,

Shira is in her second year at the university of her choice and has taken up mathematics. She is back to being an honest and happy girl.

In my religious and cultural community, no one had heard of anorexia nervosa—this was due not so much to our religion or culture but to our countries of origin, where hungry people were searching for food. In our place of prayer, Shira's illness became known when she was admitted to the children's hospital, and friends were supportive. I visited Shira daily and needed care arrangements for my other two children—I worked full-time and would go to the hospital afterwards. I would get home late, and my husband worked shift hours. Friends in our community helped take care of the younger children. Shira's tantrums were frightening; her siblings were afraid and needed company.

Since Shira's illness, another parent at our place of prayer has said to me, 'I am worried about my daughter', and I have talked with her. Another friend came to me and said her daughter was eating junk food and having dizzy spells. So, the good thing about Shira's illness becoming spoken about in our community is that more people are aware.

Some people don't realise that anorexia is a serious illness, like cancer or diabetes. Yet since Shira's illness, my mother, who is in South Asia and talks to me almost every day, has told me of a girl in her community with this same illness. You think, *'But this is in a Third World country. Why is this happening where people are starving?'* Sadly, there was no help for that child. In North America, we have been lucky to have help.

The eating disorder unit at the children's hospital is amazing. That eating disorder team took the burden off my mind. The most helpful advice was when my husband and I were told that parents were not to blame. We had been blaming ourselves, and this was destroying our relationship and family life. Through all this, I have discovered new strengths and have learnt that a support system is essential.

Chapter 23

The family stories

Reflecting on inspiring lessons

Reading the stories together is powerful. Together, they give insight into the multiple ways in which people and families recover from an eating disorder and the different ways that multi-family therapy (MFT) can help. It is striking how families and individuals within each family are impacted in different ways. What seems to help one person or family might not affect another individual or family. However, as a whole, MFT seems to support different people in many different ways.

One of the strongest themes woven throughout the stories is a sense of how much MFT can help bring people together to feel less alone. Most stories show the way that connecting with others who are going through something similar can help reduce the severe isolation people feel when struggling with an eating disorder. This is true across cultures in the stories in this book, something painfully reflected in the struggle Shira and her family faced accessing care. The way Charolette speaks about moving from a place of hiding from her illness to facing and sharing her emotions is inspiring to read. It is evident MFT has helped her and her family find new ways to connect, with less anger and frustration, and more kindness. The connection made by Lisa and Harriet, two mothers, is another heartwarming example of connection. The amount of support they are able to offer each other is incredible.

James and Marla's story speaks volumes about the importance of finding a way to partner in recovery. There is so much

DOI: 10.4324/9781003641070-26

going on for both of them, whether it is managing two households, different beliefs about parenting, or Jack's struggle with his sexuality, the bullying, and the expectations he feels from gay culture. The MFT process appears to help them to hone their partnership and learn to open up. It sounds like life is not pleasant; in fact, it is the opposite at times. However, seeing similarities and differences with others in the group seems to help them reflect on their own experiences and learn from them. Learning to collaborate, especially to take positive risks, is also at the heart of Cassandra and her mum's story. This does not always pay off, as described by Emma and her family. However, they reflect that there is always useful learning from this.

There is also a sense across many of the stories that MFT helps people to understand themselves and the illness in new ways. Rebekah talks of the way MFT helped her feel seen not just as an illness but as a person again. For Anna, MFT is a way of diluting difficult dynamics and interactions. It allowed the family members to be together and learn with each other in less direct and more manageable ways. Natalie speaks so eloquently about the hold the eating disorder had on her. For Natalie, MFT seems to help her see things from different angles, whether through the lens of time and culture, from other people's perspectives, or to see different parts of herself—sparkly Natalie. Alongside this, her dad, Dave, also seems to gain insight and to understand fully what anorexia was and how it was impacting his daughter.

For others, MFT seems to powerfully allow people to let go of guilt and truly recognise the illness is not their fault. For Amy and her parents, it was important to understand the biological basis of anorexia nervosa and the impact of isolation. The MFT experience seemed to really help them to understand and believe this is an illness that they did not cause. MFT helped them learn this is an illness from which they can help their daughter recover. It is as though once they realise she is unwell, they can manage things differently like they would with any other severe illness. MFT seems to give them confidence and skills to be on the same page together, to feel less guilty, and to set clear goals and rewards for Amy. What also underlies their whole story is the absolute determination to do what it takes and to do it as a family—they move across the world for this. As Amy's mum says, 'If we don't help our child as a family, no one can help our child'. Harriet, Cassandra's mum, speaks about how guilt, self-doubt, fear, and exhaustion can crush positive risk-taking. Addressing guilt, self-blame, and shame directly and explicitly in MFT is a key part of working together with a family and building deep trust.

For many, it is the practical support MFT offers to families. For Emily's mum, MFT brings to life the concepts she already knew about but didn't know how to implement. For her, it was something about needing to experience the method, not just read about it. The MFT process helped them to focus on the realisation that they must go through the illness; there is no way around it. This seemed especially true for Emily's dad, who reaches an important realisation that being firm and mean are not the same thing—a mental shift many parents talk about needing to make.

Another aspect of MFT that is reflected in the stories is the way MFT can speed up recovery or break through barriers in a way that seems more challenging to do in single-family therapy. For Rebekah and her family, MFT was described as 'breaking the ice' and building a more robust support network. Mathilda and her mum's story really brings home the idea that MFT can be a brief, intensive way of setting people on a new recovery-focused path. It certainly does not 'fix' everything, but it is clear from both of their accounts that it is a significant turning point in getting them working more together and having clearer goals. This seems to happen through a combination of having additional support, learning new skills, and being able to focus on where things were heading. There is a strong narrative that

MFT allowed Sarah to put her illness and current behaviours in the context of her future and the life she wants to live.

A final reflection concerns the importance of life outside the illness and treatment. Lydia's story is a lovely lesson in keeping in touch with life outside the eating disorder, that is, to be engaged in the world and have something worth going through the distress of it all for. There is this sense in this story that the cheese shop is a place where Lydia is not known as the 'ill' person. Instead, it is a place where she is expected to engage with the world and others in a non-eating-disordered way. It goes to show that safe places are not always places to be alone and to rest; rather, the safety in Lydia's story seems to come from having to engage the non-illness parts of herself and connect more with others. For Lydia, it sounds like it is just what she needs. Her part-time job in the cheese shop provides an antidote to the disconnected, lonely, and ill role people can find themselves in when they are overcome by an eating disorder.

Similarly, Shira's part-time job seems to be the key to her recovery, just like Natalie's job at the pub. These reflections teach us not to get too focused on the illness or treatment. Part of recovery is shifting beyond the illness and finding reasons to endure it and go through it. Treatment is not the only ingredient, and as Cassandra's story points out, clinicians don't always get it right. Recovery is truly about collaborating to find the best way forward.

Section III

What can parents do if they are concerned about their child?

Chapter 24

How to tell if your child has an eating disorder

Often, we get calls in our clinic from parents and loved ones who are worried about their child or adolescent. This can range from very serious food restriction and binge-purge behaviours to a more subtle change in food preferences and behaviours. Not all young people (or adults) who change their eating patterns have an eating disorder. Many people decide to change what they eat for health reasons in ways that are not damaging to them physically or psychologically. Changing our daily habits to improve well-being can be a really great way for people to feel better about themselves. Having said that, we know from decades of research that dieting behaviour and a drive towards a 'thin ideal' are risk factors for developing an eating disorder (Barakat et al., 2023). So when should you worry? In this section, we hope to outline what an eating disorder is and is not, and how to respond if you are concerned about your child.

A reminder of the diagnostic criteria

Six main eating disorders are described in the American Psychiatric Association's *Diagnostic and Statistical Manual of Mental Disorders* (DSM-5-TR; American Psychiatric Association, 2022) and the World Health Organization's *International Classification of Diseases* (ICD-11; World Health Organization, 2019). These include:

DOI: 10.4324/9781003641070-28

1. *Anorexia nervosa*: A diagnosis of anorexia nervosa is made if a person has significantly reduced the amount of food they are eating, which leads to weight loss. A strong self-evaluation of self-worth is based on weight and/or body shape. Despite being low weight, people with anorexia nervosa typically do not recognise or acknowledge this and continue either to avoid weight gain or continue to try to lose weight. There are two subtypes of anorexia nervosa. The 'restrictive' subtype is when someone loses weight primarily by reducing their daily energy intake. The 'binge-purge' subtype is for those who restrict their food intake but also binge eat, and then attempt to get rid of, or 'purge', the food by vomiting or taking laxatives.

2. *Bulimia nervosa*: For people experiencing bulimia nervosa, their difficulties are characterised mainly by episodes of binge eating followed by attempts to rid themselves of it afterwards to avoid weight gain, known as a 'purge'. The *DSM-5-TR* defines a 'binge' as repeated episodes of eating large amounts of food accompanied by a sense of loss of control. The *ICD-11* definition of binge eating emphasises the aspect of losing control without specifying that the amount needs to be large. Purging can include self-induced vomiting, excessive exercising, laxatives or other substance/medication misuse, and fasting. As with anorexia nervosa, the person's sense of self-worth is strongly influenced by their self-perception of their body weight and/or shape. People with bulimia nervosa tend to be within the healthy weight range, and if they are very low in weight, a diagnosis of anorexia nervosa binge-purge subtype is used.

3. *Binge eating disorder (BED)*: Like bulimia nervosa, BED is characterised by binge eating episodes. It differs from bulimia nervosa in that the person does not engage in compensatory behaviours afterwards. The binge eating episodes are usually quite distressing. The person may also continue to eat when full, eat very rapidly, eat when not hungry, avoid

eating with others, and feel disgusted or guilty about these behaviours.

4. *Avoidant/restrictive food intake disorder (ARFID)*: This relatively new diagnosis is only included in the most recent editions of the *DSM* and *ICD*. People with ARFID either eat very small amounts, or few types of food, or both. This can be driven by any or all of the following: a) a lack of interest in food and eating, b) food avoidance due to the sensory characteristics of the food (e.g., appearance, texture, etc.), or c) intense fear of what might happen if they eat (e.g., choking, vomiting). Importantly, people with ARFID do not describe a desire to lose weight or be thin. For diagnosis, they need to have such a limited range of food that it impacts their physical health, development, and/or well-being.

5. *Pica*: This is when someone persistently and repeatedly eats non-nutritious substances, such as non-food items (e.g., glass, soil, wool) or raw food ingredients. It is only diagnosed when the pattern of eating is severe and requires clinical intervention.

6. *Rumination disorder*: This is sometimes referred to as rumination-regurgitation disorder. It is diagnosed when someone repeatedly regurgitates food that has been swallowed. Often, the food regurgitated is then re-chewed, re-swallowed, or spat out. The bringing up of food is not associated with much effort, and people do not usually feel nauseous when it happens.

Both the DSM-5-TR and the ICD-11 include two more general categories for those who don't completely fit any of the diagnoses above, but who are experiencing significant feeding or eating difficulties that cause distress, impacting their functioning and requiring intervention. These include Other Specified Feeding or Eating Disorder (OSFED) and Unspecified Feeding or Eating Disorder (UFED). An example of an eating disorder that requires intervention but does not fully fit any of the six diagnostic criteria, and therefore is called OSFED, is 'atypical anorexia nervosa'.

This term is used when someone meets all the other criteria for anorexia nervosa including significant weight loss, but is not significantly underweight for their age, gender, and height. This is by no means less serious or less damaging to someone's health and is being seen increasingly in clinics worldwide. All eating disorders share the central core feature of a significant change in eating or eating-related behaviours with accompanied psychosocial and/or physical impairment. All can be serious and damaging conditions, irrespective of age at onset or presentation.

In this book, we have mostly focused on anorexia nervosa. It is the best known and most common eating disorder seen in clinics. Most international guidelines recommend family therapy as the first-line intervention for both conditions. For a recent review of child and adolescent bulimia nervosa treatment outcomes see Love & Baudinet (2025). While not discussed in depth in this book, it is important that population-based studies suggest BED is relatively common and is largely under-studied and under-treated. We have a long way to go in better understanding BED and the other eating disorders and developing treatments. For a recent review of treatment outcomes of BED in children and adolesents, see Brothwood & Baudinet (2025). While less common, the diagnostic criteria for Pica, rumination disorder, and ARFID are included to help you think through the range of different eating disorders and how they might apply to you or your loved one. No matter what type of eating difficulty one is experiencing, undoubtedly, having the support of loved ones around you is essential.

Now I feel confused and don't know what to do

Some of you may read the section above and think, *'That's my child!'* Others might notice several features of multiple eating disorders and feel more confused. Or, you might be thinking, *'My child is doing some of these things, but it does not feel so extreme right now.'* So, what should you do?

Whatever your experience, the first step is to try to talk to your child. This is not always easy—in fact, it can often be met with exasperation, frustration, or anger. Some things to consider when raising your concerns with your child include the following:

- They might not recognise the behaviour or its seriousness.
- They know something is not right but feel embarrassed or ashamed.
- They might be worried but are fearful that if people discover it, they will need to confront their difficulties—a very scary prospect for most.
- They have been wanting to talk about it but are struggling to know how.
- They might be worried people will judge them.
- They might be worried people will get angry with them.

When we are scared or worried, this can easily come across as frustration or anger.

This can be especially true with eating disorders, as eating is such a fundamental part of our lives. Listening is often the best starting point, rather than trying to problem-solve, criticise, or fix things. Trying to connect with your child about what is happening for them, how they are feeling, and what is happening in their world, without making assumptions or giving opinions (to start with), can help young people feel heard, listened to, and not judged.

Try to understand what emotions your child may be feeling, even if they do not make sense to you. *'Why'* questions often shut down these conversations rather than open them up, for example, *'Why would you feel like that? Everyone really likes you'* or *'Why would you care so much about what others think?'* While well intended, the subtle message from these questions can be that you think what the young person is feeling or thinking, is silly and/or you do not agree with them.

Instead, try a version of: *'I had no idea you were feeling this way. Tell me more'.* If you can make a connection with your child about their worries and changes in eating or weight, it might be useful to see if they would *then* like your help in trying to manage their worries in healthier ways. Try to be led by them if the behaviour is not significantly impacting their weight or health at that point.

Early signs and symptoms of anorexia nervosa, bulimia nervosa, or binge eating disorder

For young people with disordered eating, as opposed to an eating disorder, supportive listening and questioning may be enough. For those further along the path to an eating disorder, this will often not be enough. It is still a good starting point, but by this point, it might be hard for your child to be open and honest about what is happening to them. They may not realise the gravity of it themselves. In this case, you may likely be met with dismissal or hostility and anger. It can be very hard for a parent or loved one to know if the child's behaviour is serious or is something that will pass in time.

Signs to look for that suggest a child might be struggling with a serious eating disorder are the following:

- Eating much less or much more than usual.
- Eating alone or separate from the family.
- Excluding all foods with higher sugar and fat content.
- Showing significant weight loss or gain.
- Spending extended time in the bathroom.
- Frequently going to the bathroom after meals.
- Taking a long time to get ready and/or spending much time in the shower or in front of a mirror.
- Changing outfits often and struggling to find anything that looks 'good'.

- Wearing baggy or very tight clothing.
- Getting very upset about small comments about their appearance.

If you notice any of these signs, particularly changes in weight or physical appearance, you must act quickly and get help. Your child might not always want you to help. However, something serious might be happening to them that will not resolve without intervention. Often, seeking help can signal that you love and care for your child, even if they are not particularly keen on getting help themselves.

Where do I go from here?

If you have read this far and think you need to get some help, the next step can feel daunting. Finding the right person or service for you and your family can take a lot of work. It is essential to find a clinician who a) you connect with and b) has the proper training and expertise in eating disorders. Finding someone you connect with is difficult to gauge from a website or promotional material, and will often only come from a phone call or initial appointment. To better understand whether a person has the training and knowledge required should be an easier task. Two important things to look for are:

1. Evidence of training in eating disorder-focused family therapy (sometimes referred to as family-based treatment) (FT-AN/BN or FBT-AN/BN) and/or multi-family therapy for eating disorder (MFT-AN/BN). If the clinic or therapist emphasises individual work with young people, it is possible they will not offer family or multi-family interventions, which are currently the recommended first-line interventions for young people. Reputable training institutions include the Family Based Treatment Training Institute (https://train2t reat4ed.com) in North America; the Maudsley Centre for

Child and Adolescent Eating Disorders (MCCAED; https://mccaed.slam.nhs.uk/professionals/training/) in the UK; and the National Eating Disorders Collaboration (NEDC; https://nedc.com.au) and the Australia and New Zealand Academy for Eating Disorders (ANZAED; www.anzaed.org.au) in Australia and New Zealand.

2. An emphasis on physical health and weight restoration quickly in treatment. While the psychological aspects are essential to target and manage, a focus on physical health is often needed initially to ensure the young person is physically safe.

If neither of these things is evident from promotional material for a clinic you are attending, it is worth asking specifically about them and whether a family-based approach is available.

Some organisations offer a credentialling system for eating disorder clinicians to help people recognise who has a certain level of training and knowledge about eating disorders. ANZAED (Australia and New Zealand) and the FBT Training Institute (USA and international) offer a credential system to ensure people looking for eating disorder treatments can be confident the clinician has a certain level of training in eating disorders and their evidence-based treatments. Look for mention of these organisations or a logo in promotional material.

In countries where a public health system is in place, such as Australia, New Zealand, the UK, and much of Continental Europe, the types of treatments and services offered are not always obvious. Typically, in these countries, national guidance dictates the types of treatments, which usually include family-based treatments and sometimes MFT (see Hilbert et al., 2017, for a helpful summary of some of the major national guidelines' recommendations for the treatment of eating disorders; this chapter also provides direct links to some of the most recent published guidelines). Nevertheless, accessing services can be difficult.

In these countries with a public health system, the initial start to getting help is usually with your general practitioner (GP). They are typically the ones to make a referral to a specialist eating disorder clinic (although not always). Despite increased awareness of eating disorders, it is still common for some GPs not to be knowledgeable about the signs of an eating disorder and what to investigate. The UK Managing Medical Emergencies in Eating Disorders (MEED; Royal College of Psychiatrists, 2022) can be a helpful resource for medical practitioners in assessing and understanding medical risk. Useful observations for the GP to include in an assessment are the following:

- Weight, height, blood pressure, heart rate
- Feeling cold often; cold hands and feet; blue or purple lips
- Fine hair growing on the body, known as lanugo hair
- Dizziness, fainting, chest pain, difficulty concentrating
- Changes in eating patterns, distress at mealtimes

Any of these symptoms, in the context of changes in eating behaviours, warrants a specialist assessment with an eating dis-order clinician. Some, such as a low heart rate, chest pain, and a large postural drop in blood pressure (a big change when going from sitting to standing), might require immediate attention at a hospital emergency department. Your GP can advise on this.

If the GP has completed a thorough physical health screen and suggests that you 'watch and wait', do not wait long, particu-larly if the behaviours persist or worsen. Decades of research have shown that getting help early is one of the most effective ways of overcoming eating disorders. If nothing changes within a few weeks, seek help again.

Once referred, hopefully, you will quickly see the specialist team, and treatment can begin. When offered an appointment, ask about what types of treatment are available and whether the service provides a family-focused intervention, such as FT-AN/

BN, FBT, and/or MFT. While waiting for your initial appointment, useful things to do include:

- Making sure you provide your child with three meals and two to three snacks each day.
- Eating together to ensure you see your child is eating enough.
- Sitting with your child and supporting them through distress if needed. This often includes calm but persistent encouragement and prompting without judgement or threats.
- Limiting vigorous exercise.
- Doing things together outside of mealtimes to try to connect more.

Some recent national treatment guidelines

Australia and New Zealand
Heruc, G., Hurst, K., Casey, A., Fleming, K., Freeman, J., Fursland, A., ... & Wade, T. (2020). ANZAED eating disorder treatment principles and general clinical practice and training standards. *Journal of Eating Disorders*, *8*, 1–9. https://doi.org/10.1186/s40 337-020-00341-0

Canada
Couturier, J., Isserlin, L., Norris, M., Spettigue, W., Brouwers, M., Kimber, M., ... & Pilon, D. (2020). Canadian practice guidelines for the treatment of children and adolescents with eating disorders. *Journal of Eating Disorders*, *8*, 1–80. https://doi.org/10.1186/s40 337-020-0277-8

Germany
Resmark, G., Herpertz, S., Herpertz-Dahlmann, B., & Zeeck, A. (2019). Treatment of anorexia nervosa—new evidence-based guidelines. *Journal of Clinical Medicine*, *8*(2), 153. https://doi.org/ 10.3390/jcm8020153

United Kingdom

NICE (2017). Eating disorders: recognition and treatment. Information for the public. National Institute for Health and Care Excellence. www.nice.org.uk/guidance/ng69/ifp/chapter/Eating-disorders-the-care-you-should-expect

United States

Crone, C., Fochtmann, L. J., Attia, E., Boland, R., Escobar, J., Fornari, V., ... & Medicus, J. (2023). The American Psychiatric Association practice guideline for the treatment of patients with eating disorders. *American Journal of Psychiatry*, *180*(2), 167–171. https://doi.org/10.1176/appi.ajp.23180001

References

American Psychiatric Association. (2022). *Diagnostic and statistical manual of mental disorders (DSM-5-TR)* (5th edition, text revision). Washington DC: American Psychiatric Association. https://doi.org/10.1176/appi.books.9780890425787

Barakat, S., McLean, S. A., Bryant, E., Le, A., Marks, P., National Eating Disorder Research Consortium, ... & Maguire, S. (2023). Risk factors for eating disorders: Findings from a rapid review. *Journal of Eating Disorders*, *11*(1), 8. https://doi.org/10.1186/s40337-022-00717-4

Brothwood, P. L., & Baudinet, J. (2025). Interventions for improving psychological symptoms in binge eating disorder (BED) and loss of control (LOC) eating in childhood and adolescence: A systematic scoping review. Journal of Eating Disorders, 13(1), 44. https://doi.org/10.1186/s40337-025-01206-0

Hilbert, A., Hoek, H. W., & Schmidt, R. (2017). Evidence-based clinical guidelines for eating disorders: international comparison. *Current Opinion in Psychiatry*, *30*(6), 423–437.

Royal College of Psychiatrists. (2022). *Medical emergencies in eating disorders (MEED): Guidance on recognition and management.* www.rcpsych.ac.uk/docs/default-source/improving-care/better-mh-policy/college-reports/college-report-cr233-medical-emergencies-in-eating-disorders-(meed)-guidance.pdf?sfvrsn=2d327483_63

World Health Organization. (2019). *ICD-11: International classification of diseases (11th revision).* https://icd.who.int/

Chapter 25

Navigating the search for multi-family therapy

Given that eating disorder-focused family therapy is suggested in most international guidelines, it is more likely nowadays that eating disorder clinics and professionals are aware of FT-ED and offer it (albeit they may use different names: FT-AN, FBT, Maudsley family therapy). Multi-family therapy (MFT), on the other hand, can be harder to access. There are several reasons for this. The most common is that a service needs to be large enough to have multiple families concurrently receiving treatment to participate in the groups. For sole clinicians working in private practice, unless they are part of a large practice specialising in eating disorders, this may not be the case.

Nevertheless, many services across Australia, New Zealand, Europe, the UK, the USA, Chile, and many other countries offer MFT. MFT-AN treatment manuals have been produced in several languages, including English (Balmbra et al., 2019; Hill et al., 2022; Simic et al., 2021; Tantillo et al., 2020), French (Duclos et al., 2021), Swedish (Wallin, 2007, 2011), and German (Scholz et al., 2003). The Maudsley MFT-AN manual is being translated into Chinese, Japanese and Czech. There is a strong MFT network in Europe, and such a network is growing across Australia. See the next pages for MFT practices in different regions and how you might be able to access them.

DOI: 10.4324/9781003641070-29

MFT-AN in Australia and New Zealand

There is a strong network of MFT clinicians across Australia and New Zealand.

In Australia, MFT-AN was first implemented at the Sydney Children's Hospital Network in Westmead. The team there has been running MFT-AN for a decade and has presented and written about their experiences (Dawson et al., 2018; Wallis et al., 2015). We have provided training and ongoing consultations to teams in Melbourne (The Victorian Centre of Excellence in Eating Disorders [CEED]), Brisbane (the Child and Youth Mental Health Service [CYMS]), Perth (Child and Adolescent Eating Disorder Service, Perth Children's Hospital), and Auckland (Tupu Ora, Auckland). MFT programmes are also offered in the Central Region Eating Disorder Service in New Zealand. CEED provides training in MFT-AN for clinicians.

MFT-AN in the UK

Since 2016, England has had a network of over 70 dedicated Community Eating Disorders Services for Children and Young People (CEDS-CYP) (Scotland, Wales, and Northern Ireland have separate National Health Service provisions, but each provides some form of community-based specialist eating disorder treatment for children and young people). Many CEDS-CYP offer MFT-AN as part of routine National Health Service treatment. The team at the Maudsley Centre for Child and Adolescent Eating Disorders offers up to six groups each year for anorexia nervosa (Simic et al., 2021) and two for bulimia nervosa (Escoffié et al., 2022; Stewart et al., 2021). We have been offering training in MFT for more than a decade, and many clinicians across the country have attended. Many other child and adolescent eating disorder services in the UK offer MFT. Families can typically access these services via a general practitioner (GP) referral from a practice within their catchment area to the specialist eating disorder clinic.

MFT-AN in Europe

MFT is relatively widespread across Europe. There is a strong European MFT network and a bi-annual conference takes place. Teams in France (Cook-Darzens & Duclos, 2022), Norway (Brinchmann et al., 2019; Skarbø & Balmbra, 2020; Funderud et al., 2023), Denmark (Hollesen et al., 2012), Germany (Asen & Scholz, 2008; Born, 2012), Sweden (Dennhag et al., 2019), Belgium (Depestele et al., 2015, 2017; Terache et al., 2023), and the Czech Republic (Mehl et al., 2013), among others, have published on their work and continue to offer MFT interventions. A large MFT-AN trial is underway in France (Carrot et al., 2019).

MFT-AN in North America

Due to the predominately private healthcare provision in the USA, MFT can be more complicated to access. Treatment guidelines are not mandated, so each clinic decides its services. Given the growing evidence base, several key clinics offer MFT, and interest is building.

The University of California San Diego has a long-standing five-day MFT-AN programme called intensive family treatment (IFT), developed in collaboration with the Maudsley team (Knatz et al., 2015). More recently, they have also developed a new multi-family treatment model for adults called temperament-based therapy with supports (TBT-S). Their approach has been manualised (Hill et al., 2022) and tested with adult patients and their families (Knatz Peck et al., 2021; Stedal et al., 2023; Wierenga et al., 2018). A similar intensive five-day IFT is offered at the University of California San Francisco Eating Disorders Program. The team at the Chicago Centre for

Evidence-Based Treatment (CCEBT), a large private practice in Chicago, also regularly offers MFT-AN and has been evaluating an online version of the treatment. The team at Stanford University has been piloting online parent multi-family groups (Matheson et al., 2024), although this programme focuses on parents and does not bring whole families to work together.

Another team, at the University of Rochester, New York, has pioneered MFT with adults. They have written a treatment manual (Tantillo et al., 2020) and published several outcome studies on this model (Tantillo et al., 2015, 2019).

In Canada, MFT-AN was first developed at the Hospital for Sick Kids in Toronto (Gabel et al., 2014) as part of MFT training provided by the Maudsley team. Colleagues in this group have also developed and evaluated MFT for young adults (Dimitropoulos et al., 2015).

MFT in Asia

MFT is beginning to emerge in Asia. The team at Shinjuku University Hospital, Japan, has piloted an adapted MFT model on their adolescent inpatient unit with good outcomes (Kuge et al., 2024; Matsuo et al., 2023). In Hong Kong, Joyce Ma at the Chinese University of Hong Kong, has done much work in MFT for difficulties other than eating disorders. Joyce Ma's department may be a good place to start if trying to determine what MFT options are available in Hong Kong. A team at Zhejiang University, China, is working with Routledge to translate the Maudsley MFT-AN manual into Chinese.

MFT-AN in Latin America

We have delivered training in MFT to the team at Centro Alma in Santiago, Chile. Participants came from several South American countries, including Chile, Argentina, Uruguay, and Colombia. Our colleagues have given MFT teaching in Mexico

to Médico Comenzar de Nuevo (https://comenzardenuevo.org/
nuestro-equipo/). The team there is also very active in the Latin
America Chapter of the Academy of Eating Disorders.

MFT in the Middle East

At the time of writing, we are unaware of any teams in the
Middle East offering MFT.

References

Asen, E., & Scholz, M. (2008). Multi-Familientherapie in unter-
schiedlichen Kontexten [Multi-family therapy in day care set-
tings]. *Praxis der Kinderpsychologie und Kinderpsychiatrie*, *57*(5),
362–380.

Balmbra, S., Valvik, M., & Lyngmo, S. (2019). *Coming together, letting go*. Retrieved from: www.nordlandssykehuset.no/siteassets/
documents/Ressp/Coming-together-2019-10d-B5.pdf

Born, A. (2012). Multifamilientherapie in Deutschland. [Multi-
family group therapy in Germany]. *Praxis der Kinderpsychologie
und Kinderpsychiatrie*, *61*(3), 167–182. https://doi.org/10.13109/
prkk.2012.61.3.167

Brinchmann, B. S., Moe, C., Valvik, M. E., Balmbra, S., Lyngmo, S.,
& Skarbo, T. (2019). An Aristotelian view of therapists' practice in
multifamily therapy for young adults with severe eating disorders.
Nursing Ethics, *26*(4), 1149–1159. https://doi.org/10.1177/09697
33017739780

Carrot, B., Duclos, J., Barry, C., Radon, L., Maria, A.-S., Kaganski,
I., … & Godart, N. (2019). Multicenter randomized controlled trial
on the comparison of multi-family therapy (MFT) and systemic
single-family therapy (SFT) in young patients with anorexia nervosa: Study protocol of the THERAFAMBEST study. *Trials*, *20*(1),
249. https://doi.org/10.1186/s13063-019-3347-y

Cook-Darzens, S., & Duclos, J. (2022). Development and implementation of a relationship-focused outpatient multifamily program
for adolescent anorexia nervosa. *Family Process*. https://doi.org/
10.1111/famp.12826

Dawson, L., Baudinet, J., Tay, E., & Wallis, A. (2018). Creating community—The introduction of multi-family therapy for eating disorders in Australia. *Australian and New Zealand Journal of Family Therapy*, *39*(3), 283–293. https://doi.org/10.1002/anzf.1324

Dennhag, I., Henje, E., & Nilsson, K. (2019). Parental caregiver burden and recovery of adolescent anorexia nervosa after multi-family therapy. *Eating Disorders: The Journal of Treatment & Prevention*. https://doi.org/10.1080/10640266.2019.1678980

Depestele, L., Claes, L., Dierckx, E., Colman, R., Schoevaerts, K., & Lemmens, G. M. D. (2017). An adjunctive multi-family group intervention with or without patient participation during an inpatient treatment for adolescents with an eating disorder: A pilot study. *European Eating Disorders Review*, *25*(6), 570–578. https://doi.org/10.1002/erv.2556

Depestele, L., Claes, L., & Lemmens, G. M. D. (2015). Promotion of an autonomy-supportive parental style in a multi-family group for eating-disordered adolescents. *Journal of Family Therapy*, *37*(1), 24–40. https://doi.org/10.1111/1467-6427.12047

Dimitropoulos, G., Farquhar, J. C., Freeman, V. E., Colton, P. A., & Olmsted, M. P. (2015). Pilot study comparing multi-family therapy to single family therapy for adults with anorexia nervosa in an intensive eating disorder program. *European Eating Disorders Review*, *23*(4), 294–303. https://doi.org/10.1002/erv.2359

Duclos, J., Carrot, B., Minier, L., Cook-Darzens, S., Barton-Clegg, V., Godart, N., & Criquillion-Doublet, S. (2021). *Manuel de Thérapie Multi-Familiale* (p. 168). www.researchgate.net/publication/350906742_Manuel_deTherapie_MultiFamiliale_approche_integrative_pour_la_prise_en_charge_d%27adolescents_souffrant_d%27Anorexie_Mentale_etdeleurs_familles

Escoffié, A., Pretorius, N., & Baudinet, J. (2022). Multi-family therapy for bulimia nervosa: A qualitative pilot study of adolescent and family members' experiences. *Journal of Eating Disorders*, *10*(1), 91. https://doi.org/10.1186/s40337-022-00606-w

Funderud, I., Halvorsen, I., Kvakland, A. L., Nilsen, J. V., Skjønhaug, J., Stedal, K., & Rø, Ø. (2023). Multifamily therapy for adolescent eating disorders: a study of the change in eating disorder symptoms from start of treatment to follow-up. *Journal of Eating Disorders*, *11*(1), 92. https://doi.org/10.1186/s40337-023-00814-y

Gabel, K., Pinhas, L., Eisler, I., Katzman, D., & Heinmaa, M. (2014). The effect of multiple family therapy on weight gain in adolescents with anorexia nervosa: Pilot data. *Journal of the Canadian Academy of Child and Adolescent Psychiatry*, *23*(3), 4.

Hill, L. L., Knatz Peck, S., & Wierenga, C. E. (2022). *Temperament based therapy with support for anorexia nervosa: A novel treatment*. Cambridge: Cambridge University Press. https://doi.org/10.1017/9781009032063

Hollesen, A., Clausen, L., & Rokkedal, K. (2013). Multiple family therapy for adolescents with anorexia nervosa: a pilot study of eating disorder symptoms and interpersonal functioning. *Journal of Family Therapy*, *35*, 53–67. https://doi.org/10.1111/1467-6427.12000

Knatz, S., Murray, S. B., Matheson, B., Boutelle, K. N., Rockwell, R., Eisler, I., & Kaye, W. H. (2015). A Brief, Intensive Application of Multi-Family-Based Treatment for Eating Disorders. *Eating Disorders: Journal of Treatment and Pevention*, 23, 315–324. https://doi.org/10.1080/10640266.2015.1042318

Knatz Peck, S., Towne, T., Wierenga, C. E., Hill, L., Eisler, I., Brown, T., … & Kaye, W. (2021). Temperament-based treatment for young adults with eating disorders: Acceptability and initial efficacy of an intensive, multi-family, parent-involved treatment. *Journal of Eating Disorders*, *9*(1), 110. https://doi.org/10.1186/s40337-021-00465-x

Kuge, R., Kojima, K., Shiraishi, K., Sasayama, D., Honda, H., Simic, M., & Baudinet, J. (2024). Adaptation of multi-family therapy for children and adolescents with anorexia nervosa in Japan. *Journal of Family Therapy*, *46*, 374–387. https://doi.org/10.1111/1467-6427.12468

Matheson, B. E., Van Wye, E., Whyte, A., & Lock, J. (2024). Feasibility and acceptability of a pilot studying investigating multi-family parent-only guided self-help family-based treatment for adolescent anorexia nervosa. *International Journal of Eating Disorders*. https://doi.org/10.1002/eat.24182

Matsuo, Y., Morino, Y., Oka, T., Kuge, R., Fujimoto, A., Tominaga, T., … & Yamada, R. (2023). [Multiple family therapy for adolescents with anorexia nervosa: A pilot study to investigate its feasibility for use in Japan]. *Japanese Journal of Psychiatric Treatment*, *38*, 1083–1091.

Mehl, A., Tomanova, J., Kubena, A., & Papezova, H. (2013). Adapting multi-family therapy to families who care for a loved one with an eating disorder in the Czech Republic combined with a follow-up pilot study of efficacy. *Journal of Family Therapy, 35*(Suppl 1), 82–101. https://doi.org/10.1111/j.1467-6427.2011.00579.x

Scholz, M., Rix, M., & Hegewald, K. (2003). Tagesklinische multifamilientherapie bei anorexia nervosa – manual des Dresdner modells [Outpatient multifamiliy therapy for anorexia nervosa – manual of the Dresdner model]. In B. Steinbrenner & C. S. Schönauer (Eds.), *Essstörungen: Anorexie – Bulimie – Adipositas; Therapie in Theorie und Praxis* [Eating disorders: Anorexia – bulimia – obesity; therapy in theory and practice] (pp. 66–75). Vienna: Maudrich Verlag.

Simic, M., Baudinet, J., Blessitt, E., Wallis, A., & Eisler, I. (2021). *Multi-family therapy for anorexia nervosa: A treatment manual* (1st edition). London, UK: Routledge. https://doi.org/10.4324/978100 3038764

Skarbø, T., & Balmbra, S. M. (2020). Establishment of a multifamily therapy (MFT) service for young adults with a severe eating disorder – experience from 11 MFT groups, and from designing and implementing the model. *Journal of Eating Disorders, 8*(1), 9. https://doi.org/10.1186/s40337-020-0285-8

Stedal, K., Funderud, I., Wierenga, C. E., Knatz-Peck, S., & Hill, L. (2023). Acceptability, feasibility and short-term outcomes of temperament based therapy with support (TBT-S): A novel 5-day treatment for eating disorders. *Journal of Eating Disorders, 11*(1), 156. https://doi.org/10.1186/s40337-023-00878-w

Stewart, C. S., Baudinet, J., Hall, R., Fiskå, M., Pretorius, N., Voulgari, S., … & Simic, M. (2021). Multi-family therapy for bulimia nervosa in adolescence: A pilot study in a community eating disorder service. *Eating Disorders, 29*(4), 351–367. https://doi.org/10.1080/10640266.2019.1656461

Tantillo, M., McGraw, J. S., Hauenstein, E. J., & Groth, S. W. (2015). Partnering with patients and families to develop an innovative multifamily therapy group treatment for adults with anorexia nervosa. *Advances in Eating Disorders, 3*(3), 269–287. https://doi.org/10.1080/21662630.2015.1048478

Tantillo, M., McGraw, J. S., Lavigne, H. M., Brasch, J., & Le Grange, D. (2019). A pilot study of multifamily therapy group for young adults with anorexia nervosa: Reconnecting for recovery. *International Journal of Eating Disorders*, *52*(8), 950–955. https://doi.org/10.1002/eat.23097

Tantillo, M., McGraw, J. S., & Le Grange, D. (2020). *Multifamily therapy group for young adults with anorexia nervosa: Reconnecting for recovery*. New York: Routledge.

Terache, J., Wollast, R., Simon, Y., Marot, M., Van der Linden, N., Franzen, A., & Klein, O. (2023). Promising effect of multi-family therapy on BMI, eating disorders and perceived family functioning in adolescent anorexia nervosa: an uncontrolled longitudinal study. Eating disorders, *Journal of Treatment and Prevention*, 31(1), 64–84. https://doi.org/10.1080/10640266.2022.2069315

Wallin, U. (2007). *Multi-family therapy with anorexia nervosa. A treatment manual.* Lund, Sweden: Lund University.

Wallin, U. (2011). *Multifamiljeterapi vid anorexia nervosa* [Multifamily therapy of anorexia nervosa]. Lund, Sweden: Behandlingsmanual.

Wallis, A., Baudinet, J., Dawson, L., Tay, E., Greenwood, D., McMaster, C., & Miskovic-Wheatley, J. (2015). Multiple family therapy for anorexia nervosa at the Eating Disorder Service, the Children's Hospital at Westmead. *Journal of Eating Disorders*, *3*(S1). https://doi.org/10.1186/2050-2974-3-S1-O11

Wierenga, C. E., Hill, L., Knatz Peck, S., McCray, J., Greathouse, L., Peterson, D., … & Kaye, W. H. (2018). The acceptability, feasibility, and possible benefits of a neurobiologically-informed 5-day multi-family treatment for adults with anorexia nervosa. *The International Journal of Eating Disorders*, *51*(8), 863–869. https://doi.org/10.1002/eat.22876

Abbreviations

ANZAED	Australia and New Zealand Academy for Eating Disorders
ARFID	Avoidant/restrictive food intake disorder
BED	Binge eating disorder
CCEBT	Chicago Centre for Evidence-Based Treatment
CEED	Centre of Excellence in Eating Disorders
CYMS	Child and Youth Mental Health Service
CEDS-CYP	Community Eating Disorders Services for Children and Young People
DSM-5-TR	*Diagnostic and Statistical Manual*, 5th edition, text revision
FBT	Family-based treatment
FBT-AN	Family-based treatment for anorexia nervosa
FBT-BN	Family-based treatment for bulimia nervosa
FBT-ARFID	Family-based treatment for avoidant/restrictive food intake disorder
FT-AN	Family therapy for anorexia nervosa
FT-BN	Family therapy for bulimia nervosa
FT-ED	Eating disorder-focused family therapy
FU	Follow-up
GP	General practitioner
IFT	Intensive family therapy
MCCAED	Maudsley Centre for Child and Adolescent Eating Disorders
MEED	Managing Medical Emergencies in Eating Disorders

MFT	Multi-family therapy
MFT-AN	Multi-family therapy for anorexia nervosa
MFT-BN	Multi-family therapy for bulimia nervosa
NEDC	National Eating Disorders Collaboration
NICE	National Institute for Health and Care Excellence
OSFED	Other Specified Feeding or Eating Disorder
PFT	Parent-focused treatment
RCT	Randomised controlled trials
SickKids	Hospital for Sick Children in Toronto
TBT-S	Temperament-based therapy with supports
UCSD	University of California San Diego
UFED	Unspecified Feeding or Eating Disorder

Overview of FT-ED

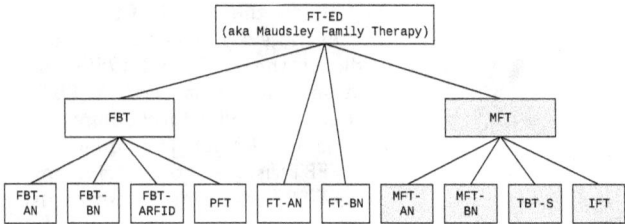

```
                    FT-ED
        (aka Maudsley Family Therapy)

        FBT                          MFT

FBT-   FBT-   FBT-   PFT   FT-AN  FT-BN  MFT-   MFT-   TBT-S   IFT
 AN     BN   ARFID                        AN     BN
```

Key:

☐ Single-family therapy interventions

☐ Multi-family therapy (group-based) interventions

Table O.1

Term	Definition
Family-based treatment (FBT)	FBT is a term used for the manualised form of eating disorder-focused family therapy developed by Jim Lock, Daniel le Grange, and colleagues in the USA. The first edition of the FBT-AN manual (Lock et al., 2001) was developed in consultation with the Maudsley team and reflects the model of treatment used in the early Maudsley research studies in the 1980s and 1990s. In addition to anorexia nervosa, FBT has been manualised for bulimia nervosa and ARFID. The generic term (FBT) is used to describe any form of FBT including parent-focused treatment.
Family-based treatment for anorexia nervosa (FBT-AN)	FBT-AN is a term used to refer specifically to FBT for anorexia nervosa. FBT-AN has been manualised and is currently in its second edition (Lock et al., 2001; Lock & Le Grange, 2012).
Family-based treatment for bulimia nervosa (FBT-AN)	FBT-BN is a term used to refer specifically to FBT for bulimia nervosa. FBT-BN has been manualised (Le Grange & Lock, 2007).
Family therapy for anorexia nervosa (FT-AN)	FT-AN refers to the current version of eating disorder-focused family therapy for anorexia nervosa used at the Maudsley Hospital. There is a treatment manual (Eisler et al., 2016) which describes the current practice at the Maudsley. The manual is widely used by eating disorder services in England and other teams that have trained at the Maudsley.

Table 0.1 (Continued)

Term	Definition
Family therapy for bulimia nervosa (FT-BN)	FT-BN refers to the current version of eating disorder-focused family therapy for bulimia nervosa used at the Maudsley Hospital and elsewhere. FT-BN has been manualised. The manual is due to be published in 2025 (Baudinet & Simic, 2025).
Eating disorder-focused family therapy (FT-ED)	FT-ED is an umbrella term used to describe all the closely related family therapies for eating disorders that have evolved from the original Maudsley approach. This includes FBT and all its specific versions, including parent-focused therapy, as well as FT-AN and FT-BN. It also includes both the single-family and multi-family therapy approaches.
Intensive family therapy (IFT)	IFT is an intensive, five-day, stand-alone multi-family therapy programme used at the University of California San Diego and the University of California San Francisco.
Multi-family therapy (MFT)	MFT is the umbrella term used to refer to all formats of multi-family therapy, regardless of the specific model or patient group.
Multi-family therapy for anorexia nervosa (MFT-AN)	MFT-AN is the term used to refer specifically to MFT for anorexia nervosa developed at the Maudsley Hospital. The treatment has been manualised (Simic et al., 2021).
Multi-family therapy for bulimia nervosa (MFT-BN)	MFT-BN is the term used to refer specifically to MFT for bulimia nervosa developed at the Maudsley Hospital.

(Continued)

Table O.1 (Continued)

Term	Definition
Parent-focused treatment (PFT)	PFT refers to a parent-only version of FBT developed and evaluated by Daniel le Grange and colleagues (Hughes et al., 2015). It is based on the principles of FBT.
Temperament-based therapy with supports (TBT-S)	TBT-S refers to a five-day stand-alone multi-family therapy programme developed at the University of California San Diego for adults with anorexia nervosa. The model has been manualised (Hill et al., 2022).

Eating disorder-focused family therapy manuals

English language manuals

Child and adolescent manuals

FBT-AN

Lock, J., Le Grange, D., Agras, S., & Dare, C. (2001). *Treatment manual for anorexia nervosa: A family-based approach* (1st edition). New York: Guilford Press.

Lock, J., & Le Grange, D. (2012). *Treatment manual for anorexia nervosa: A family-based approach* (2nd edition). New York: Guilford Press.

FBT-BN

Le Grange, D., & Lock, J. (2007). *Treating Bulimia in Adolescents: A Family-Based Approach* (1st edition). New York: Guilford Press.

FBT-ARFID

Lock, J. (2022). *Family-based treatment for Avoidant/Restrictive Food Intake Disorder*. New York: Routledge/Taylor & Francis Group.

FT-AN

Eisler, I., Simic, M., Blessitt, E., Dodge, L., & MCCAED Team. (2016). *Maudsley Service Manual for Child and Adolescent Eating Disorders.* https://mccaed.slam.nhs.uk/professionals/resources/books-and-manuals/

FT-BN

Baudinet, J., & Simic, M. (*in press*). *Integrated Family Therapy for Adolescent Bulimia Nervosa: A Treatment Manual.* London, UK: Routledge.

MFT-AN

Simic, M., Baudinet, J., Blessitt, E., Wallis, A., & Eisler, I. (2021). *Multi-Family Therapy for Anorexia Nervosa: A Treatment Manual* (1st edition). London, UK: Routledge. https://doi.org/10.4324/9781003038764

PFT

Hughes, E. K., Sawyer, S. M., Loeb, K. L., & Le Grange, D. (2015). Parent-Focused Treatment. In K. L. Loeb, D. Le Grange, & J. Lock (Eds.), *Family Therapy for Adolescent Eating and Weight Disorders* (1st edition, pp. 59–71). New York: Imprint Routledge.
Adult manuals

TBT-S

Hill, L. L., Knatz Peck, S., & Wierenga, C. E. (2022). *Temperament Based Therapy with Support for Anorexia Nervosa: A Novel Treatment.* Cambridge University Press; Cambridge Core. https://doi.org/10.1017/9781009032063

MFT FOR YOUNG ADULTS

Tantillo, M., McGraw, J. S., & Le Grange, D. (2020). *Multifamily Therapy Group for Young Adults with Anorexia Nervosa: Reconnecting for Recovery* (1st edition). Routledge.

MFT FOR ADULTS

Balmbra, S., Valvik, M., & Lyngmo, S. (2019). *Coming together, letting go*. Retrieved from: www.nordlandssykehuset.no/siteassets/documents/Ressp/Coming-together-2019-10d-B5.pdf

Non-English language manuals

Child and Adolescent

FRENCH MFT MANUAL

Duclos, J., Carrot, B., Minier, L., Cook-Darzens, S., Barton-Clegg, V., Godart, N., & Criquillion-Doublet, S. (2021). *Manuel de Thérapie Multi-Familiale*. Retrieved from: www.researchgate.net/publication/350906742_Manuel_de_Therapie_Multi-Familiale_approche_integrative_pour_la_prise_en_charge_d%27adolescents_souffrant_d%27Anorexie_Mentale_et_de_leurs_familles

SWEDISH MFT MANUAL

Wallin, U. (2007). *Multi-family therapy with anorexia nervosa. A treatment manual.* Lund: Lund University.

Wallin, U. (2011). *Multifamiljeterapi vid anorexia nervosa* [Multifamily therapy of anorexia nervosa]. Lund, Sweden: Behandlingsmanual.

GERMAN MFT MANUAL

Scholz, M., Rix, M., & Hegewald, K. (2003). Tagesklinische multifamilientherapie bei anorexia nervosa – manual des Dresdner models. In B. Steinbrenner & C. S. Schönauer (Eds.), *Essstörungen: Anorexie – Bulemie – Adipositas; Therapie in Theorie und Praxis* (pp. 66–75). Vienna: Maudrich Verlag.

Index

Note: Page numbers in **bold** refers to Tables.

Alexander, June, story of 2–13
American Psychiatric
    Association (APA) 25, 285
anorexia nervosa: characteristics
    of 23–24; cultural and social
    factors in 30; diagnosis of 286;
    early signs and symptoms
    of 290–291; families as key
    in overcoming 43; historical
    definitions of 22–23; impacts
    of 24; portraits of 59–60;
    presentation of 24; prevalence of
    26; temperament, neurobiology,
    and genetics of 27–28, 36
anxiety 27, 34, 67, 110, 177,
    203, 220–221, 225–226;
    calming of 130; effects
    on families 34, 50; food
    restriction in blunting 28,
    29; incidents of extreme 86;
    over missing school 191–192;
    perfectionist traits and 28,
    161; provoked by mealtimes
    63, 97; psychoeducation for
    49; quick spiraling of 96;
    social 95, 98; therapeutic
    relationship and 50
Asia, multi-family therapy
    (MFT) in 299

avoidant/restrictive food intake
    disorder) (ARFID) 22, 23, 25,
    288; characteristics of 25–26;
    diagnosis of 287; prevalence
    of 26

binge eating 23, 97, 105; in
    bulimia nervosa 24–25, 286
binge eating disorder (BED)
    288; defined 25; diagnosis
    of 286–287; early signs
    and symptoms of 290–291;
    prevalence of 26
Binswanger, Ludwig 22
Bruch, Hilde 32
bulimia nervosa: characteristics
    of 24–25; diagnosis of 286;
    early signs and symptoms of
    290–291; historical definitions
    of 22–23; prevalence of 26

caring environment at home,
    creation of 245–254
Charcot, Jean-Martin 31
Christmas survival guide 131
contracting, multi-family therapy
    (MFT) 62
cultural and social factors in eating
    disorders development 29–31

Diagnostic and Statistical Manual of Mental Disorders (DSM-5) 25, 285–288

eating disorder-focused family therapy (FT-ED) 45; empirical evidence on 63–67
eating disorders: defining 22–26; development of 27–37; diagnostic criteria for 285–288; family interventions for 44–52; family role in development of 31–33; family therapy manuals for 311–313; impact on family and family reorganization around the illness 33–37; national treatment guidelines for 294–295; prevalence of 26; public awareness of 21; recognizing 16; role of culture and social factors in 29–31; role of family in recovery from 1–13, 21–22, 43, 99–112; signs and symptoms of 290–291; steps to take in addressing 291–294; temperament, neurobiology, and genetics of 27–29; understanding 14–15
Europe, multi-family therapy (MFT) in 298
externalisation 47–48

family interventions: empirical evidence on 63–67; Maudsley approach (*see* Maudsley family therapy for anorexia nervosa); multi-family therapy (MFT) (*see* multi-family therapy (MFT))

family role: in development of eating disorders 31–33; in recovery from eating disorders 1–13, 21–22, 43, 99–112; in reorganization around illness 33–37; *see also* parents
family sculpt exercise 60–61
family stories 15–16, 81–82; anorexia does not care who you are or where you are 273–277; 'Can I have some fries, Mummy?' 258–272; creating a caring environment at home to support recovery 245–254; on everyone in the family having a role in recovery 99–112; on the getting of communication skills leads to breakthroughs 240–244; 'I am not my mother; I'm me' 227–232; on importance of being treated with respect 83–98; on job in cheese shop providing a lesson in recovery 136–140; mother and son 152–162; mothers and friendship 119–135; 'Oh, my sister does that, too' 255–257; reflecting on inspiring lessons in 278–281; reshaping daughter-mother dynamics 141–151; sparkle behind a belly button piercing 215–226; that 'there is no cookie cutter for this illness' 189–196; understanding the illness helps mother take charge 233–239; when dad is the primary carer 113–118; when 'doing' with others makes a difference 197–214; when MFT is the

last in a long list of therapies 163–177; when patients believe 'only I can get myself out of this illness' 178–188

fathers: belief that 'there is no cookie cutter for this illness' in 189–193; 'Can I have some fries, Mummy?' and 265–266; creating a caring environment at home to support recovery 252–254; as primary carers 113–118; respect in multi-family therapy and 86–91; when 'doing' with others makes a difference 201–205; when MFT is the last in a long list of therapies 166–170

friendships between mothers 119–135

genetics and eating disorders development 14, 27–29

Girl Called Tim, A 5–6, 9

guilt and blame 29, 34, 59, 172, 188, 243, 260, 279–280; parents and 34, 187, 188, 190, 235, 252, 275; reduced by externalisation 48

Gull, William 31

International Classification of Diseases (ICD)-11 25, 285–288

Janet, Pierre 22

Kagawa, Shutoku 22

Laqueur, Peter 53

Lasègue, Charles 31

Latin America, multi-family therapy (MFT) in 299–300

Maudsley family therapy for anorexia nervosa 15, 21–22, 43; central aim of 44–45; development of 44–46; ending treatment, discussion of future plans and discharge in 51–52; engagement in treatment and development of therapeutic alliance in 46–48; exploring issues of individual and family development 50–51; helping family to manage eating disorder 48–49

meal plans 48, 49, 50, 97, 160, 185, 186, 190

meals, multi-family 62–63

mealtime role reversal 60

Middle East, multi-family therapy (MFT) in the 300

Minuchin, Salvador 32–33, 44

Morton, Richard 22

mothers: anorexia does not care who you are or where you are and 273–277; belief that 'there is no cookie cutter for this illness' in 193–196; 'Can I have some fries, Mummy?' and 258–265; creating a caring environment at home to support recovery 245–252; friendships between 119–135; and the getting of communication skills leads to breakthroughs 240–244; and a job in a cheese shop providing a lesson in recovery 136–139; recovery role of 106–111; reshaping daughter-mother dynamics and 141–146; respect in multi-family therapy and 83–86; and sons 152–158; on sparkle behind a belly button piercing 221–226; understanding the illness helps them take charge 234–239; when 'doing' with others

makes a difference 197–201;
when MFT is the last in a
long list of therapies 163–166;
when patients believe 'only
I can get myself out of this
illness' 183–188
multi-disciplinary team (MDT) 51
multi-family therapy (MFT)
1, 43, 52–59; activities in
59; anorexia does not care
who you are or where you
are and 273–277; in Asia
299; belief that 'there is no
cookie cutter for this illness'
and 189–196; 'Can I have
some fries, Mummy?' and
258–272; contracting 62;
creating a caring environment
at home to support recovery
245–254; empirical evidence
for 13–14, 63–67; in Europe
298; everyone in the family
having a role in recovery
in 99–112; family sculpt
in 60–61; family stories of
(see family stories); and the
getting of communication
skills leads to breakthroughs
240–244; history of use for
anorexia 53–55; 'I am not my
mother; I'm me' and 227–232;
importance of respect in
83–98; job in a cheese shop
providing a lesson in recovery
and 136–140; as last in a long
list of therapies 163–177;
in Latin America 299–300;
mealtime role reversal in
60; in the Middle East 300;
mothers and friendship in
119–135; mothers and sons
in 152–162; multi-family
meals in 62–63; navigating
search for 16–17, 296–300; in

North America 298–299; 'Oh,
my sister does that, too' and
255–257; portraits of anorexia
in 59–60; reshaping daughter-
mother dynamics 141–151;
for schizophrenia 53; sparkle
behind a belly button piercing
and 215–226; themes covered
in 55, **56–58**; timelines in
61–62; in the UK 297–298;
understanding 15–16;
understanding the illness helps
mother take charge 233–239;
when dad is the primary carer
113–118; when 'doing' with
others makes a difference
197–214; when patients
believe 'only I can get myself
out of this illness' 178–188

nasogastric tubes (NGTs) 83,
94, 260
neurobiology and eating
disorders development 27–29,
36
North America, multi-family
therapy (MFT) in 298–299

obsessive compulsive disorder
(OCD) 88, 96, 233, 234
Other Specified Feeding or
Eating Disorder (OSFED)
287–288

parents: anxiety in 34; with
closer relationships with
children 34–35; feeling
confused and not knowing
what to do 288–290; and
how to tell if child has eating
disorder 285–294; relationship
with each other 35–36; steps
for 291–294; see also family
role

patients: believing 'only I can
   get myself out of this illness'
   178–183; 'Can I have some
   fries, Mummy?' and 266–267;
   'I am not my mother; I'm me'
   and 227–232; and a job in a
   cheese shop providing a lesson
   in recovery 139–140; mothers
   and sons as 158–162; recovery
   role of 99–106; reshaping
   daughter-mother dynamics
   and 146–151; respect in multi-
   family therapy and 94–98;
   on sparkle behind a belly
   button piercing 215–221;
   understanding the illness helps
   mother take charge 233–234;
   when 'doing' with others
   makes a difference 210–214;
   when MFT is the last in a long
   list of therapies 172–177
perfectionism 27–28, 161, 186,
   201, 203, 233, 239
pica 287, 288
portraits of anorexia 59–60
psychoeducation 14, 47, 49

reshaping daughter-mother
   dynamics 141–151
respect in multi-family therapy:
   fathers and 86–91; mothers
   and 83–86; patients and
   94–98; siblings and 91–93

rumination disorder 287, 288
Russell, Gerald 22

siblings: 'Can I have some fries,
   Mummy?' and 267–272; 'Oh,
   my sister does that, too' and
   255–257; recovery role of
   111–112; respect in multi-
   family therapy and 91–93;
   when 'doing' with others
   makes a difference 205–210;
   when MFT is the last in a long
   list of therapies 170–172
signs and symptoms of eating
   disorders 290–291

temperament and eating
   disorders development
   27–29
therapeutic alliance 46–48
timelines in multi-family therapy
   (MFT) 61–62
travelling tips 131

United Kingdom, multi-family
   therapy (MFT) in the
   297–298
Unspecified Feeding or Eating
   Disorder (UFED) 287

World Health Organization 25,
   285
Wulff, Moshe 22

For Product Safety Concerns and Information please contact our EU
representative GPSR@taylorandfrancis.com
Taylor & Francis Verlag GmbH, Kaufingerstraße 24, 80331 München, Germany

www.ingramcontent.com/pod-product-compliance
Lightning Source LLC
Chambersburg PA
CBHW070245290326
41929CB00047B/2609